WITH THE WORLD TO CHOOSE FROM

Edward Beatty, chancellor of McGill University from 1920 to 1943. *Used with permission of McGill University Archives, PL007704.*

With the World to Choose From

Celebrating Seven Decades of the Beatty Lecture at McGill University

EDITED BY
BRETT HOOTON, ROBIN KONING,
AND MEAGHAN THURSTON

Published for Research and Innovation, McGill University
by
McGill-Queen's University Press
Montreal & Kingston • London • Chicago

© McGill-Queen's University Press 2021

ISBN 978-0-2280-0800-2 (cloth)
ISBN 978-0-2280-0801-9 (ePDF)

Legal deposit third quarter 2021
Bibliothèque nationale du Québec

Printed in Canada on acid-free paper that is 100% ancient forest free (100% post-consumer recycled), processed chlorine free

We acknowledge the support of the Canada Council for the Arts.
Nous remercions le Conseil des arts du Canada de son soutien.

Library and Archives Canada Cataloguing in Publication

Title: With the world to choose from : celebrating seven decades of the Beatty Lecture at McGill University / edited by Brett Hooton, Robin Koning, and Meaghan Thurston.
Names: Hooton, Brett, editor. | Koning, Robin, editor. | Thurston, Meaghan, editor.
Description: Includes bibliographical references.
Identifiers: Canadiana (print) 20210208147 | Canadiana (ebook) 20210208279
 | ISBN 9780228008002 (cloth) | ISBN 9780228008019 (ePDF)
Subjects: LCSH: Speeches, addresses, etc.
Classification: LCC PN6121 .W58 2021 | DDC 808.85—dc23

This book was typeset in Minion Pro.

McGill University is on land that has long served as a site of meeting and exchange amongst Indigenous peoples, including the Haudenosaunee and Anishinabeg nations. We acknowledge and thank the diverse Indigenous peoples whose presence marks this territory on which peoples of the world gathered for these lectures.

Contents

Foreword xi
Suzanne Fortier

Acknowledgments xiii
Martha Crago

Introduction 3
Brett Hooton, Robin Koning, Meaghan Thurston

Sir Edward Wentworth Beatty: A Life of Service 27
Robin Koning

Past Beatty Lectures 41

A Note on the Selection of Lectures 45

The Interplay of East and West,
Points of Conflict and Cooperation (1955) 47
Barbara Ward
Introduction by Glenda Sluga

Asia Today: Revolutionary Change in
the Twentieth Century (1968) 59
Han Suyin
Introduction by Laifong Leung

How Long Have We Got? (1971) 79
Peter Ritchie-Calder
Introduction by Catherine Happer

Genetic Engineering: Ambush or Opportunity? (1972) 91
Robert Sinsheimer
Introduction by Françoise Baylis

The Emergence of Intelligent Life in the Universe (1975) 103
Fred Hoyle
Introduction by Victoria Kaspi

Interpretation in Music and in Life (1975) 113
Yehudi Menuhin
Introduction by Nora Chastain

A Swing to the Right?
Socio-political Changes in the Western World (1981) 125
Ralf Dahrendorf
Introduction by Helmut K. Anheier

Apartheid: Dying or Resurgent? (1982) 141
Gwendolen Carter
Introduction by Shireen Hassim

The New World Order (1993) 157
Mikhail Gorbachev
Introduction by Kathryn Stoner

Right of Interference: Progress and Failure in Conflict Prevention
in an Age of Global Anxiety (1996) 175
Bernard Kouchner
Introduction by Payam Akhavan

Lessons in Living from the Dying (1997) 187
Cicely Saunders
Introduction by David Clark

Canada in the World: The Challenges Ahead (2005) 201
Michael Ignatieff
Introduction by Christopher Sands

Building Social Business: The New Kind of Capitalism
that Serves Humanity's Most Pressing Needs (2010) 213
Muhammad Yunus
Introduction by Dax Dasilva

The Challenge of Regressive Democracy (2017) 229
Charles Taylor
Introduction by Rowan Williams

Difficult Women, Bad Feminists, and Unruly Bodies (2018) 239
Roxane Gay
Introduction by Debra Thompson

Permissions 247

Foreword

On 4 October 1954, two thousand faculty, students, and Montrealers gathered in the Sir Arthur Currie Memorial Gymnasium, eager to hear Sarvepalli Radhakrishnan, India's first vice president, deliver the inaugural Beatty Lecture. Sixty-seven years later, the Beatty Lecture has become one of McGill University's signature annual events, a distinguished lectureship, and one of Canada's longest running lecture series. The Beatty Lecture is celebrated for bringing internationally renowned thought leaders to the McGill stage and for the diversity of topics those lecturers cover. Above all, the Beatty Lecture is known for inspiring audiences to think deeply, and sometimes critically, about their world.

I am honoured to introduce this anthology of select past Beatty Lectures – particularly during McGill's bicentennial year. In 2021, we celebrate this great university's 200th anniversary, a remarkable milestone to reach, and a unique time for reflection. Our past can serve as a guide to help us address present challenges and direct us toward a better future. This anthology shines the spotlight on fifteen standout lectures spanning the past seven decades. In doing so, it serves as a tangible record of the Beatty Lecture's reach and influence, as well as our own collective history.

The lecturers who have stood at the Beatty podium have brought their unique perspectives to help us understand some of the most significant moments and discoveries of our time, and to stimulate public discussion around them. This anthology features Han Suyin's 1968 lecture about the communist revolution in China; Robert Sinsheimer's 1972 lecture exploring the implications of genetic engineering; Gwendolen Carter's reportage on apartheid in South Africa in 1982; and Mikhail Gorbachev's imagining of "a new world order" in 1993, just two years after the dissolution of the Soviet Union. More recently, Roxane Gay's 2018 lecture about the #MeToo movement – in which she describes "a reckoning, one that has been a long time coming" – seems destined to serve as a cultural touchpoint for those studying today's world in the years ahead.

Although decades have passed since some of these lectures took place, the topics covered in many of them remain startlingly relevant today. In these pages, journalist Peter Ritchie-Calder warns us about the devastating effects of climate change in his lecture delivered fifty years ago. Cicely Saunders, in 1997, described how the modern palliative care movement that she pioneered arose as a "protest against the pain, isolation, and neglect suffered by dying people," – much-needed work that continues to this day. I appreciate that the greatest lesson Saunders says she learned during her incredible career was "simply to listen."

I hope readers, too, will find valuable insights in this collection by discovering or rediscovering these important historical voices through their Beatty Lectures. There is much in these pages that we should listen to, take to heart, and be inspired by. I point not only to the lectures, but also to the prefaces that introduce us to each talk, authored by emerging or established luminaries in their own right. Vicky Kaspi, a world-renowned astrophysicist and McGill professor, provides the preface to astronomer Fred Hoyle's lecture. Dax Dasilva, a technology CEO who helps other entrepreneurs become leaders in their communities, introduces Mohammad Yunus's lecture on building social businesses. And the acclaimed violinist Nora Chastain introduces us to the lecture delivered by her former teacher, Yehudi Menuhin.

The Beatty Lecture honours an important figure in both McGill and Canada's history: Sir Edward Beatty, who served as chancellor of McGill from 1920 to 1943 and the president of the Canadian Pacific Railway from 1918 to 1942. The Beatty Lecture was endowed through a generous gift made by Sir Edward's brother, Dr Henry A. Beatty, in 1952. Thanks to this gift, McGill has had the privilege of welcoming speakers of singular distinction each year to the Beatty Lecture podium for seven decades – and this act of generosity will continue to allow us to do so far into the future.

Please join me in treasuring these past Beatty Lectures and in anticipating all the thought-provoking talks still to come.

Professor Suzanne Fortier
Principal and Vice-Chancellor and McCall MacBain Professor
McGill University

Acknowledgments

I wish to express my most sincere gratitude to all those individuals whose generous support made this anthology possible. The idea to publish a collection of the Beatty Lectures arose during a conversation between the editors of this anthology with McGill Queen's University Press (MQUP) in 2018. MQUP was one of the Beatty Lecture's earliest partners, having published several of the lectures from the 1950s to the early 1970s. The university is thrilled to work with them again to bring the Beatty Lectures to a wide audience. Our gratitude to MQUP and Natalie Blachere who encouraged this project from the outset.

The publication of this anthology was made possible by many individuals at McGill University. The Office of the Vice-Principal, Research and Innovation, organizes the Beatty Lecture and spearheaded the creation of this book. Though too many to thank individually, I would also like to acknowledge the indispensable contribution of staff and volunteers who manage the logistical production of this signature event on an annual basis, in particular the McGill Alumni Association and University Advancement.

Staff at the McGill University Archives and McGill Library located and digitized the textual, photographic, and audiovisual records required to bring this project to life. Special thanks are due to Julien Couture, Frédéric Giuliano, and Gregory Houston.

To provide historical context and comment on the contemporary relevance of the included lectures, fifteen individuals – renowned in their own right – provided prefaces. I am extremely grateful for their contribution. A sincere thank you to each for such insightful introductions to the lectures. Thanks are due to the rights holders, relatives, and in some cases the lecturers themselves with whom the editors had the pleasure of corresponding and who permitted us to publish the Beatty Lectures included in this anthology.

McGill wishes to thank the Canadian Broadcasting Corporation (CBC) for their recent participation as moderators of the Beatty Lecture live events and for their ongoing support.

For turning the transcripts, as well as the historical background on the series and on the life of the series' namesake, Sir Edward, into polished texts, my thanks to the anthology's editors, Brett Hooton, Robin Koning – also our in-house Beatty Lecture expert – and Meaghan Thurston. The editors wish to acknowledge the additional editorial support from Junji Nishihata, Nancy Ross, and Harry Thurston.

Finally, I thank you – readers and audiences of the Beatty Lecture – for your ongoing enthusiasm for one of Canada's most renowned lecture series.

Martha Crago, c.m., Phd., DSc,
Vice-Principal, Research and Innovation
McGill University

WITH THE WORLD TO CHOOSE FROM

INTRODUCTION

"With the World to Choose From": Seven Decades of the Beatty Lecture

Brett Hooton, Robin Koning, Meaghan Thurston

On a cool and rainy October evening in 2018, a crowd began to gather at the entrance to Pollack Hall on McGill University's downtown campus. Soon, a line snaked around the block from the box office. When the audience was finally seated, an anticipatory hush filled the room. As the #MeToo movement dominated headlines and newsfeeds around the world, Roxane Gay, the American cultural critic and bestselling author, was set to deliver the sold-out Beatty Lecture. Gathered to hear her speak was an audience eager to be informed and challenged, to hear words that might change how they think about the world, and to be inspired to make change. When Gay took to the stage, the audience rose to their feet and burst into loud cheering and applause.

As though describing the very same evening seven decades earlier, in October 1955, McGill Principal F. Cyril James wrote of renowned economist Barbara Ward's Beatty Lecture: "the best indication of the interest that her lectures evoked is the simple statement that more than 2,500 people – students, professors, and other citizens of Montreal – turned up on three evenings in singularly wintry weather … The ovation that she received was sincere and heartwarming."[1]

Since the first Beatty Lecture – as Principal Suzanne Fortier remarks in her foreword – eager audiences have flocked to McGill to hear from an incredible roster of influential thinkers from around the world. One of the longest running lecture series in North America, and uniquely international in scope, the ninety Beatty Lectures delivered to date reflect not just the narrative of the ideas of the past, but the importance of these ideas to present day and future generations. This anthology brings a collection of fifteen of these captivating talks to print – many for the first time.

A LASTING GIFT

McGill established the Beatty Lecture in 1952 in honour of Sir Edward Beatty, who had served as president of the Canadian Pacific Railway from 1918 to 1942 and as McGill's chancellor from 1920 to 1943. The program was made possible thanks to a $100,000 gift to the university from Edward Beatty's brother, Dr Henry A. Beatty. This endowment enabled McGill to invite a "distinguished scholar or scientist" from outside Canada to deliver a series of three public lectures on a topic of their choice during a month-long stay on campus. The Dean of Graduate Studies and Research, David Thomson, and Noel Fieldhouse, Dean of Arts and Science, led the charge to choose the first Beatty Lecturer, an exciting but challenging mission. "With the world to choose from, it becomes difficult to select for the Beatty Lectureship,"[2] wrote Thomson to James on 29 August 1952.

Their choice, Sarvepalli Radhakrishnan, was then two years into his role as the first vice president of India, a country that had just undergone a monumental transition from British rule into independence. Radhakrishnan had also recently served as India's ambassador to Russia during a period of expanding Soviet totalitarianism. James was so eager for him to be the first to speak at the Beatty podium that he delayed the launch of the Beatty Lecture until the vice president's schedule could permit the visit in 1954. The wisdom of James' decision was confirmed when the high demand for tickets forced him to change the venue from Redpath Hall to the much larger Sir Arthur Currie Memorial Gymnasium just days before the lecture. Since that first night, the Beatty Lecture has been one of McGill's signature annual public events, filling auditoriums year after year.

A ROSTER LIKE NO OTHER

This anthology presents a selection of fifteen of the most outstanding Beatty Lectures since its launch. To read this anthology is to travel back in time and revisit pivotal moments in history through the words of those who played a large role in shaping them. The prefaces before each lecture, written by the leading academics and public intellectuals of our day, forge links between eras and across generations.

The 1955 Beatty Lecture series, delivered by one of the twentieth century's most influential visionaries, the English economist Barbara Ward, opens this anthology. As a journalist, prolific author, and an adviser to world leaders including John F. Kennedy and Kwame Nkrumah of Ghana, Ward had already gained worldwide recognition as a pioneer for sustainable development. It was an unfortunate sign of the times that despite Ward's many accomplishments, which included her post as the first female foreign editor of *The Economist*, a headline in *The Montreal Gazette* the week before her first lecture trumpeted, "Woman to Give Sir Edward Beatty Memorial Talks."[3]

In her third Beatty Lecture, which is featured in this anthology, Ward called for the creation of institutions "which transcend national sovereignty sufficiently to give mankind a form of general political order without which we are all but certain to plunge into totally destructive war." It was a timely message. Just a month later, the Vietnam War erupted in a world already divided by the Cold War. Ward saw beyond the dangers inherent in an increasingly interdependent world to the possibility of global equality and prosperity. In the 1970s, she established the International Institute for Environment and Development and played a leading role at landmark United Nations conferences on the environment, food security, and urbanization.

In the 1960s, Beatty Lecture organizers invited another influential speaker to address the big issue of the decade. British author Han Suyin, widely known as one of the early and notable supporters of Mao Zedong, was the Beatty lecturer in 1968, two years after Mao launched the Cultural Revolution in China. Over the course of three lectures, she extolled the communist nation's role as "the self-proclaimed vanguard and leader of revolutionary change" in Asia and Latin America. Her words sparked controversy on campus. The staff and faculty journal, the *McGill Reporter*, ran the headline, "Dr Han Suyin Delivers Shock Treatments"[4] and described her lectures as, "distasteful to some, unsettling to others."[5] Conversely, editors at McGill's student paper, *The McGill Daily*, scoffed at those critics who "foamed over this display of 'Maoist propaganda.'"[6]

In the 1970s, the selection of Beatty lecturers shifted gears, focusing primarily on researchers and writers working at the forefront of science. The decade also saw a change in the format of the Beatty Lecture: lecturers gave only one talk rather than a series, but up to four different Beatty lecturers might speak throughout a single year. From this period, the anthology presents Peter Ritchie-Calder's 1971 lecture on the impact of global warming; biophysicist Robert Sinsheimer's lecture, delivered the following year, which predicted the profound implications that human genome research would have on science and humanity; and finally, astronomer Fred Hoyle's 1975 lecture that explored the emergence of intelligent life in the Universe. In the 1970s, Canadians would be welcomed at the Beatty podium for the first time. Renowned author Saul Bellow, who was born in Lachine, Quebec, and moved to Chicago, Illinois, as a youth, inaugurated this initiative in 1973.

Political scientist Gwendolen Carter ushered the Beatty Lecture into the 1980s, and once again shone the spotlight on political upheavals, this time in apartheid-era South Africa. A frequent visitor to the country, Carter's extensive scholarship provided policymakers and academics with an understanding of the extreme inequality happening there. Her 1982 lecture spoke to the emerging decade of increased domestic and international strikes, sanctions, and demonstrations held against the apartheid government. Canada's largest anti-apartheid conference took place that year in Ottawa. Carter, who was born in Hamilton, Ontario, became known as the founder of African Studies in the United States.

In the 1990s and early 2000s, the Beatty continued to feature leading voices in global politics. In Mikhail Gorbachev's 1993 lecture, which is available to view in English, French, and Russian on the Beatty Lecture Digital Archive website, the former Soviet leader envisioned a "new world order" in the wake of the fall of the Russian Federation. Three years later, Médecins Sans Frontières co-founder Bernard Kouchner called for "a new kind of intervention" as he reflected on recent wars in Yugoslavia and Rwanda. Closer to home, in 2005, future Liberal Party leader Michael Ignatieff called for a new era of "federalism based on respect and recognition," stating that, "we can't mean anything to the world unless we stay united."

In the Beatty Lecture's most recent decade, a range of powerful movements and revolutions are reflected in the speakers who took to the stage. In 2010, Beatty Lecture organizers invited Nobel Peace Prize Laureate Muhammad Yunus to speak about social enterprises and the microcredit banking system he pioneered – a groundbreaking concept that changed the way we think about poverty and about the ability and willingness of the poor to help themselves. "Every human being is packed with unlimited capacity," Yunus told his audience, and "to ask them to not to use that capacity is criminal."

In 2017, Canadian philosopher and McGill Professor Emeritus Charles Taylor, winner of the Kyoto Prize and Berggruen Prize, delivered an impactful lecture on "The Challenge of Regressive Democracy," shortly after the Brexit vote in England and the victory of Donald Trump in the United States' presidential election. We close this anthology with Roxane Gay's 2018 lecture on #MeToo activism, delivered to a packed auditorium, and her declaration that "we talk about resistance, when what we actually need is a revolution."

INSIDE THE ARCHIVES

This anthology – which for the first time brings to publication lectures from each decade of the Beatty Lecture's existence – would not exist without the help of McGill's dedicated archivists. Though the Lecture has been an important part of McGill's history for more than sixty-five years, much of its history was forgotten, even by the team dedicated to its annual production.

In 2018, McGill's Office of the Vice-Principal, Research and Innovation, engaged a full-time project manager and the McGill University Archives to unearth the rich story of the lecture series. McGill's archivists identified over fifteen boxes of content related to the Beatty Lecture held in their vaults. Inside were audio cassettes of lectures dating back to the 1960s, fortunately all still in working condition, and manila folders holding transcripts dating back to the 1950s. Careful examination of the contents by the Beatty Lecture history project lead, Robin Koning, revealed rare recordings of lectures delivered by Nobel-winning scientists, such as Richard Feynman and Francis Crick, as well as the 1979 lecture delivered by world-renowned primatologist Jane Goodall, in addition to a number of the lectures featured in this anthology.

Also meticulously stored away in the Archives were boxes holding black and white photographs, press clippings, and promotional posters. Several boxes contained folders full of administrative documents from the Beatty Lecture's early years when Principal James oversaw the program. This included a letter from Canada's then Prime Minister Louis St Laurent, congratulating James on the success of the first lecture. Several folders contained contracts with book publishers. During the first two decades, some of the lectures were published in book form, first by W.W. Norton & Company and then by McGill University Press (now McGill-Queen's University Press).

Committee meeting minutes from 1967 presented a list of potential speakers to invite including names familiar to this day: Buckminster Fuller, Barbara Tuchman, U Thant, Jean Paul Sartre, Chou En-lai, Norman Mailer, Arthur Miller, Lewis Mumford, and Martin Luther King. Stowed away in a folder of correspondence from the late 1950s was a letter signed by T. S. Eliot, politely declining McGill's invitation to lecture, with the excuse that his "visits to the New World are primarily to visit old friends and relatives."[7]

Other unearthed ephemera included an expense sheet for the British historian Arnold Toynbee's lecture series in 1961, noting the £655 cost for a return steamship fare from Liverpool to New York to Montreal for him and his wife, as well as "train fares, tips and sundry expenses."[8] Some of these ephemera are now featured here in the pages of this anthology.

An unfortunate gap in the records also revealed itself: neither recordings nor transcripts existed for every lecture, particularly those from the mid-1980s to the early 2000s. This was the early era of digital transformation, which likely resulted in the hasty disposal of analogue forms of documentation, such as paper printouts and cassette tapes. Yet, during these years a steady stream of Nobel Prize winners delivered the Beatty Lecture, including physiologist Luc Montaigner, biologist Gerald Edelman, environmental activist Wangari Maathai, writer Saul Bellow, and chemists Paul J. Crutzen and Rudolph A. Marcus.

Other notable lost recordings include lectures delivered by authors Margaret Drabble and Oliver Sacks, by Queen Noor of Jordan, and by tennis legend Arthur Ashe, whose 1992 lecture on "Living with AIDS" was delivered just two months before his death from AIDS-related pneumonia. From the records, we do know that a standing-room only crowd of over one thousand people turned out to hear Ashe speak. "You know, the scientists and physicians who work on AIDS know much more about this subject than I do, but I guess you would rather hear about it from me,"[9] he told the rapt audience, as reported in *The Montreal Gazette* that week. Fortunately, a treasure trove of recordings and transcripts do exist, and these can be accessed in the Beatty Lecture Digital Archive website, launched in 2019.

INSPIRING AUDIENCES TODAY AND TOMORROW

In its eighth decade, and in this, McGill's bicentennial year, the Beatty Lecture is expanding its reach through this first print anthology of past lectures, created in partnership with McGill-Queen's University Press (MQUP). The fact that MQUP has opted to publish these lectures echoes McGill University's strong desire to retain and disseminate them in a permanent form. This anthology now serves as a tangible addition to the live event – hosted by a CBC journalist since 2018 – which has been a national and global forum of ideas for more than sixty-five years.

Bringing this eclectic group of voices – with all the power inherent to oration – to print was no easy task. Using audio recordings, or where none existed, historical transcripts, video files or past publications, we sought in our editing to preserve the integrity of the spoken word while also ensuring readability and enjoyment of the texts.

One of the unanticipated joys in compiling this collection was the discovery of connections or unintentional exchanges transmitted across the decades and between lectures. In 1968, Han Suyin decried the political, social, and economic inequities in wealth distribution between East and West, referencing, and challenging, the worldview of the dominant economists of the day, including Barbara Ward who had spoken at the Beatty Lecture podium a decade before. In 1993, at the height of the Russian constitutional crisis, McGill professor Charles Taylor moderated the lecture delivered by Mikhail Gorbachev; twenty-four years later, there are echoes of this discussion in Taylor's 2017 Beatty Lecture on the threats of regressive democracy. Indeed, over the course of seven decades, Beatty lecturers – from peace advocate and science journalist, Peter Ritchie-Calder (1971) to the father of microcredit, Muhammed Yunus (2010); and from political scientist Gwendolyn Carter (1982) to author Roxane Gay (2018) – have anticipated, or reflected upon, the times of their fellow lecturers in their calls to envision a world redefined by cultural diversity and the adoption of a global perspective.

We hope the reader takes the time to enjoy these lectures that we feel fortunate to have engaged with in the editing process. In a digital era, when information is relayed immediately and too often defined by short sound bites, the Beatty Lecture is more remarkable and relevant than ever before as a space for ideas, for discussion, and for informed debate. The stage is set, and we hope you will be inspired to join in the conversations to come.

NOTES

1 James, F. Cyril, Introduction to *The Interplay of East and West, Points of Conflict and Cooperation* by Barbara Ward (New York: W.W. Norton & Company, Inc., 1957), 5–6.
2 Correspondence from David Landsborough Thomson to F. Cyril James, 5 May 1952, RG2_C170_5944, McGill University Archives, Montreal, Quebec, Canada.
3 "Woman to Give Sir Edward Beatty Memorial Talks," *The Gazette* (Montreal, Quebec), 19 October 1955: 22.
4 Tom Perlmutter, "Beatty Lecturer: Dr Han Suyin Delivers Shock Treatments," *The McGill Reporter*, 18 November 1968: 4.
5 Ibid.
6 Mark Starowicz, "Kosher," *The McGill Daily*, 12 November 1968: 4.
7 Correspondence from T.S. Eliot to F. Cyril James, 2 December 1958, McGill University Archives, Montreal, Quebec, Canada.
8 Statement of expenses from Arnold Toynbee, 31 January 1961, RG2_C262_7857, McGill University Archives, Montreal, Quebec, Canada.
9 Mark A. Wainberg and Norbert Gilmore, "When AIDS Victim Arthur Ashe Spoke, They Listened," *The Gazette* (Montreal, Quebec), 13 March 1993: B6.

American writer Roxane Gay delivered the 2018 Beatty Lecture.
Used with permission of Joni Dufour.

An audience member asks Roxane Gay a question during the question-and-answer session after her 2018 Beatty Lecture. *Used with permission of Joni Dufour.*

Principal Cyril F. James, photographed in 1937, was appointed in 1940 by Chancellor Beatty and led the Beatty Lecture series during its first decade. *Used with permission of McGill University Archives, PR009604.*

McGILL UNIVERSITY
MONTREAL

MAY 20 1952

Faculty of Arts and Science

May 19, 1952.

Dr. F. Cyril James,
Principal and Vice-Chancellor,
McGill University.

Dear Mr. Principal:

Herewith a list of "possibles" for our Sir Edward Beatty Memorial Lecturer. I have left out Butterfield because he was at Queen's this winter and Oakeshott, because he has gone to London so recently that I doubt whether he will be able to get away. There are people such as Moberley, of whom you will have thought, and there are scientists, such as Schroedinger, about whom David will know more than I do. I have put an asterisk against some names for a possible short list.

Respectfully yours,

H. N. Fieldhouse
Dean

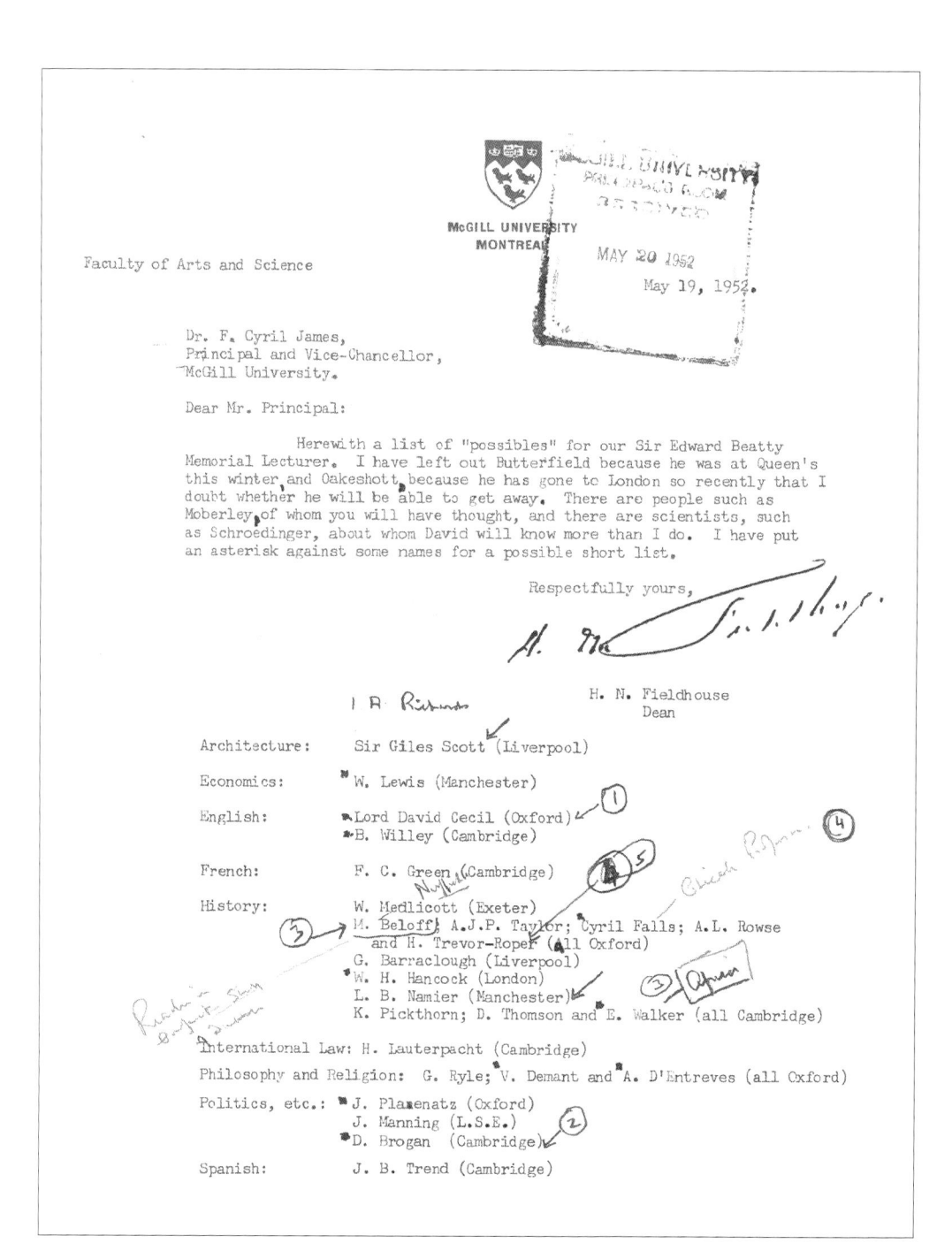

Architecture:	Sir Giles Scott (Liverpool)
Economics:	W. Lewis (Manchester)
English:	Lord David Cecil (Oxford)
	B. Willey (Cambridge)
French:	F. C. Green (Cambridge)
History:	W. Medlicott (Exeter)
	M. Beloff; A.J.P. Taylor; Cyril Falls; A.L. Rowse and H. Trevor-Roper (all Oxford)
	G. Barraclough (Liverpool)
	W. H. Hancock (London)
	L. B. Namier (Manchester)
	K. Pickthorn; D. Thomson and E. Walker (all Cambridge)
International Law:	H. Lauterpacht (Cambridge)
Philosophy and Religion:	G. Ryle; V. Demant and A. D'Entreves (all Oxford)
Politics, etc.:	J. Plamenatz (Oxford)
	J. Manning (L.S.E.)
	D. Brogan (Cambridge)
Spanish:	J. B. Trend (Cambridge)

Dean H.N. Fieldhouse provided Principal James with suggestions of lecturers from faculty members in a letter dated 19 May 1952. From this list, A. L. Rowse and Max Beloff would deliver the Beatty Lecture in 1963 and 1967 respectively. *Used with permission of McGill University Archives,* RG7_C105_132_2.

Sarvepalli Radhakrishnan, India's first vice president, delivered the inaugural Beatty Lecture on 4 October 1954. *Used with permission of Getty Images.*

SIR EDWARD BEATTY LECTURER: The first Sir Edward Beatty Memorial Lecturer at McGill University, Dr. Sarvapalli Radhakrishnan, vice-president of India and world-famed philosopher, chats with McGill Chancellor B. C. Gardner (right) and Principal and Vice-Chancellor F. Cyril James (left) shortly before delivering his lecture at McGill's Sir Arthur Currie Memorial Gymnasium last night.
(Gazette Photo Service)

Discord Between Mind and Spirit Bar Peace, Radhakrishnan Says

There will be no peace or safety in the world until man can heal the discord between his mind and his spirit, Dr. Servapalli Radhakrishnan, Vice-President of India and noted philosopher, told an audience of about 2,000 Montrealers last night.

In an address inaugurating the Edward Beatty Memorial lectures at McGill University, Dr. Radhakrishnan spoke of the religious and spiritual heritage of India, saying it formed the basis of the philosophic and religious thought of the East. The second lecture in the series, to be given Thursday, will deal with the West, and the third, scheduled for Friday, will deal with the meeting of East and West.

The H-bomb, said Dr. Radhakrishnan, is the symbol of man's intellectual achievement, but man must learn to put this and other achievements to good purpose, to reconcile the mind and the spirit.

"One of the great lessons of the spiritual heritage of India," he said, "is that man's intellectuality must grow to spirituality." Spiritual intuition and awareness is a greater source of light than discursive reason, he said.

Dr. Radhakrishnan traced the history of civilization in India back to the third millenium B.C. Recent archaeological discoveries, he said, had showed there was a highly developed culture flourishing in the valley of the Indus river about 3,000 B.C.

He traced the impact of various cultures which invaded India through the centuries—Arabic and Islamic, early Christian, later European Christian. Characteristic of the tradition of the East, he said, is religious tolerance.

"Dogma and doctrines are mere

Sarvepalli Radhakrishnan is flanked by Principal James to his left, and Chancellor B.C. Gardener to his right, in this *Montreal Gazette* photo taken the day after his inaugural lecture. *Used with permission of McGill University Archives, RG2_C170_5943_2.*

The Sir Edward Beatty Memorial Lectures

October 4, 7 and 8, 1954

Dr. Sarvepalli Radhakrishnan, the Vice-President of India, will deliver the first series of The Sir Edward Beatty Memorial Lectures in Redpath Hall at 8.30 p.m. on Monday October 4th, Thursday October 7th, and Friday October 8th.

These Lectures were established by the generous gift of the late Dr. H. A. Beatty to enable the University each year to invite a distinguished scholar to come as our guest and discuss one of the outstanding problems that confront our generation. Dr. Radhakrishnan has chosen the difficult subject of *East and West*, a problem that has many facets reflected in each day's newspaper, and he brings a unique background of experience to its consideration.

Immediately after his graduation from Madras Christian College, Dr. Radhakrishnan entered upon his chosen career of philosophy and became in succession a Professor at the Universities of Madras, Mysore and Calcutta. Administrative responsibilities as Vice-Chancellor of Andhra University from 1931 to 1936 did not interrupt his studies or dim the greatness of his international reputation, so that, in 1936, he was called to England by Oxford University as the first Spalding Professor of Eastern Religion and Ethics. Personal friend of Mahatma Gandhi and of the present Prime Minister of India, Dr. Radhakrishnan served Oxford, and the whole western world, for more than a decade by his brilliant exposition of Indian ideals and philosophy until his country, with the great challenge of independence confronting it, called him back to public service. As the first Indian Ambassador to Moscow, he established the present pattern of diplomatic relationships between the two countries and after his return to Delhi was, without opposition from any other candidate or party, elected to the Vice-Presidency.

No man in our time is better qualified to help us attain an understanding of the eastern world, and all who heard him deliver the Convocation Address at McGill University in May 1953, will remember the brilliance of his presentation. I am happy to extend to you a cordial invitation to attend these Lectures.

Since the seating accommodation in Redpath Hall is limited, no more than two tickets can be allotted to each recipient of this letter, and I should appreciate it if you would fill in the attached application at once, and either send it, or present it personally, to the Registrar's Office.

F. CYRIL JAMES.

To: The Registrar
    McGill University

Please deliver to bearer (or send to me at the address below) .... tickets for The Sir Edward Beatty Memorial Lectures to be delivered by Dr. Radhakrishnan.

Signed......................................

Address......................................

....

Announcement for the inaugural Beatty Lecture series in October 1954.
Used with permission of McGill University Archives, RG2_C170_5943.

Telegram dated 12 March 1954 from Sarvepalli Radhakrishnan to Principal James stating that his Beatty Lecture series can be announced. *Used with permission of McGill University Archives, RG2_C170_5943_P.*

English economist Barbara Ward delivered the 1955 Beatty Lecture.
Used with permission of the International Institute for Environment and Development (IIED).

McGILL UNIVERSITY

THE SIR EDWARD BEATTY MEMORIAL LECTURES
BY
BARBARA WARD

EAST AND WEST:
Contrasts and Elements of Collaboration

SIR ARTHUR CURRIE MEMORIAL GYMNASIUM-ARMOURY

8.30 p.m.
24, 27 and 31 October, 1955

A card used to promote Barbara Ward's Beatty Lecture series.
Used with permission of McGill University Archives, RG2_C170_5944_3.

Telegram from Barbara Ward (Lady Jackson) to Principal James stating, "Speeches now in shape after hard work." *Used with permission of McGill University Archives,* RG2_C170_5943_P.

Han Suyin delivered the Beatty Lecture in the Sir Arthur Currie Memorial Gymnasium in October, 1968. *Used with permission of McGill University Archives, PR013240.*

Han Suyin (*centre*) with Mrs Wilder Penfield (*right*) in the Osler Library. *Used with permission of McGill University Archives, PR013231.*

Former Soviet leader Mikhail Gorbachev at a press conference on campus before his 1993 Beatty Lecture. *Used with permission of McGill University Archives, PR050788.*

Canadian philosopher and McGill Professor Emeritus Charles Taylor delivered the 2017 Beatty Lecture on "The Challenge of Regressive Democracy." *Used with permission of Joni Dufour.*

Conservationist Jane Goodall delivered the Beatty Lecture in 1979 and in 2019, becoming the first repeat Beatty lecturer to date. *Used with permission of Joni Dufour.*

Personal   Ottawa, October 13, 1954.

F. Cyril James, Esq., Ph.D., F.R.E.S.,
   Principal and Vice-Chancellor,
      McGill University,
         Montreal, Quebec.

Dear Dr. James:

        I wish to thank you for your letter of October 12 and for transmitting the kind farewell message of Dr. Radhakrishnan to me.

        I was very pleased to learn that the lectures proved so successful and that he enjoyed his stay in this country. It is my sincere hope that this visit of an eminent Eastern scholar and statesman will have increased still further the friendship and understanding between the people of India and Canada.

        With kind personal regards,

              Yours sincerely,

              Louis S. St Laurent

A letter of congratulations from Prime Minister St Laurent to Principal James dated 13 October 1954. *Used with permission of McGill University Archives, RG2_C170_5943.*

Sir Geoffrey Faber, Chairman. Richard de la Mare, Vice-Chairman. Morley Kennerley (U.S.A.), T.S.Eliot, W.J.Crawley,
P. F. du Sautoy, Alan Pringle, David Bland, Charles Monteith

FABER AND FABER LTD PUBLISHERS

FABBAF, WESTCENT, LONDON
MUSeum 9543 (4 lines) 24 Russell Square London WC1

TSE/AM 2nd December, 1958.

The Vice-Principal,
McGill University,
Montreal, 2,
Canada.

Dear Mr. Vice-Principal,

I thank you for your letter of November 25th and I much appreciate the honour of being invited to lecture on the Beatty foundation at so distinguished a university. I have thought your proposal over carefully, but have come to the conclusion that it is so very unlikely that I should be able to visit America for a long enough period to spend three or four weeks in Montreal, that I am obliged, regretfully, to decline your invitation. My visits to the New World are primarily to visit old friends and relatives and, unless I were able to spend a number of months at a time in the States, a visit of four weeks would be out of the question. My visits have of necessity to be centred about the vicinity of Boston, Massachusetts, and I cannot go further afield for very long, when I am on your side of the water for only from four to six weeks.

I am most interested to know that Ted Spencer and Eloise were friends of yours and also that you know the family of Miss Macfadyen, who has actually typed this letter for me.

Yours sincerely,

T. S. Eliot

Irish poet T. S. Eliot politely declined McGill's invitation to lecture in 1958.
Used with permission of McGill University Archives.

Australian economist Douglas Copland, photographed here meeting the press before his Beatty Lecture series in 1961 (*he is seated on couch, left*). *Used with permission of McGill University Archives, PR050788.*

American tennis champion and activist Arthur Ashe stood at the Beatty Lecture podium in 1992 to speak about "Living with AIDS." *Used with permission of McGill University Archives, PR050788.*

Polish composer Witold Lutoslawski, photographed here with McGill students, delivered the Beatty Lecture in 1993 and received an honorary degree from McGill's Faculty of Music. *Used with permission of McGill University Archives, PR051207.*

Tanzanian diplomat Anna Tibaijuka delivered the Beatty Lecture in 2007. *Used with permission of Owen Egan.*

Among the notable Canadians to have delivered the Beatty Lecture, author Margaret Atwood in 2016. *Used with permission of Owen Egan.*

Audience members line up to ask Muhammad Yunus questions during the question-and-answer session for his 2010 Beatty Lecture. *Used with permission of Stephane Desjardins.*

Sir Edward Wentworth Beatty: A Life of Service

Robin Koning

When the president of the Canadian Pacific Railway (CPR), Edward Wentworth Beatty, officially became McGill University's sixth chancellor in 1920, the event took place with little fanfare, just as he wanted. According to the *McGill News*, "there was no installation ceremony, little publicity, and no ballyhoo ... anything even faintly dramatic or theatrical rang false in his ear and worried him."[1]

A year later, Beatty made his first public appearance as chancellor of McGill, presiding over the university's great Centenary Convocation. In the one hundred years since its founding, McGill had grown into an institution that newspapers heralded, "the pride of Canada."[2] In his speech, Beatty spoke about the great purpose of the university, namely, to uphold the life and intellectual needs of the people. The celebrations that day were filled with much pomp and circumstance – fifty-four honorary degrees were conferred, including upon Canada's Governor General Sir Julian Byng. The new chancellor received high praise in the *McGill News*, which declared, "Our rookie Chancellor stepped straight into a world-series convocation and calmly hit a home run."[3]

As both the president of the world's largest privately owned transportation system and as McGill's chancellor, Beatty spent the better part of his life in the public eye. Despite reaching great heights of success, he carried himself without pretension or grandiosity. He had the reputation of being entirely natural with everyone he spoke to, from porters to pastors, professors to prime ministers. At his core, Beatty was a man of service who simply wanted to roll up his shirtsleeves and get down to the duties of the day.

At McGill, Beatty is best remembered for his life-long devotion to the university's students. On Saturday afternoons, he could be found sitting in the bleachers with students and cheering on McGill's football team. As McGill's Principal F. Cyril James recalled, "At Convocation, the jaunty angle of his cap was somehow more important than the solemn formality of the gold laced gown, and his message to the graduating class was the counsel of an elder brother who understood his fellows and loved them."[4]

EARLY YEARS (1877–1900)

Edward Wentworth Beatty was born in Thorold, Ontario on 16 October 1877, the third son and fourth child of Henry Beatty and his wife Harriet M. Powell. Harriet was from Coburg, Ontario and a relative of the Masseys, a prominent Canadian family who built their fortune manufacturing farm tools. Another major lecture series, the CBC's Massey Lectures, was created in 1961 in honour of Vincent Massey, heir to the family business and Canada's governor general from 1952 to 1959.

Henry immigrated with his family from Ireland to Thorold at the age of nine, and later worked as an apprentice in a hardware business. People described him as a man of unusual executive ability and vision, qualities his son Edward would inherit. Henry followed the gold rush to California and then British Columbia, returning to Thorold with $40,000 in his pockets. He then joined his uncle's steamship business, the Beatty Line of Sarnia, but left the company in 1882 to join the CPR's lake shipping interests as a manager.

In 1887, the Beatty family moved to Toronto so that the children – Edward, his sister Mary, and brother Henry – could pursue higher education. Back then, few would have predicted young Edward Beatty's future rise to great heights. More at home on a rugby pitch than behind a stack of books, Edward was expelled from his first preparatory school, managing to complete his education only with the help of a tutor at Upper Canada College.

While newspapers would one day proclaim Beatty a born-leader of the CPR, his early ambitions had nothing to do with the railways or the steamships that his father managed. "I really wanted to be a doctor but my older brother, with not the slightest regard for my own feelings, decided that he was to be a doctor, and that left the law for me since I felt not the call for the Church, and I couldn't think of any other profession,"[5] he is quoted as saying.

In 1898, Beatty graduated with a degree in political science from the University of Toronto. He continued his studies at Osgoode Hall Law School and then apprenticed at a Toronto law firm. In June 1901, Beatty was called to the Ontario bar. A month later, a partner in the firm became general counsel to the CPR and Beatty moved with him to Montreal to work as his assistant at the national headquarters located at Windsor Street Station. "I thought a year's work in Montreal would be a useful experience," Beatty recalled, "but the work was fascinating. I was learning new things all the time."[6]

LEADING THROUGH BOOM, BUST, AND WAR (1901–1942)

Fiercely devoted to his new job, Beatty quickly rose in the ranks at the CPR, from assistant solicitor, to general counsel, to vice president. "In my first ten years I took ten days holidays, there was too much to do,"[7] he said. Despite his promotions, Beatty once considered an offer to leave and become a partner in a major Toronto law firm. As Beatty would often recall, CPR President Lord Thomas Shaughnessy persuaded him to stay by cajoling him with the question, "Do you want to be an ordinary lawyer all your life, or do you want to be president of the CPR?"[8]

In 1918, Shaughnessy retired and offered Beatty the job as president. Just days before his forty-first birthday, Beatty became the first Canadian-born head of the CPR. He now oversaw nationwide and international train lines that ran from London to Hong Kong, a global steamship line, a telegraph system, a hotel chain, 15 million acres of land and a billion dollars in investments. No wonder the press described Beatty as "the man with the world's biggest job."[9] Though Beatty's youth and lack of practical railway experience made his presidency a controversial decision among company ranks, he rapidly proved his merit.

One year later, McGill University elected Beatty as a governor. At the time, Prime Minister Robert Borden served as chancellor, but when he resigned due to poor health in 1920, the university appointed Beatty to the position. McGill and the CPR traditionally had close ties, and Beatty held personal interest in youth work, but few could have predicted the long relationship Beatty and the university were forging together.

Beatty's first ten years at the helm of the CPR saw tremendous growth across the company, including line extensions, hotel construction, and the expansion of shipping fleets. From 1925 to 1929, the CPR's earnings reached the peak in its history. But when the 1920s boom turned bust, Beatty faced the daunting task of steering the CPR through the Great Depression. Thanks to his sound fiscal management, the CPR entered the economic downturn debt free, unlike its rival the Canadian National Railway.

In his role as chancellor, Beatty also sought to ensure the financial health of the university. From 1935 to 1939, Beatty created the Governor's Guarantee Fund, which required McGill's governors to provide enough funds to balance the university's books. And despite the great challenges facing McGill's graduating class of 1934, Beatty bolstered them with an optimistic convocation address: "What are the qualifications for success? What will be the evidence that the years spent within these walls have not been wasted? Not wealth. Not visible and material success as the world has measured it in my lifetime. I suggest to you that your generation will be wiser than those who preceded you, and that you will know that success is but another name for happiness and that happiness lies within the reach of every human being."[10]

In a rare bright moment during this period of economic depression, on 23 June 1935, King George V recognized Beatty's achievements in public services, educational activities, and philanthropy, making him a Knight Grand Cross of the Most Excellent Order of the British Empire. As the *Montreal Gazette* reported, "Sir Edward ranks easily among the foremost citizens of the Dominion and the honor that has been bestowed upon him by His Majesty could not be better placed."[11]

After weathering the Great Depression, Beatty faced yet another challenge: leading the CPR through World War II. As the Canadian representative for the British Ministry of War Transport, he organized the operation of the Atlantic Bridge, a colossal undertaking that flew CPR Air Service transport bombers between Canada and Britain. The CPR ultimately shipped 307 million tons of freight and 86 million passengers by land, including 280,000 military personnel. Twenty-two CPR ships went to war, twelve of which sunk in combat.

"MCGILL WAS TRULY IN HIS HEART" (1940–1943)

During the course of his tenure as chancellor of McGill, Beatty oversaw many important milestones in the life of the university: the opening of the Montreal Neurological Institute and the Research Institute of Endocrinology; the establishment of the Faculty of Graduate Studies and Research, the Faculty of Music, and the School of Graduate Nurses; the construction of the Sir Arthur Currie Memorial Gymnasium – the future first home of the Beatty Lecture; the completion of a new wing of the Royal Victoria College; and the enrollment of over six thousand McGill women and men in the Canadian Armed and Auxiliary Forces at the start of World War II.

However, by the 1940s, Beatty's health had declined, likely a result of years of overworking. In 1941, he suffered a massive stroke. His doctors persuaded him to resign as CPR president, but he maintained his position as the company's chairman and refused to give up his duties as McGill's chancellor. On one notable occasion, an ill and hospitalized Beatty briefly left his sickbed to watch a McGill convocation ceremony through his car window. As described in the *McGill News*, "McGill was truly in his heart. Anything that affected the University was a matter of deep concern to him, and he was tremendously proud in an unobtrusive way of his Chancellorship."[12]

Edward Beatty died from heart failure at the Royal Victoria Hospital in Montreal on 23 March 1943, at the age of 65. His funeral took place at the Church of St Andrew and St Paul in downtown Montreal. The funeral did not feature a eulogy of Beatty's life, only prayers and two hymns, as he had instructed. The proceedings for Beatty's funeral, however, reflected his reputation as a national hero. Thousands of people lined the streets to pay their respects. McGill cancelled all afternoon classes so that students and faculty could honour their former chancellor. Montreal's

CPR offices closed at noon. Prime Minister Mackenzie King and Quebec's premier, Joseph-Adélard Godbout, attended the funeral. Among the pallbearers were McGill's Principal James and Donald Cuthbert Coleman, the latter who succeeded Beatty as CPR president. Vincent Massey, then Canadian High Commissioner to the United Kingdom, led a memorial service held in London, England.

Addressing the press, Prime Minister King stated, "From the time of his appointment as president of the CPR in 1918 to his resignation of that office about a year ago, Sir Edward Beatty held a position in public esteem second to none among those who have been foremost in the life of Canada … To the zeal for great causes to which he gave of his time and talents so unsparingly, he brought exceptional gifts of scholarship, broad-mindedness and high-principled leadership."[13]

The glowing obituary in the *McGill News* for Beatty underscored his unwavering devotion to the university that he called home: "Finally when the doctors ordered him to drop as much as possible of the voluntary burden he carried, McGill was something he would not yield, and he died our Chancellor."[14]

A PHILANTHROPIC LEGACY

Beatty died unwed and without heirs. On his deathbed, he left half of his estate to various charities. He had given generously to McGill in his lifetime, including through two annual scholarships, one for Greek and Latin and one for mathematics, for which he personally selected the beneficiaries.

Beatty's philanthropic and educational work extended beyond McGill. He also served as trustee and president of the Royal Victoria Hospital in Montreal, president of the Shawbridge Farm School, governor of Lower Canada College in Montreal, president of the Boy Scouts of Canada, chairman of the Rhodes Scholarship selection committee for the Province of Quebec, and chancellor of Queen's University.

In 1952, McGill received a $100,000 gift from Dr Henry A. Beatty in memory of his brother, to establish a lecture in his name. In the century since Beatty first donned the McGill chancellor's cap, his legacy has grown, thanks in large part to his family's generous gift. The Beatty Lecture is now one of Canada's oldest and most renowned lectureships. It is an enduring chapter in the story of a man devoted to the country he served and to the exchange of big ideas.

NOTES

1 T.H. Matthews, "Sir Edward Wentworth Beatty," *McGill News*, Summer 1943: 7.
2 "McGill University and its New Chancellor," *The Morning News* (Coffeyville, Kansas), 15 November 1921: 3.
3 Ibid.

4 F. Cyril James, "Sir Edward Beatty," *McGill Yearbook*, 1943: 8.
5 "Railway Chief Meant to be a Doctor," *The Winnipeg Evening Tribune* (Winnipeg, Manitoba), 4 February 1928: page unknown.
6 Ibid.
7 Ibid.
8 Don Nerbas, *Dominion of Capital: The Politics of Big Business and the Crisis of the Canadian Bourgeoisie, 1914–1947* (Toronto: University of Toronto Press, 2013), 119.
9 "The Man With The World's Biggest Job," *The Malayan Saturday Post* (Singapore), 20 June 1931: 18.
10 Edward W. Beatty, "Playing the Game," *Saturday Night*, 19 July 1934: page unknown.
11 "Noted Canadians Honored by King," *The Gazette* (Montreal, Quebec), 3 June 1935: 10.
12 Matthews, "Sir Edward," 7.
13 "Leaders of Nation," 1.
14 Matthews, "Sir Edward," 8.

Edward Beatty, McGill chancellor from 1920 to 1943, photographed at a 1942 convocation ceremony. *Used with permission of McGill University Archives, PR029085.*

Athletically rather than scholarly inclined, Beatty captained the University of Toronto rugby team, as photographed here in 1897. *Used with permission of Exporail, Canadian Pacific Railway Company Fonds.*

Beatty at the CPR headquarters in Montreal in 1919, a year after his appointment as the company's first Canadian-born president. *Used with permission of Queen's University Archives.*

EDWARD WENTWORTH BEATTY, B.A., K.C.
President, Canadian Pacific Railway

A photoengraving by Quebec political cartoonist Arthur George Racey dated 1922.
Used with permission of the McCord Museum, M20111.9.

Beatty circa 1920s, location unknown.
Used with permission of Exporail, Canadian Pacific Railway Company Fonds.

Beatty and CPR staff at Cameron Lake, British Columbia, date unknown. *Used with permission of Exporail, Edward Beatty Fonds.*

Photographs from Beatty's "Annual Inspection Trip" scrapbook in 1929 shows a CPR train stationed in Field, British Columbia. *Used with permission of Exporail, Edward Beatty Fonds.*

A CPR tourist postcard of McGill's downtown campus in 1928.
Used with permission of McGill University Archives, PU023162.

Beatty stands to the left of British Prime Minister Ramsay McDonald at his honorary degree ceremony in 1929. *Used with permission of McGill University Archives, 2014-0031.04.3.*

Beatty resigned from the CPR due to failing health in 1942 but remained Chancellor until his death one year later. *Used with permission of McGill University Archives, RG2_C87_2410.*

One of the few portraits of Beatty in his later years, circa 1940s. *Used with permission of McGill University Archives, 1940_0481.04.155.*

A caricature of Beatty in his chancellor's cap and gown that hangs on the walls of McGill's Faculty Club, dated 1935. *Used with permission of McGill University Archives, PR028124.*

Past Beatty Lectures

2020   Steven Pinker, "Progress and Enlightenment in the 21st Century"
2019   Jane Goodall, "Journey from the Jungle"
2018   Roxane Gay, "Difficult Women, Bad Feminists, and Unruly Bodies"
2017   Charles Taylor, "The Challenge of Regressive Democracy"
2016   Margaret Atwood, "Humanities in an Age of Environmental Crisis"
2015   John Wood, "Whose Version of the Future is Going to Win?"
2014   Karl Deisseroth, "Illuminating the Brain"
2013   Witold Rybczynski, "Architecture and the Passage of History"
2012   Kerry Courneya, "Physical Activity in Cancer Survivors: A Field in Motion"
2011   Alfred Brendel, "Does Classical Music Have to be Entirely Serious?"
2010   Muhammad Yunus, "Building Social Business: The New Kind of Capitalism that Serves Humanity's Most Pressing Needs"
2009   Marc Tessier-Lavigne, "Brain Development and Brain Repair: The Life and Death of Nerve Cells"
2008   James Gustave Speth, "Capitalism and the Environment: From Crisis to Sustainability"
2007   Anna Tibaijuka, "Divided Cities: Caught Between Hope and Despair"
2006   Richard Dawkins, "Queerer Than We Suppose: The Strangeness of Science"
2006   Deepak Chopra, "Religion and Spirituality"
2005   Michael Ignatieff, "Canada in the World: The Challenges Ahead"
2004   Steven Sanderson, "Global Poverty Alleviation and the Impoverishment of Wild Nature"
2004   Shirin Ebadi, "Democracy: The Precondition to Peace"
2003   Herman E. Daly, "Uneconomic Growth and The Illth of Nations: Defining the Optimal Scale of the Macro Economy"
2002   Sandra Steingraber, "Protecting the First Environment: The Ecology of Pregnancy and Childbirth"

2002	Richard John Neuhaus, "Liberal Democracy and Acts of Faith"
2002	William Galston, "Religion and Liberal Society"
2002	Queen Noor of Jordan, "Creating a Culture of Peace"
2002	John Maddox, "What Remains to be Discovered"
2002	Wangari Maathai, "Standing up for the Environment"
2000	Vartan Gregorian, "Libraries and Reading in the Computer Age"
2000	Jonathan Miller, "Laughing Matters: Humour and Comedy"
2000	Paul Crutzen, "The Importance of the Tropics in Atmospheric Chemistry"
1999	Steven Mithen, "Becoming Human: The Evolution of Mind and Language"
1999	Paul Ewald, "What's Catching: The Darwinism of Disease"
1999	Eugenie C. Scott, "The Great Controversy"
1999	Carl Djerassi, "Science-in-fiction is Not Science Fiction"
1998	Luc Montagnier, "AIDS on the Threshold of the Year 2000: Merging Western Experiences and African Realities"
1997	Cicely Saunders, "Lessons in Living from the Dying"
1997	Oliver Sacks, "Neurology and the Soul"
1997	John Horgan, "The End of Science"
1996	Bernard Kouchner, "Conflict Prevention in An Age of Global Anxiety"
1996	Roger Schank, "Why Most Schooling is Irrelevant: Computers and the Future of Learning"
1995	Yves Coppens, "From Africa, the Cradle, to America, the New World: The Prehistory of Man and the Peopling of the Earth"
1995	Catherine Bertini, "Women Eat Last"
1994	Paul Sacher, "Paul Sacher Remembers Béla Bartók"
1994	Nancy Wexler, "Huntington's Disease: Member of an Expanding Family of Disorders"
1994	David Akers-Jones, "Hong Kong Horizons"
1994	Rudolph Marcus, "Life in Science: Interaction of Theory and Experiments"
1994	Margaret Drabble, "The Corpse in the Garden: Concealments and Disclosures in Fiction and Biography"
1993	Barbara Ehrenreich, "Can Feminism Change the World?"
1993	Witold Lutoslawski, "About the Element of Chance in Music"
1993	Mikhail Gorbachev, "The New World Order"
1993	Jacques Attali, "Europe on the World Stage in the Twenty-First Century"
1992	Arthur Ashe, "Living with AIDS"

1991	Pierre Boulez, "Répons: How to Develop a Musical Idea"
1991	C. N. Yang, "Symmetry and Physics"
1990	Daniel Boorstin, "America: Discovery, Invention, or Creation?"
1990	Francis Bretherton, "Understanding the Earth System"
1990	Norman Myers, "Safeguarding the Biosphere: What Cost? What Payoff?"
1990	Gerald Edelman, "Morphology and Mind"
1989	Sally Falk Moore, "Nationalism, Cultural Pluralism, and the State"
1988	Kirk Varnedoe, "Fine Disregard: Inventions in Early Modern Art"
1987	Christopher Hill, "Milton and the English Revolution"
1987	John Mortimer, "The Art of Advocacy" and "Clinging to the Wreckage"
1985	Francis Crick, "How Do We See Things?"; "The Search-Light Hypothesis"; and "The Problem of Awareness"
1984	William McCarthy, "The Limits of Trade Union Power"
1983	I. F. Stone, "The Trial of Socrates Revisited: What Plato Doesn't Tell Us"
1982	Gwendolen Carter, "Apartheid: Dying or Resurgent?" and "The African States Seek Economic Liberation"
1981	Saunders Mac Lane, "How Mathematicians Get New Ideas" and "Distortion of Science by Politics"
1981	Ralf Dahrendorf, "A Swing to the Right? Socio-political Changes in the Western World" and "The European Community at the Beginning of the 1980s"
1979	Ved Mehta, "Mahatma Gandhi and Modern India"
1979	Richard Feynman, "Light and Matter, The Modern View: Photons Particles of Light"; "Quantum Behaviour"; and "Interaction of Light and Matter"
1979	Jane Goodall, "Chimpanzees in the Wild: Perspectives on Primate Behaviour"
1977	E. O. Wilson, "The Evolution of Social Behaviour"
1977	Edwin Reischauer, "Japanese-American Relations"
1976	Derek de Solla Price, "Craftsmanship and Jigsawpuzzling in Science"
1976	Alexander King, "A New Economic Order: Is it Necessary or Feasible?"
1975	Yehudi Menuhin, "Interpretation in Music and in Life"
1975	Fred Hoyle, "The Emergence of Intelligence in the Universe"; "Cosmological Theories and Controversies"; and "The History of Matter"
1974	Robert N. Bellah, "Relevance of Man's Religious Experience"

1973	Saul Bellow, "Joyce's Ulysses: A Personal View"
1972	Robert Sinsheimer, "Genetic Engineering: Ambush or Opportunity?"
1971	Peter Ritchie-Calder, "Science and Social Change: Science and International Relations"; "Science and Human Rights"; and "Science and Posterity"
1968	Han Suyin, "Asia Today"; "Asia Yesterday"; and "Asia Tomorrow"
1967	Max Beloff, "Commonwealth Weakness, Britain"
1964	E. E. Rich, "Montreal and the Fur Trade: The French Background"; "The American Frontier"; and "The Northwest Company"
1963	A. L. Rowse, "The Political Uses of History"; "The Role of Germany in Modern History"; and "The Responsibility of the Historian"
1961	Douglas Copland, "The Changing Structure of the Western Economy"
1961	Arnold Toynbee, "The Present Day Experiment in Western Civilization: The Experiment in Hellenization"; "The Attraction of the Western Way of Life"; and "Parliamentary Democracy on Trial"
1959	Morris Bishop, "The Great River at the White Man's Coming"; "The Missionary and the Coureur du Bois: Sagard and Brandûlé"; and "Champlain"
1956	Julian Huxley, "The Possibilities of Life, Mind, Man"
1955	Barbara Ward, "The Interplay of East and West, Points of Conflict and Cooperation"
1954	Sarvepalli Radhakrishnan, "India and World Affairs"

A Note on the Selection of Lectures

At the time of publication, ninety incredible individuals have delivered the Beatty Lecture at McGill University. Until 2005, more than one Beatty Lecture could occur in a year. Only recently has the Beatty Lecture become a singular annual event. The lectures herein selected for this anthology represent the past seven decades of the Beatty Lecture series' history and scope, which included science, healthcare, social development, literature, political science, the arts, and music. The texts have been slightly edited for readability and clarity, and in some cases, certain spelling has been modified. Unfortunately, some of the lectures we had hoped to include in the anthology are missing, due to the fact that recordings or transcripts do not exist for every lecture, particularly those from the 1980s to the early 2000s. In other cases, although the lecture transcript exists, the copyright permission could not be secured. Finally, other recent lecturers used slides, or, as in the case of Austrian pianist and writer Alfred Brendel's 2011 Beatty Lecture, included performance to a degree that is difficult to capture in print. Fortunately, a recording of Brendel's lecture and many others can be accessed at the Beatty Lecture Digital Archive website (www.mcgill.ca/beatty).

Barbara Ward. *Used with permission of the International Institute for Environment and Development (IIED).*

1

The Interplay of East and West, Points of Conflict and Cooperation

31 October 1955

Barbara Ward

INTRODUCTION

In 1955, Barbara Ward saw a world riven with fractures. Europe was in decline, America was on the rise, Eastern Europe was under Communism, and the Far East was in revolt. With her assessment of an unbalanced world order, it is hard not to hear in Ward's Beatty Lecture of that year the tones of our own existential discomfort more than half a century later. Equally, the argument Ward puts in the Beatty Lecture is embedded in her historically specific sense of the "profound political dilemma," what she describes as the relationship between "the great civilizations of the Orient and ourselves." Weighing up the relative influence of nationalism, communism, and internationalism, her theme is the "interplay" between the West and the East, both Eastern Europe or Asia. The tensions in her approach here – between the claims of nation and the promise of the international, between her vision of cultural diversity and a "planetary" perspective – echo across the next two decades of her public career.

Born in 1914, educated at Oxford, where Arnold Toynbee[1] was among her mentors, Barbara Ward lived at the nexus of extraordinary personal and institutional networks, particularly for a woman. As a relatively young woman, she worked at the UK Ministry of Information, and at *The Economist* she rose to foreign editor. At the time of Ward's visit to McGill University, she was married to Robert Jackson, a man closely associated with the United Nations, and living on the Gold Coast, still a British colony, where she characteristically built strong local connections. As important to the fashioning of Ward's intellectual outlook was her active Catholicism, to the extent that it motivated her anti-communism as much as the defence of a "Western" political and economic way of life. Not uncoincidentally, in the full version of her lecture, Ward insists that the rediscovery of "the purpose of life" was the only solid foundation of the moral as well as economic unity of East and West.

Much in Ward's message rehearses the idiosyncrasies of her personal views, education, and experiences. This includes now outdated conceptions of nationalism as a natural feeling that evolved from ancient tribal forms, and the superior functionality of linguistically hegemonic states, with Britain, France, and Spain as the ideal. As importantly, Ward is future-looking, as she notices that science and technology, communication and travel, "the whole organization of economic life" are "making complete nonsense of any nation's claim, even the largest, to be totally sovereign and self-contained." Indeed, because the world is "so small and so integrated … it must find some form of social and political order which transcends all these supposedly sovereign units."

Yet, Ward is surprisingly wary of investing in the relatively new inter-national institution, the United Nations, as still too infant to have proven its worth. Instead, she offers "minimal" institutions to be used for peaceful arbitration and economic governance. She even confirms the relevance of the World Bank, International Monetary Fund, and an organization that she imagines might deal with world trade (the World Trade Organization was invented in 1995). Arriving at the view that this is "a perfectly new situation," Ward goes so far as to suggest the necessity for "institutions for mankind as a whole – a planetary system, if you like." Her later books, *Spaceship Earth* (1966), *Only One Earth* (1972), and *Progress for a Small Planet* (1979), will take this suggestion to a fuller conclusion, by insisting on the ineluctability of global interdependence and the mutually entangled future of economics and the earth.

In 1955, Ward's Beatty Lecture only glimpses these ambitions. However, if we read it from the confusion of our own international order in crisis, it stands as a reminder that even when "parochialism and national myopia" are at their peak, people and ideas, not determinism, decide history; that we should rise to the obligation of asking ourselves, "if there is anything else upon which we can draw to raise our sights a little, and give an international order some kind of wider backing, some greater vision and stronger ideal."

*

Glenda Sluga is Professor of International History and Capitalism at the European University Institute in Florence, and also Professor of International History, and ARC Kathleen Fitzpatrick Laureate Fellow at the University of Sydney. In 2020, she was awarded a European Research Council Advanced Grant, overseeing a five-year research program on "Twentieth Century International Economic Thinking and the Complex History of Globalization."

LECTURE

W. W. Norton & Company published Barbara Ward's three Beatty Lectures in 1957 in a book titled *The Interplay of East and West, Points of Conflict and Cooperation*. The following is an excerpt from the third lecture presented on 31 October 1955.

When we turn to consider the political relations between East and West, we have to admit that today, as indeed for the last hundred years, they are dominated by the fact of nationalism. Indeed, one could argue that the master institution produced in the political life of the West in the last six hundred years is the nation state. It has drawn its strength from many roots. First of all, it goes back to the tribe itself and to the sense of protection which man, faced with fear of an unknown and largely hostile universe, felt from gathering together with his kin. In the protective, co-operative group of clan or extended family he could defend himself against his neighbour, establish his control over hunting fields and fishing rights and generally carve out a small area of certainty and security.

Perhaps this tribal feeling is the deepest of all our aspirations. It is certainly one of the oldest. From the very beginning of organized political life among mankind the sense of belonging to one group and not belonging to another has been enormously strong. Then, as civilizations developed, the old feeling of the tribe or clan developed into the idea of loyalty to the clan chief and loyalty to the dynasty. History witnessed a whole series of dynastic states in which the sense of "belonging," in so far as it was felt at levels higher than the village community, was linked to the person of the king. But, admittedly, this positive loyalty of owing allegiance to one monarch was stimulated most fiercely in times of dynastic war. Patriotism was no doubt a high virtue but its strongest expression was often the readiness to maim and kill those who did not accept the same loyalties.

In our modern world these old, long-established, deep rooted political institutions have taken a new and what I fear one can only call a more virulent form. The reason may partly be a matter of coincidence. Three states which, on a dynastic basis, were established most early in Western Europe also offered a unique coincidence of language and frontier. In Spain, in France, and in Britain, three of the first kingdoms to develop from medieval dynastic politics to what we would now call the modern nation state, the linguistic and geographical frontiers overlapped to a degree which is far from usual in the world at large. A more usual pattern in human history has seen many different language groups ruled together by a single dynasty. This pattern was broken in Western Europe. The idea therefore grew up that a man who spoke the same language was a brother and fellow citizen and anyone who did not was an alien.

This extreme concept of solidarity by tongue has lain at the root of a great many troubles in Europe ever since the first crystallization of modern nationhood in Britain, France, and Spain. It has not only added a lethal edge to war. It is totally inappropriate to areas of mixed language such as the old Austro-Hungarian Empire, for example, where there was no possibility of making frontiers and languages coincide.

Nationalism has been further enhanced by the growth of democracy. If everyone has a right to participate in the political control of the state, then everyone tends to feel that there is far more at stake in the state than the fortunes of this or that dynasty. A citizen's own private and personal fortunes are involved in what happens to the community. His sense of oneness with his own society is inevitably reinforced, and democracy and nationalism grow together.

Last of all – and this is perhaps the most serious of all developments – modern industry has grown up and drawn the whole community into a web of production, trade, and commerce. Local differences in the economy vanish. A man's whole livelihood no longer depends entirely on the village or the valley, or a local type of agriculture. It is bound up with the fortunes of the national market. Each citizen shares in the economic interests of the state and the state becomes the representative of the total economic life and interests of the people. Trade is no longer a fringe activity conducted by a few merchants; trade is the life-blood of the nation and if the country cannot trade or prosper, the life of every citizen is exposed. Thus, as Professor Arnold Toynbee has pointed out with extraordinary vividness, into the old institution of the dynastic state, with its limited political loyalty, we have poured two enormously powerful molten-lava streams of political energy. One is the identification of the citizen with his stake in democracy. The other is the total identification of his interests with the industrial and economic life of the country.

The new wine in the old bottles has proved an intoxicating brew. The modern nation state virtually admits no rule beyond its own, no interest beyond its frontiers, and no check, even theoretical, upon its sovereignty. And this, first produced in the Western world, was the instrument through which Western life has, in the last four hundred years, been carried out into Asia, and, as pointed out above, it came in a highly aggressive form. The spirit of nationalist aggression first came to the notice of men in the East in the shape of bitter national struggles between different trading groups, between Portuguese and Dutch, between French and British. Serious Eastern observers, accustomed to the "live and let live" policies usually pursued by earlier traders, particularly the Arab traders, were amazed and indeed disgusted to see that there was virtually nothing that a merchant of one European nation would not do to a merchant of another nation provided he could get rid of his competition. At the next stage of Western encroachment, the nations of Europe had developed their industrial strength, and national rivalry was now used as part of a pattern establishing colonial and imperial control over Asian lands. Indeed, one of the reasons why the Japanese excluded all foreigners for over two hundred years was because they had come to the conclusion that the merchants from Europe were always the entering point, the wedge, for the coming of political control exercised by a European nation. At the same time, although the impact of Western economic policies on Asia was in many ways progressive and dynamic, it also involved a large element of exploitation and the sacrificing of the interests of the local people to that of distant Western European nations; capitalism and exploitation, capitalism and imperialism, became synonymous in the minds of Eastern peoples.

Today, we have entered a new phase. Nationalism in the exclusive arrogant Western sense has become the guiding star of Asia. The habit of intense nationalism has been caught from us because Asians came to believe that this was the only way in which they could ever meet us on our own terms. For the last fifty years and more, Asia has been undergoing the type of national revolution which occurred a century or so earlier in Europe. The concept of the dynastic state has largely disappeared. In its place Asian peoples are enshrining the nation state. The Japanese, for all their theoretical devotion to the Emperor, led the way. In India, the spirit of exclusive nationalism led to the tragic split between Hindu and Muslim in which religion served as the new determinant of nationalism and divided the subcontinent into two states. In areas like Kashmir, nationalism determines a government to impose its will upon a local people even if the local people are not particularly anxious to receive that form of political control. In Indonesia, Javanese nationalism suppressed a federal form of structure and imposed a unitary state. But perhaps the most remarkable illustration of the strength of this new nationalism that has swept Asia lies in the fact that it is proving in many ways stronger than Communism itself. I do not mean to suggest that nationalism, as such, is sufficient to counter Communism. We have seen in China how the nationalistic dictatorship of General Chiang Kai-shek was in fact defeated by the Communists. But the Communism of Mao Tso Tung is a thoroughly national Communism. A first step after victory in 1949 was to send Chinese troops into areas such as Tibet, once loosely under Chinese national control. Another instance is the attempt to mobilize the overseas Chinese in Southeast Asia in the interests of Communism. In short, China is following the example of the Soviet Union where Communism began as an international movement but has tended more and more to become subordinate to the interests of Great Russian policy. We can surely say that any force that is strong enough to master the great supernational ideology of the twentieth century must be a very formidable force indeed.

This development may mean that Communism has the best chance of exploiting nationalism to the fullest. But it also means that once we are confronted with a Communist revolution, we should not think for one moment that we are rid of nationalism. One need only cite the example of Tito in Yugoslavia and his long feud with his large Communist neighbour. Communism can exploit nationalism but nationalism can also penetrate and completely permeate Communism. One consequence, incidentally, of this development is to refute the Communist claim that Communism alone provides a basis for world order. When it comes to the crucial point, Communism becomes one more instrument in the hands of aggressive nationalism.

This frantic development of nationalism may have been set on its way quite inadvertently by us (the number of things that the West has inadvertently started is really startling), but it has now reached its climax with the attempt of virtually all states in the world to organize themselves on the basis of the nation state. And, by history's greatest and potentially most tragic ironies, this worldwide opting for total, unfettered national sovereignty has come at a time when science and technology are making complete nonsense of any nation's claim, even the largest, to be totally sovereign and self-contained. Think of changes that have occurred in communications, in travel, in the whole organization of economic life in the last hundred years. They point in one direction only, towards a world so small and so integrated that it must find some form of social and political order which transcends all these supposedly sovereign units. We have reached the quintessence of nationalism just when, from the point of view of industrial, economic, and social organization, exclusive nationalism has become completely impracticable.

This is the profound political dilemma with which we are living and it is a dilemma not only of the West. It is a dilemma of East and West together and at this point there is not much difference between the problems that lie ahead for either sector. We can say perhaps that we in the West who have lived with nationalism rather longer are possibly less excited by it than those new nations in Asia or those emergent nations in Africa for whom nationalism is a new strong drink only tasted in this century. But from the point of view of any kind of sane world order, it is nonsense in West or East to suppose that all these various competing and anarchical sovereignties can prosper without any form of organization which transcends them, or any form of order which coordinates their activities and helps them to avoid the gravest forms of clash. The fact that the notion is nonsense does not, of course, mean that mankind is not going to attempt to perpetrate it. But nonsense it remains and potentially violent, dark, destructive nonsense at that.

However, the scale of the folly may now help to induce new ideas. Our grandchildren may look back upon this age and be grateful to the atomic bomb and the hydrogen bomb because they realize that in no other way could it be demonstrated to a blinded humanity just what folly its arrogant parochialism had become. If weapons can now blow up a whole continent, if even a quite limited use of modern weapons can extinguish the human species, then, clearly, men have some overriding interest in common, however unwilling mankind as a whole may be to admit this fact. Perhaps we need something as horrifying as the hydrogen bomb to startle our imaginations into realizing that in a world as close, integrated, and tiny as our world today, the uncontrolled competition of anarchic national sovereignty is a condition which, literally, we must overcome or perish.

So often before, we have said that we must overcome national rivalries or be destroyed. But, this time, there is a literal sense to the words. It is highly doubtful whether our planet could stand more than a certain amount of hydrogen warfare; this generation certainly could not, and it is even doubtful whether the human species as such could either. So we face, at the moment of our extremest nationalism, the fact that it is the high road not simply to disaster but probably to extinction. We may hope that this fact will dawn upon more and more of us (although, I am afraid, at present it seems to dawn every time there is an atomic test and "undawn" the moment the test is over). However, let us suppose, as a supreme act of faith, that the dawn stays and develops into a broad day of intelligence. Then I do not think there will be much doubt about the task that lies equally before both East and West. It is to devise those institutions – they can be minimum institutions – which transcend national sovereignty sufficiently to give mankind a form of general political order without which we are all but certain to plunge into totally destructive war. The task is common to East and West, yet the West must give a lead in this matter. We have been extreme nationalists longer and therefore should by now be growing out of that painful malady, whereas the East has caught the fever of nationalism only recently and is in a more virulent stage of the disease. We who should be getting more immune to the old ideas are, therefore, the only group from which a lead can come in constructing a general order of security for mankind.

Formal constitution – drafting is not the right approach. For one thing, we are dealing with a perfectly new situation. To devise institutions for mankind as a whole – a planetary system, if you like – is very far, in its complexity and scale, from even the greatest experiment made in federation so far, that of the Founding Fathers. For another, any form of international government, being as remote as any government can be from the people it governs, runs desperate risks of being oppressive and intolerable to average human beings. Government is never very pleasant but the further it is removed the worse it can become. Obviously, anything as remote as a system of general international order must be the minimum compatible with our not blowing ourselves up. Much of the value in human life lies in its variety and richness and diversity. We do not want to ensure survival from extinction at the cost of extinguishing everything that made life worth living in the first place.

What we are looking for is, then, a minimum plan for international order, the minimum necessary to prevent atomic war with the maximum amount of variety and diversity that is possible within such a framework. The starting point must,

I believe, be the nation state. Nationalism has been pushed to a lunatic extreme but nations have, nonetheless, a continuing and organic identity. World order, for instance, need no more abolish the nation state than the existence of a French state implies calling all Frenchmen Dubonnet. The state, as historically developed, has staying power, it has unity in diversity, it has a common loyalty. All these are very valuable things. What is wrong is that modern nationalism is like cancer in a healthy body: it has gone so far in its pretensions and claims that it threatens to destroy the whole social order. But that does not mean that the national community, like the organic cell, is not basically a healthy thing. So let us not conceive a world order in which everyone is called something like XY2Z.

Now, is there any analogy in history which we might take to guide us in moving towards a balanced world order? One might discuss the problem in terms of the United Nations since it seems the nearest institution we have to an instrument of general government. But there are two reasons for hesitating. The first is that absolute state sovereignty is still enshrined in the Charter. The second is that ten years' practical functioning is a very short time for judgment. I do not say that the United Nations might not be the embryo of world order but it does not tell us what functions the nation states have to surrender to a higher authority. For guidance on that point, we must look elsewhere.

One of the most remarkable institutions in the whole history of mankind was the old Chinese Empire. It held together a vast mass of mankind living with every kind of climate and geography and including a broad range of tribal loyalties and historical traditions. It also maintained its unity in diversity over a longer period than any other system we have known. The interesting point about the Chinese imperial structure was that it touched very few things. It defended the frontiers and dealt directly with the punishment of violence, in other words, external or internal aggression; it concerned itself with the maintenance of the very elaborate irrigation system which was necessary to ensure Chinese food supplies. It was also charged with countering disaster and famine and undertook the control of foodstuffs in times of shortage. Thus the imperial government performed what one might call the minimum task of keeping order. It dealt with aggressive crimes. It attempted to keep some sort of overall economic balance of stability. Within that framework, the provinces, the family, the clans, the provincial organizations, the lawyers, the merchants – all enjoyed a high degree of autonomy and were strongly encouraged to settle most of their internal affairs by mediation and agreement. Here, then, is a possible analogy with the kind of minimum institutions that we might employ in order to prevent ourselves from destroying life permanently on this planet. On the one hand, we must accept institutions and processes which ensure the peaceful settlement of disputes. On the other, a central authority needs some powers to ensure general economic stability.

First, the peaceful settlement of disputes – this may seem difficult enough if we look round the world and think of the number of disputes that are going on now. On the other hand, it is equally legitimate to look at conditions in a rather more optimistic way and remember the areas within which nobody any longer thinks of settling disputes by force. A large part of the world today does not intend to use force. What is needed is to institutionalize that intention – to formalize means of arbitration and conciliation, and to strengthen the International Court of Justice, and to back these institutions by some international method of using police powers if methods of peaceful conciliation are put aside by one or other of the contestants. This last point is the most difficult for nationalism to accept. Yet it is the only means of removing sanctions from the individual decision of the powers, great or small.

Such minimum political arrangements would, of course, be greatly reinforced by the existence of functioning international economic institutions. One of the obvious ways of underpinning an international system, based on law, not force, would be to prevent conflicts and disputes from reaching such a pitch of embitterment that they can only be settled by violence. Not all disputes begin in economics (very far from it), but nevertheless, certain forms of economic stress and stringency are such that nations and groups involved in them no longer behave in a rational manner. For instance, it is reasonably certain that Germany could have solved its problems without Hitler had it not been for the despair and misery caused by the 1929 depression. The disintegration of the German economy in that crisis created conditions of desperation and political extremism of which the Nazi Party was able to take advantage.

Therefore, if we are to have much hope of settling our disputes peacefully, we must have the means to make sure that conflicts do not reach an extreme point. We have to ensure that nations are not driven to violence by overpopulation, by too much pressure on resources, by inability to feed themselves, by inability to trade – by all these classical pressures which, for instance, started Japan out on its path of imperialism after the nineteen twenties. Nor is the outlook for such action too discouraging. At least the technical and economic means are available. One of the vast changes brought about by industry, technology and science in this century is that once we abandon the purely national approach, our power to deal with extreme economic pressures is almost infinitely great. Again and again, when we say that we cannot cope with a certain economic situation, what we really mean is: "If I were to cope with it effectively, I should have to do something beyond my frontiers, which I am not prepared to do." Europe's dilemma in 1947 – between rising demands and falling dollar reserves – would have been insoluble if America had not decided to act beyond its frontiers in the Marshall Plan.

There is no shortage of information on what international economic institutions are needed to reinforce the peaceful settlement of disputes. In fact, the reports that have been written on the subject within the Atlantic area since 1947 now number upwards of a dozen, and all point more or less in the same direction. The score of this particular orchestral piece has been prepared again and again and again; the only trouble is that the orchestra will not play. Now, if you want, as I say, to see what kind of minimal institutions are needed in our economic life, I would recommend the Grey Report, the Bell Report, the Rockefeller Report, the Paley Report, the vast documentation of the Organization for European Economic Co-operation and so many more. But the point is that most of these studies support more or less the same conclusion: that we need probably three master institutions for regulating our economic life in the international sphere. The first is an extended version of the International Monetary Fund to deal with the exchange and convertibility of currencies; the second is an organization to deal with the problems of balancing international trade at the highest and not at the lowest level. The proposed Organization for Trade Co-operation might be the embryo of such an agency. The third is an organization for ensuring the movement of capital, and possibly of population as well. Part of its functions are already covered – although on too modest a scale – by the World Bank for International Reconstruction and the new International Finance Corporation. These are minimum economic institutions which may perhaps be said to correspond to the public works, irrigation, and famine relief undertaken by the Chinese imperial government. They are the least onerous institutions we need to create some form of economic stability in our world and to prevent disputes and difficulties becoming embittered by the pressure of economic want and the envy, hate, and spite which want creates.

Let us now suppose that, by some miracle of insight and courage, we do enhance, extend, and make effective such institutions. What then? How can they be effective, for is not our world split down the middle between the Communists and the free? It is all very well to talk about functioning international organizations. It may be fun to draw up minimum blueprints (I would underline that word, minimum. I have tried to suggest the minimum in this field, for the maximum would be intolerable). But at the end of it all, the Communists can sabotage the whole attempt.

The first thing to be said is that over large areas of this world's surface, what the Communist will or will not do has absolutely no bearing on this problem. Nationalism is worldwide; but Communism is confined, and we hope it continues to be so, to perhaps one-third of the world's surface, perhaps a bit more: too much, in fact, but still not even half the world. Within the area where the Communist writ does not run, we are cooperating under a free system of sovereign national states; and nobody is going to thwart us if we set to work in this area to make experiments in the sacrifice and pooling of sovereignty. When I look at this field of free-world sovereignty I am reminded of a lot of bathers standing round a very cold pond and constantly putting in a toe to test the temperature. They all know that at some point they have to get into that pond, and it probably will not be so bad when they do, but as long as they go on touching the problem of sovereignty with one toe, and shrinking back, how very unpleasant it seems!

Schemes like NATO, our adherence to the United Nations, plans like the Colombo Plan or the Marshall Plan, are the toes we put in to feel out the water. It seems pretty cold; and we draw back. Then come second thoughts: "Oh well, we have to get in." So back we come and feel the water with yet another plan. But we postpone the real decision, which is to get in and say: "All right, together with all nations sufficiently like-minded to make this experiment, we will recognize that the day of unlimited national sovereignty is past. We will set up a functioning international order in a world which is now as small as the continental United States a hundred years ago." Once we have reached that point, the objection that half the world is Communist will be irrelevant, because we shall have begun to act in the areas in which we are already free to act now, if only we can make up our minds.

Incidentally, to pursue our own policies in our part of the world would also prove the best way of dealing with Communism. One of the great troubles in our present policy towards Communism is that we seem to spend our time saying: "What is Uncle Khrushchev doing? Let us go and try to prevent it." It seems to me that if we had a policy of our own for developing the kind of institutions we need for sane international living, we might experience the reverse process and find the Russians actually wanting to know what *we* were up to: frankly, since the great days of the Marshall Plan, they have not had to show a flicker of interest. They have the idea and we encourage it – that they hold the centre of the stage and everyone else will more or less dance to their tune. So, quite apart from the survival of humanity, even the short term interest of waging the cold or cooling war would be served if we tried to establish the kind of political and economic order by which we can hope to avoid extinction. We should soon maneuver the Communists into the position of having to find out what we were doing, and possibly even asking if they might do it too.

A new approach of this kind is of particular importance in our relations with Asia. The first reason is political. If international relations continue to be conducted on the base of raw national interest, the chief aspect of Western policy will continue to recall all the centuries when Western nationalism was the equivalent, in Eastern minds, of imperialism and colonialism. The suspicion will persist that behind Western national interest still lies a propensity to control and exploit Eastern lands[2].

The second reason concerns economics – or rather, the point where politics and economics overlap. If we were to accept seriously the aim of using international cooperation to check the world's potential disasters before they reach the explosive stage, we would find, inevitably, that much of our effort was being directed to Asia. There the hopes for capital growth and development are far more uncertain than in the West, and the pressure of population and need infinitely greater.

Moreover, Asia would be the great beneficiary if, as one of the main lines in our international policy, we were to adopt the social principle which has been of such immense service within our own communities, the principle of the wealthy helping the not-so-wealthy and using capital creatively to bring up conditions of living on all sides. In the first stages of our international economic cooperation, we would find that a large part of the work we had to do would consist of the wealthier Western nations undertaking a long-term co-operative effort to raise the standards of Asia: and they would be doing so through international agencies – a method which would remove still further the taint of "Western exploitation." In short, a policy of international economic co-operation, based on the traditional principles of the democratic West, leads inevitably to the most effective method of defeating the Communist conspiracy in Asia and of creating, East and West together, the kind of world in which humanity may yet hope to survive.

NOTES

1 Arnold Toynbee (1889–1975) was an English historian and a philosopher of history whose research and writing explored the rise and fall of civilizations. He delivered the Beatty Lecture series in 1961 on "The Present Day Experiment in Western Civilization."
2 The Anglo-French intervention at Suez, however interpreted in London and Washington, seems in Asian eyes a conclusive demonstration that colonial attitudes persist in the West. The Communists are also trying with all possible emphasis to pin the colonial tag on President Eisenhower's definition of American interest in a non-Communist Middle East. The crisis and the aftermath of Suez thus illustrates the urgency of giving as strong an international orientation as possible to Western initiatives in Asia and the need to separate, as much as may be, purely Western interests of a strategic or even economic kind from broad policies of aid and reconstruction in Eastern countries.

2

Asia Today: Revolutionary Change in the Twentieth Century

22 October 1968

Han Suyin

INTRODUCTION

Han Suyin, the pen name of Rosalie Matilda Kuanghu Chou, was born in 1916 in Henan province, China, to a Chinese father of Hakka origin and a Belgian mother. She studied medicine in Brussels on a scholarship, and, in 1938, she returned to China and married Tang Pao-Huang, a Nationalist officer. While he was temporarily stationed in England as a military attaché, Suyin went to join him and completed her medical degree. In 1947, Tang died while fighting the Communists in Manchuria. Two years later, Suyin moved to Hong Kong where she fell in love with Ian Morrison, a married Anglo-Australian journalist who was killed covering the Korean War. Her novel based on the affair, *A Many-Splendoured Thing*, became an international bestseller and was made into an Oscar-nominated film.

Suyin was a prolific author whose writing was often derived from her life experiences, as found in the bestselling novels *Destination Chungking* (1942) and *Birdless Summer* (1968). She was also a controversial cultural activist due to her outspoken support of Mao Zedong; however, her books that sympathized with Mao's Cultural Revolution gradually lost their readership following his death in 1976. After the student-led, pro-democracy demonstrations held in Tiananmen Square in Beijing on 4 June 1989, she changed her position.

Suyin delivered her Beatty Lecture in 1968 when China's Proletarian Cultural Revolution (1966–76) was at its height. With that spirit in mind, Suyin began her lecture by asserting that the fundamental fact of historical development is change. After World War II, ex-colonial Asian countries became independent, yet they were unable to escape the manipulation and control by Western imperialists and their masses continued to be suppressed and exploited by the dominant class. The wealthy shrunk in number but grew richer, the poor poorer. As Suyin noted, this polarity ironically also existed in the United States, "A nation where it is impossible

Han Suyin. *Used with permission of McGill University Archives, PR036633.*

for Congress to appropriate $50 million to eradicate rats in the slums, but which appropriates $7 billion more for the war in Vietnam."

According to Suyin, the world was in crisis. In the Soviet Union, despite Stalin's achievements, the failure of its revolution and its reversal to the exploitative ruling class were obvious. The notion of "peaceful coexistence" was only an important step to global exploitation. Toward the end of her speech, she turned her focus to China's ongoing Proletarian Cultural Revolution and suggested that the world could learn from it.

Over fifty years have passed since Han Suyin's enthusiastic lecture. China's Proletarian Cultural Revolution has been condemned, the Soviet Union has collapsed, and China has dropped the ideology of class struggle. Deng Xiaoping's get-rich reform has elevated China to become a rival with the United States, forming a new "Big Two." The political, social, and economic issues affecting the world that Suyin raised in her lecture still exist. Unforeseen by her, however, in this age of information technology, historical change is happening at a much faster speed and on a wider scale.

*

Laifong Leung is Professor Emerita of the University of Alberta in the Department of East Asian Studies. Her books include *Morning Sun: Interviews with Chinese Writers of the Lost Generation* (1994) and *Contemporary Chinese Fiction Writers: Biography, Bibliography and Critical Assessment* (2016).

LECTURE

McGill-Queen's University Press published Han Suyin's three Beatty Lectures in 1969 in a book titled *Asia Today: Two Outlooks*. The following is an excerpt from the first lecture presented on 22 October 1968.

Robert Gomer, Chairman of the Board of the Bulletin of the Atomic Scientists, once wrote that mankind today is caught up "in an evolutionary stream of its own making, but beyond its control. We shall have to accept the fact," he adds, "that even under the best of circumstances, man must change to meet changes that he himself has set off."

I find the regret implicit in this sentence both surprising and revealing; surprising for an atomic scientist; revealing in that Gomer shows he is not prepared to cast off the outdated and deliquescent social structures which imprison man in a mental cage of the tenth century, while his science and techniques carry him to the stars.

The fundamental fact of historical development is change, the most constant factor of mankind's forward course; both in the social fabric, the institutions and structures of the systems that are evolved, and in the individual, the social being and his consciousness. Whether circumstances are best or worst makes no difference to the relentless march of history; and no wishful thinking can stop it.

The creation of systems and structures is accomplished by revolutionary and violent change; partly conscious, partly unconscious in that it escapes our awareness; at the same time as the systems yield to new social frameworks, man's values, attitudes, beliefs are destroyed, and new ones arise. This is not done by a slow continuous evolution. It happens in leaps, in crises explosive and violent. The old is repudiated, with all its beliefs, attitudes, its literature and art and ways of being; man assumes a new psyche, new mores, and new goals; and this is not done in vacuo, but depends upon changes in the material basis, the means of production, the relation between these and man, and the classes evolved. Class society, in which a ruling class imposes its philosophy, ideas, and values upon the rest, has been until today the constant characteristic of historical development. Thus the slave society, the feudal, and the capitalist; each with its dominant class and its submissive, serving, exploited ones, its economic structure corresponding to (and indeed the foundation of) this mental superstructure, which at the same time reinforces and moulds it. In this to and fro between economic basis, social system, and mental superstructure, all human relationships are moulded and stamped.

In turn the new system, once progressive, becomes rigid, inadequate, as material processes and changes make it unable to cope with new realities. But the dominant class owes its position and its very soul, all its conditioned reflexes, to the system, and its place in it. It possesses hierarchies and mores, laws and apparatus of suppression, to guarantee its domination. To relinquish it is to cease to exist; therefore, it will battle for the maintenance of the status quo, and against the new philosophy, new ideas, which threaten it. The new is labelled hostile and alien; the old invokes morality, law and order, warns that change will mean confusion and crime. Yet the law and order imposed are the law and order of its own supremacy; as time goes on, and its decrepitude has lost the capacity of reform and adaptation, it refuses to perceive, because it has refused a priori the evidence, that what it has tried to label alien, and different, is indeed nurtured within its own system, born within its own structures. For it is internal conflict, internal contradiction, internal disintegration which proceed apace and proceed to destroy it by self-destruction, not an imposition from the outside.

Thus revolutionary change begins, and our twentieth century is rife with it, an epoch of internal disintegration and splits, of new organizations, new structures and concepts. Confusion, as it is called, is the herald of a new order emergent.

Because of the acceleration imprinted upon events by the technological level of our epoch, changes are accelerated; the leaps into awareness, the speed of inter-communication, spread far more swiftly a knowledge of conflict than they did a century ago. Time has taken wing, the jet, not the oxcart, is its hallmark. Change is upon us before our minds have accepted that the solid base of our accepted social framework is no longer solid. Violence characterizes this enormous birth of new structures and systems, violence on a world scale, not due to an infiltration of alien ideas and subversion, but due to the internal disintegration of the social framework itself. Violence is always attributed to the side of the new emergent forces, but is actually the outcome of the growing inability of the old to make adaptation and reform, its increasing and eventually total recourse to suppression and repression, called maintenance of law and order; a violence increasingly directed toward its own conflicts, because it is from within that revolutionary changes arise.

In the twenty-three years since the end of World War II, the emergence of ex-colonial countries into what is called independence, and their struggle for survival both economic and political, has provided the world arena both with a plethora of new governments. And this has provided the press with repeatedly disillusioning hopes that conferences of experts, aid, the adoption of Western scientific methods and other gimmicks, would solve the problems of what has been called underdevelopment. These problems are really the passage or change from the system both political and economic under which these nations laboured, a semi-colonial, semi-feudal state, in which their economies were monopolized and directed to the benefit of the Western metropolitan dominant power, to another system, which assures both survival and growth in an independent form.

Because for so long these areas in the world were treated as "objects," the study of their conditions continues to be directed, not by the historical concepts which would reveal their true condition, and the necessity for revolutionary change which is evident, but with the aim of justifying past interests and present policies toward them. Thus it is being accepted that they are "underdeveloped," and the change from this term to the word "developing," intended to convey a more hopeful note, does not alter the fundamental fact that they are, with the exception of China, in the throes of a revolutionary change which began in the previous century and is going on; and that no amount of placebo conferences, or pious illusions, can conceal this process.

Twenty years ago Asian destinies were decided in the West; today the emergence of China and the increasing momentum of change elsewhere in Asia – as in Latin America and Africa, areas of the world where wants and needs become more vast, the clamour of revolt more strident – mark this universal upheaval as an epoch of world revolution. With the development of China replacing Japan as the first non-white power to grow strong on her own resources and efforts, and today the self-proclaimed vanguard and leader of revolutionary change, a new pattern emerges, though we refuse to see it except to label it violence, or subversion. The shaping of alliances and military pacts and policies designed to contain this new force cannot do so; for it stems from within, from the relentless process of historical forces within the nations themselves. The history of Asia must be reappraised, reinterpreted within the context of the present century and its independence movements. Because in many cases the latter are still weak and in the process of change, the great waves of resistance to colonial expansionism, which turned Asia in the nineteenth century into the most intensive battlefield and caused millions of deaths and led to the most savage reprisals, have not been properly studied. The pattern of the peasant uprisings which mark the nineteenth century is still passed over in silence, chiefly because similar uprisings threaten many of the elitist ruling classes in the unstable Asian governments of today.

In the nineteenth century, uprisings all over Asia had an interlinked effect, coalescing in their timing. The Taiping and Nien uprisings in China (1851–67) and the uprisings in India (1857–59) and in Persia (1844–52) formed a "wave" of revolt; there was no concerted, conscious move; but they happened within the same period of time because they were responses to similar conditions heralding the bankruptcy of the feudal agricultural base. At the end of the nineteenth century a second upsurge of such struggles took place: in Persia (1890–91), in Assam and Manipur (1891), in India (1895–97), in (at the time) French Indochina (1891–98), in Korea (1893–95), in Turkey and the Philippines (1896–98), and again in China (1899–1900). The abortive Russian Revolution of 1905 was followed by a third series of Asian revolts: the revolution in China led by Sun Yatsen (1911), the revolts led by the All-India National Congress (1905–8), and the revolts in Persia and Turkey (1908–9).

The October Revolution in Russia in 1917 heralded yet another series of upsurges: in China, the Great Revolution (1925–27); in Africa, in Vietnam, in India. Indeed, since the turn of the twentieth century, there has been one constant feature in the Asian world, that is, upsurges and national-liberation struggles with periods of quiescence in between, which were the result of massacres and repression by the colonial powers. But this dampening was only temporary; soon, and in an even more progressive, more organized way, the revolutionary "wave" went on; for this is historical change; mass-powered and inner-directed, it cannot be stemmed, short of massive and total genocide.

The triumph of the Communist Revolution in China in 1949 occurred in the midst of yet another series of armed uprisings, in Malaya, in Burma, in Indonesia, in Vietnam, in the Philippines, in Africa, not to mention Latin America. What we are witnessing today all over the world is yet another series, but this time the features which characterize it are its extension to those hitherto apparently safe centres of wealth and power, Western Europe and the United States itself.

The illusion, therefore, that a peaceful evolutionary change for the so-called undeveloped countries of Asia (and other parts of the world) is in process or can be manipulated is a vanishing one; indeed, the example of Latin America, which is "Asian" by all standards except in name, is appropriate: a vast and exploited peasant semi-proletariat, living in subhuman conditions; cities which are examples of shocking wealth and glaring poverty side by side, crowded and crammed with refugees from hunger fleeing the countryside; and a few enormously rich families, 3 per cent of the population owning 87 per cent of the national wealth; an economy completely satellite and dependent upon foreign capitalism and gravitating more and more to it; violent seething revolt spearheaded by youth movements and by the beginnings of peasant guerilla movements in the countryside. It is a picture with which we are now familiar; as is the conspicuous failure of all glowing blueprints which purport to transform this state of affairs into prosperous stability through such devices as the Alliance for Progress, which turns out to be an alliance between foreign interests and the local ruling class to protect their interests at the expense of the people. It is now forty years since 1928, when Herbert Hoover first mooted grandiose schemes for Latin America, and in these forty years all that has happened is increased exploitation and poverty for the masses, increased wealth for the few, a familiar polarization. Half of Latin America has suffered from military coups and all democratic liberties have been eroded or have disappeared one by one; enormous profits have, however, been reaped by foreign capital, many times what has been invested; but the peoples of Latin America have not profited from it, and the clamour for revolutionary change is now gathering head.

In Asia too something similar to the Alliance for Progress, but called by other names, is being tried; and it is similarly designed to delude and to delay, but not to solve the pressing economic problems of the nations. It holds up to them the glowing prospects of emulating and resembling the wealthy Western nations, while at the same time exploitation, more wholesale, efficient, and merciless than in colonial days, still continues, and in the same way: by an alliance between monopoly interests and the local "elite" or ruling class, the latter increasingly reliant upon suppression and repression to maintain its unstable rule.

In the years from 1955 to 1968, the conspicuous feature of two-thirds of humanity, Asia (excepting China), Africa, and Latin America, has been growing poverty and growing revolt and dissent, and a youth movement spearheading and verbalizing protest at the same spot in time, not because of common and concerted action, but because of common and similar historical factors. The disappearance in Asia of copies of Western "parliamentary" governments left in place by European colonial powers in their withdrawal, the withering of economic dreams of progress, the emergence of arbitrary and oppressive and dictatorial militarist regimes, are fully documented steps in a disintegration which is an inevitable process in the emergence of a new order. The backing of the most regressive and repressive militarist rulers by the "Western democracies" makes, as in China in the past, a mockery of pretensions to democracy, and duplicates what happened in China and what so relentlessly and irrevocably led the youth of China to the only road left, the road to socialism and communism. The situation is paradoxical; Western capitalism has been its own worst enemy; for it is not because of China's emergence (though all is done to create China psychosis everywhere in the world) that the unrest, upheavals, and economic deterioration occur, but because the policies of domination, under the forms of economic stranglehold and military suppression, have outlived the passing of old-type colonialism, continue, and are reinforced.

The overall aspect of the economic deterioration of Asian countries (save for small exceptions, due to the temporary boom of the Vietnam war, in Japan, South Korea, and other small and satellitic economies bound to United States monopoly enterprise) has been fully documented. Not only Gunnar Myrdal and Barbara Ward, but a host of other economists, leave us with nothing but bleakness of prospect. And the sooner it is realized that the hoax being played by expensive economic conferences is at the expense of the needy, the sooner perhaps the peoples whose gathering revolt storms the very bastions of capitalism will organize their own destiny and take in hand the power that is theirs to create a better future for themselves.

The famed economist Barbara Ward argues that it is the lack of capital to realize the essential technological transformations in the so-called undeveloped two thirds of the world which explains the lag; and she pleads with the wealthy nations for more largesse; to redress the balance disparities which are ever growing and increasing. The milch cow economy under which the undeveloped nations suffered did not disappear after 1945, despite the presence of local capital; in fact, Miss Ward points out that about 80 per cent of the capital devoted to development is provided locally; but this local capital is tied to the overall control of foreign investment capital, and profits derived are often withheld from those very sectors in public demand which would provide the infrastructure for progress. The progress, if there is any, is localized to the cities, which develop an urban middle class; the cities become a target for hungry rural hordes pouring out of stagnant countrysides. In these city ghettos, a 60 per cent unemployment rate among the young people is not unusual; it is almost the rule.

Miss Ward has asked long enough for 1 per cent of the gross national product of wealthy countries in assistance; and she notices, with disheartened matter of factness, that this is not forthcoming and will be less forthcoming than ever. For it is the policies, the ideas behind the manipulations of wealth and the world market which have not changed. Hence to ask the needy nations to look to the West for a shining example of what they ought to do is to add insult to injury. And recently the example has begun to lose its lustre in a singular manner. The Asian picture of revolt and uprising is no longer confined to Asia; today Asia is everywhere in the world, and in the heart of the Western powers themselves.

Arthur Schlesinger, Jr, writes in "America 1968: The Politics of Violence" (*Harper's Magazine*, August 1968) that the proudest, most technologically advanced country in the world, the United States, whose capitalist expansion, in the form of monopolies, stretches to almost every economy in the world, is also the greatest failure in human terms, and the most violent country in the world. "We must recognize that the evil is in us," he writes, "that it springs from some dark, intolerable tension in our history and our institutions ... perhaps when we first began the practice of killing and enslaving those whom we deemed our inferiors because their skin was another color."

In writing this, Schlesinger is not far from repeating what Mao Tsetung wrote, that American imperialism, its wealth and power system, was founded upon the Black slavery it had imposed, and that as the Blacks rose and challenged this power, its decline and fall would begin.

For the past decade scientists, economists, religious personalities have been urging American society and its ruling apparatus to a change of mind, a change of heart, more vision; a moral betterment; greater concern for the deprived, the exploited, the growing poverty both within the wealthiest nations and in the rest of the world. "The reason for the failure of any long-term Atlantic strategy [for aiding economic development in the world of the underprivileged] to emerge has nothing to do with resources. It is rooted in something much deeper, the manner of thinking about the world still dominant in our societies ... drift is carrying us towards the rapids ... if we are ready for something like the sustained practice of welfare and justice, we are likely to make progress ... if we cannot, we must face the fact that the technology which might have united and enriched our world is much more likely to blow it up." Thus says Miss Ward. And Philip Hauser writes: "If we are not prepared to make the investment in people, in human resources, we will be forced to increase our investment in police and National Guard, the army and possibly ... it can happen here in America ... resort to concentration camps and even genocide." A gloomy, "Asian type" prospect indeed.

There seems a determinism in the processes of disintegration of a social system when its time is up, which baffles all rationality, all intelligent assessment; hysteria and fear, self-destructive paranoia, dominate as the contradictions become more acute, as the problems increase in scope and scale. There is more and more recourse to brutality and suppression, to the apparatus of police and army, to shooting and jailing. Society becomes increasingly polarized between the haves and the have-nots; the class struggle, which is always present, and is indeed the fundamental characteristic of societal development (in spite of those who deny it), becomes increasingly clear, overt, and militant; and violence seems the only way out because the peaceful processes of protest and dissent have been ignored or put down. A paranoid obtuseness acts as a rigid armour-proof to reason and common sense, and gaudy and gorgeous blueprints for alleviation of poverty remain glib bafflebab. Increasingly the wealthy get fewer but wealthier, the poor poorer, more pauperized but more numerous; the liberties acquired in earlier times, the safeguards against tyranny, go one by one or two by two; the United States arrogates to itself more power as it feels its hold less stable; and all that is reinforced is the apparatus of police and army; the latter increasingly powerful in the running of the country; that way lies fascism and military take-overs, as in China before 1949, as in Asia today. A nation where it is impossible for Congress to appropriate $50 million to eradicate rats in the slums, but which appropriates $7 billion more for the war in Vietnam; where it is impossible to ban weapons, to combat what is euphemistically called an epidemic of violence, but where it is possible to vote another billion for research into anti-riot weapons, has become morally deficient. And without being metaphysical, we can still augur that it is mental and moral bankruptcy which signals the beginning of the end.

Perhaps the most traumatic failure of the capitalist system, the one most noticed in Asia, is in the sector of science and technology. Why is it that with all the resources of science, with the great technological advances which accompanied the expansion of capitalism, especially during wars which took place between capitalist states, why is it that with the production of the greatest wealth, the vastest power, the most fabulous technological miracles, mankind suffers more from hunger, poverty, and bloodshed than at any other time in history, and on a vaster scale? If this poverty were "Asian," confined to what is described as the "have-not nations," one could always (as is done) continue to evade the real causality by talking of "natural aptitudes," but it is not so, since within the richest country on earth 30 per cent of the population live within a growing matrix of want. Is there no remedy offered that can work, save the ever growing sums expended in violent suppression of the signs of dissent and discontent?

The fault is not that of science and technology; or even of scientists. Science and the scientists are taken over, monopolized, acquired, commodity whose value is based upon what is called the market, the law of supply and demand; as all else, they become a tool, and the goals are the goals of the system, whose end motivation is profit. Profit for the sake of profit, increased dividends, the rise of market value of stocks, an elusive triumph, an octopus possession which drains the world of real prosperity even as it creates more wealth for selected sectors; a society in which waste is a component of consumption and where artificial needs rather than real want are catered for. The prices of manufactured capital goods to be sold to Asian countries are raised, while the commodities from these countries are lowered in price; the experts travelling round the world to find "a solution" to these man-created problems cannot do so, because any rational and real solution is rejected, since it would not enter within the motivation of profit and superprofit by the already wealthy at the expense of the poor.

Science and technology are bought and sold, as is brain power, a commodity, a product; the goal of science to build prosperity and happiness for mankind, to eradicate ignorance and superstition, is forgotten while technique is increasingly devoted to the arts of death, not life; the talents of the ablest brains go to the Pentagon, the biggest employer, the biggest single user of advanced technologies and of technologists and scientists; the world is combed for brains which can be bought and used to produce lethal weapons and fabricate foolproof ways of massive genocide. The creation of a plague bacillus ten thousand times more deadly than anything nature devised has received the attention of a goodly number of geniuses; and this degradation of science to the uses of extermination, not peace, this paranoid frenzy is regarded as normality, spoken of as "security." Science can make the deserts flourish, produce strains which can multiply crops; but these uses of science are restricted to limited areas and for reasons tied to strategic ends. With the invasion by American capital of every national economy, the industries of Europe are also held in bondage, as are their scientists; dependent, paying royalties for patents, becoming subsidiaries of the gigantic parent monopoly; increasingly funds and resources are devoted to the military-industrial complex, because in that sector the profits are the greatest. And where does all this lead us? To Watts, Chicago, Vietnam – parallels are becoming increasingly striking. And Asia watches and says: "They are becoming like us!"

And so the world is in crisis, its peoples seized in the grip of a new awareness. Dissent, an intellectual movement, particularly marked among the young, is questioning the structure and aims of education, because education is directed toward serving this kind of society, and this is no longer good enough. The young are becoming aware of the larger issues inherent in the structure of society itself. For man lives not by bread alone, or as Khrushchev once claimed, for goulash. Never did Khrushchev, that short-sighted careerist, go more wrong than in this contemptuous estimation of the human being as quite satisfied when his material needs were minimally satisfied. This crisis of awareness has been brought about by the contradictions within the system, by Vietnam, by the rising opposition of two-thirds of the world to exploitation, and by the emergence of China. The ferment in educational institutions is manifest, for the first spark of a new consciousness is usually found among students and young intellectuals; as happened in China in 1919, as is happening all over Asia and Latin America today. This is the prelude, but not the full-fledged start of a revolutionary movement. It fulfils a useful purpose: to define and verbalize revolt, to provide the spark which later finds its own kindling to turn into a prairie fire.

"Revolt is good, revolt is clean, is healthy," Camus said; "revolt is the very movement of life; we cannot deny it without renouncing life itself." And Mao Tsetung said: "Revolt is justified." This repudiation is the first step; the expansion of revolt from universities to the streets is another; but it is only when there comes about the alliance and integration of these youth movements with the pauperized, the exploited, the oppressed – as in China, the workers and the peasants – that revolution truly has a reality, a motive force, a power of change. And eventually the leadership must pass to them, to the proletariat, and the proletariat, too, must be defined, and must educate itself, and be educated, into the theory and practice of revolution. Both in France and in Latin America, we have seen the students march under the slogan: "We must suppress ourselves as a class, integrate ourselves to the proletariat, accept its leadership." This is a new development, an unambiguous short cut to the organization of a revolutionary force. And it is fear of this alliance between intellectual and worker which, in Mexico, Latin America, and other countries, is evoking such savage suppression. At this juncture, we do well to quote the words spoken by Mao Tsetung in 1962: "The next fifty or a hundred years or so, beginning from now, will be a great era of thoroughgoing change in social systems everywhere in the world, an earthshaking era without compare in all previous history. Living in such an era, we must be ready to engage in great struggles, the form of which will have many different features from those of the past."

Prophetic words, for in the unfolding future we see no hope of peaceful evolution or peaceful transition, in Asia, or anywhere, evolving out of the system of monopoly imperialism which is today's capitalism in the West. On the contrary, the expansion of this imperialism (for it will continue to expand for a while yet) creates and extends everywhere a real proletariat at the same time as export of capital disdains investment in human resources in its own national boundaries and internal pauperization also extends. Disintegration from within, militant movements of national liberation, of armed struggle in the exploited regions abroad, will therefore grow and continue to grow. For a while yet, perhaps a decade or so, the gigantism of monopoly capital will increase as exploitation increases and as increasing ways of repression are devised and found. But this is not forever; and the day will come when from within the heart and bowels of this great colossus will come its own revolution; and no amount of Wallaces or Mace, no increase of National Guardsmen or voting of repressive weapons can eradicate the ferment within the hearts of men, the growing class struggle, however disguised, in every country of the world today.

This is the prospect and the choice has already been made; Chicago in September 1968 was a turning point. The Vietnam war points up the lesson, as Robert Heilbroner writes: "The great lesson of the Vietnam war is that the mightiest nation on earth has not been able to defeat the forces of revolutionary nationalism in one of the smallest and poorest Asian nations in the world ... the ultimate purpose of our intervention was not to beat a national enemy, but a revolutionary force, to demonstrate that wars of national liberation would end in disaster for the revolutionaries. Now, by a supreme irony, we have shown the opposite. The prospect is one of worldwide upheaval, in which the Vietnam war will have been only ... one campaign." In 1965 President Johnson, confident of winning, proclaimed the intention of the USA to interfere everywhere with armed might wherever the interests of the USA called to do so (the way he put it was the defense of freedom). Today the uprisings have shifted and occur in the heart of America's great cities, and it is to tackle the revolt in the streets of America that the soldiers must go home. This is the picture of the West which the Asian nations see and which they are beginning to understand.

But I can hear many in my audience say that: you have denounced and condemned the deeds of capitalism, pointed out its inability to solve the contradictions within, pointed out the growing hatred and revolt against its exploitation abroad. But what of socialism? What of the conflicts and contradictions within the socialist world? What of Soviet Russia, and its totalitarian ways, not only within, but also as applied to its satellites? What about Czechoslovakia, and the students of Prague and Warsaw? And how shall we interpret China's Cultural Revolution? Is it not the certain sign that China is divided, in chaos, and crumbling within? Are those the models of revolutionary change and the patterns to follow?

The man who most clearly and first of all analyzed and denounced the new imperialism arising out of what was once the first socialist country in the world is Mao Tsetung. The explanation is based on dialectical materialism, social and historical, but we must remember that the true course of science and scientific method from the beginning was based upon dialectical concepts. As Benjamin de Leon writes in the *Bulletin of the Atomic Scientists*, June 1968: "We are compelled [in science and technology] to recognize the dialectical concept that change in quantity transforms into change in quality." The law of contradiction, basic to dialectics, the unity of opposites as essence of all things, is also basic to science. Mao Tsetung has expanded and developed, based on the accumulated experience of the Chinese Revolution, the knowledge of contradiction and of qualitative change. Mao says that "although in the general development of things the material determines the mental, and social being determines social consciousness, yet we also, and indeed we must, recognize the reaction of *mental* on *material* things, of the social consciousness on social being, of the superstructure on the economic base." The whole course of the Chinese Revolution under Mao and the direction of the Cultural Revolution, exhorting to combat selfishness and personal interest as a political as well as a moral attainment, are of significance in that they open to us a greater dimension of understanding, giving due place to mental and conscious processes, and taking us away from rigidly mechanical materialism. Mankind on the march is not only materially determined, but idea-propelled. It is also ideas, accepted and put into action by the masses of the people, which move it forward; historical development is always a mass action in its final analysis. The saying by Mao that "the people, only the people, are the motor force of history" embodies this concept; as does the one which says that "correct ideas [relevant to reality and to the class whose interest it represents, the class which holds the key to future development] … once absorbed by the masses become an immense material force," which can change heaven and earth, which can transform the world.

It is from this point of view, of the mental superstructure, that we shall trace part of the reversal phenomenon in Russia, and also envisage the Cultural Revolution in China.

Each economic and political system contains within itself the seeds of its opposite, as does each situation, each thing, and the play of these opposites, their relative ascendancy and mutual interaction, is the source of motion, development. Hence it is obvious that, within each system, its opposite becomes manifest when the dominant aspect of its contradiction begins to head toward decrepitude. With young capitalism (and capitalism at its inception was a progressive force as compared with the feudalism it destroyed and replaced) was also born the working class; the first machine saw the first proletariat. In the nineteenth century, in the full flush of capitalist expansion and colonial conquest, the working class also evolved; from a class in itself, initiating spontaneous revolts against exploitation, to a conscious class for itself, with its own philosophy, Marxism, with the beginning of a leadership, the communist party. The twentieth century was to see the expansion and organization of revolutions based on Marxism led by communist parties, vanguards of the working class; and great gains by the working class, undreamt of in the nineteenth century. But it was also to see, as Lenin described, its opposite, counter-revolutionary revisionism, in its theoretical and practical aspects. In practical terms this begins with conciliation and compromise, and even more, within the Marxist parties, the rise of a new class, a new bourgeoisie, cut off from the masses it once led as vanguard, anxious to take the place of the class it once overthrew, not to transform the world, but to enjoy it in the same exploitative way. Along with the development and spread of revolutions under the banner of socialism also comes this internal dichotomy; which in the final analysis represents the counter-current of ideas, attitudes, values, which emanate from the capitalist system; for, at the present stage, it makes for a return to capitalism, the phenomenon of reversal, or restoration of the past. Lenin was well aware of this when he said that "the socialist revolution is not a single battle on a single front, but a whole epoch of struggles on many and varied, indeed, on all fronts" and that the consolidation of socialist power, which is the power of the proletariat, the working class, cannot come unless there is, at the same time, *the fullest democracy in practice* which alone can guarantee the stability of this power and its success.

This saying of Lenin's we must ponder in its full significance, for it enables us to understand a little more the processes at work, the patterns of the future along which Asian and other nations may move.

Even after the violent revolutionary overthrow of the capitalist system, the mental superstructure is not overthrown. It is easy to cut off heads, say the Chinese, but that does not solve anything, for it is the ideas inside the heads that must change. This phenomenon of reversal has its inception in minds, a phenomenon which the Chinese have studied very deeply, especially during the last decade. And it is curious that the anguished cries of economists today, as well as the youth movements, also accent this point. If we trace what happened in Russia, we must go back to the Stalin era, and that very excellent pamphlet "On the Question of Stalin" by the Chinese is forthright and clear on the subject.

Emotional abhorrence provoked by the repetitive recital of Stalin's purges should not obviate the fact that Stalin did have great achievements. The Chinese list both. There have been lesser men than Stalin, in less difficult situations, who have exerted a great tyranny, and though Stalin's rule was incredibly harsh it is undoubtedly due to Stalin and not to his successors that Russia is today a great industrial power. Stalin's rule did lift the Russian people from feudal serfdom into the modern age, from abysmal ignorance and poverty into education, comparative well-being. In the leadership of his people during World War II, Stalin performed an immense, gigantic task. We often forget how threatened, invaded, surrounded by enemies Soviet Russia was in its early years. If Stalin became suspicious he often had good reason to. He became increasingly arbitrary in his methods, write the Chinese, leading to what they call "a partial disruption of socialist legality." In his purges he made no distinction between enemy and non-antagonistic contradictions, the normal run of difference that exists within a social system, a distinction which Mao Tsetung was to make in 1957, but had already applied in practice all through the long and complex course of the Chinese Revolution. "He showed a tendency toward great nation chauvinism," the Chinese say (and they ought to know for they too had to deal with it).

Stalin neglected the most important element in the advance and maintenance of a genuine communist party, the constant and continuous necessity for study, practice, rectification, criticism and self-criticism, the constant integration with the people, linking theory to practice and paying attention to what the Chinese call the working style, or methods of work. "He even mistakenly," write the Chinese, "intervened in the internal affairs of certain fraternal countries and parties ... and he wronged and purged many loyal communists and good people.... All this had surviving bad effects." All this had indeed. A bureaucracy, unprincipled, opportunistic, parroting Marxist slogans but without comprehending them, corrupt with rampant factionalism and intrigue, fed Stalin with flattery and made no attempt to promote political education, either among party members and cadres or among the people. And Khrushchev, who during Stalin's lifetime had been one of the most addicted to the personality cult (witness what he wrote and said), was a product not of socialism, but of this personal careerism. The thick verbal confusion which calls any abandonment of socialism "liberalization" was only the abandonment by Khrushchev, under the guise of condemning Stalin at the 10th Congress, in 1956, of any principles of socialism, or even just principles. A new class of domineering bureaucrats without anything in view but their own advancement, allied to the new managerial and technocratic elite, took the place of the overthrown Czarist bourgeoisie, but since the ideas of personal profit and the disregard of working class and peasantry remained, and cultural attitudes and reflexes of the past survived, the phenomenon of reversal in all its manifestations asserted itself. Soviet Russia today has gone back to Czarism, and already the rifts and contradictions within are showing, despite the tremendous power that is the Soviet Union today.

This reversal is often pointed out to Asian nations as proof that socialism has failed; that socialism could not work, and so Russia, in order to advance, had to go back to the market stimulus, material incentives, capitalist methods, et cetera. Actually the evidence is to the contrary. It was under Stalin, whatever his defects, and because of socialist economic policies (even though only partly realized) that Russia's formidable and accelerated growth, especially in industry, occurred in the 1930s, a growth rate unequalled in the world except today by China.

But the increasing stranglehold of an authoritarian bureaucracy, the censorship, the purges, which were the bad side of Stalin's reign, have been chiefly remembered so that socialism became equated with tyranny rather than bureaucracy.

A truer verdict would be that the failure of Russia's revolution and its reversal to an exploitative ruling class are due not to the failure of socialism, but to not enough socialism, to socialism insufficiently consolidated or developed, certainly not developed to the stage Lenin had in mind when he wrote of full democracy for the working masses.

The word "liberalization," so freely applied to Russia until the aggression against Czechoslovakia, is inappropriate. It does not indicate or guarantee democracy for the proletariat, for the masses of the people; the treatment of writers and intellectuals (always put forth as symbolic and significant of greater freedom), as the recent trials have shown, is Czarist in behaviour. What is "liberalized" is ways and means of getting rich for the elite class, the new bourgeoisie; but the apparatus of power becomes even more concentrated in the hands of fewer people, and it is a neo-fascist state which then emerges, or, as Chou En-lai called it, a social imperialism. Toward other countries, there is the same kind of exploitation as practised by any exploiting colonial power. The societal ethics have become self-interest, material incentive, and profit. The working class is once again betrayed. However, the depoliticization of workers and intellectuals is marked; and there is a long way to go before the failed revolution of these areas finds its way back to original aims. Meanwhile the rise of the new class, ever more perceptible class differentiations, as regards salaries, amenities, and educational opportunities between peasant and worker on the one hand and bureaucrat manager on the other, are reproducing the pattern of ruling class and exploited. Indeed, Sir Alec Douglas-Home pointed all this out when he congratulated Russia upon becoming "one of us," and predicted that the abandonment of revolutionary aims and of socialism would be of infinite value to the cause of capitalism, for thus the "brushfires" of liberation movements and revolutionary uprisings in Asia and in the rest of the world would be well controlled. And the hierarchized communist parties of Europe which follow the pattern and the orders of Moscow have shown the same degeneration, away from revolutionary staunchness; they have become ensconced in a hierarchy afraid of trouble, hostile to the real interests of the working class, useful in canalizing grievances into demands for higher wages. The last thing that Russia wishes, therefore, is revolutionary change anywhere in the world today, and so do these erstwhile communist parties. And today Russia is being looked at with hope for containing China; her introduction into India, into Southeast Asia, is welcomed as a factor for reinforcing the status quo. Overshadowing all else today is the complicity and collusion between the Soviet Union and the United States, and the epitomes of this process and of compromise and entente with capitalism are the Nuclear Non-Proliferation Treaty, Vietnam, and the occupation of Czechoslovakia.

Of this diarchy, this dual hegemony over a world to be exploited, à deux, Asia is fully aware as events follow each other; but when the Chinese started denouncing it eight years ago, very few people understood what the so-called Sino-Soviet dispute was all about; and indeed China was called bellicose, aggressive, et cetera, in that usual confusion of terminology and labels which characterizes much of what passes for information today.

This entente, this collusion, guarantees a second imperialism in the world. And the process continues. This is called liberalization. But Alexander Werth, an expert who has devoted two decades to Russia, writes in *The Nation* in 1968 that Russia is a police state, and that it is getting worse. And India, once so expert at balancing between the Big Two, now goes in fear of being also divided to serve the rapacity of her "friends."

The external policies of this new imperialism are guided by self-interest; but self-interest depends on values and appraisals and goals; those of Russia today are founded upon this dual hegemony of power in all its ambivalence. This was at first called "peaceful coexistence," which meant that Russia was no longer desirous of supporting revolutionary movements, but intent on coming to an entente with the USA. But peaceful coexistence with the United States did not mean a peaceful world; it was a phrase designed to mask the bilateral division of the world into spheres of influence; henceforth there could not, it was surmised, be any war possible between the Big Two; for war between them would be mutual destruction; but wars by proxy, for many reasons, would become rife; and indeed be a sine qua non for the continuation of the *entente à deux*. The Big Two would mutually agree on terrain and war, for such occasions would also be occasions for reinforcing their power, for getting export markets for armaments, obtaining privileges, and putting the weaker countries who depend on them in permanent debt.

Thus every moment of crisis in the world has been a step further in closer mutual agreement on carving up the world: Cuba has led to the hot line; the test ban, designed not to allow any other country to test atomic weapons, while the Big Two, having tested all they needed in air, now resorted to underground tests, was, as Stewart Alsop wrote, clearly directed against China. The Vietnam war did not prevent closer and yet closer meetings; including cultural, technical, economic agreements. The six-day war between Egypt and Israel served to reinforce Russia's hold upon the Mediterranean, and was notice of her interests there; the Pakistan-India war heralded Russian implantation in the subcontinent. The Treaty on the Non-Proliferation of Nuclear Weapons has received no dent from the Czechoslovak invasion, nor has there been a single effective gesture of protest by the United States, even though it was the self-proclaimed champion some three years ago of freedom anywhere in the world.

The nations of the world have now learnt the true meaning of "peaceful coexistence," under which they can prepare themselves to be partitioned and even, if needs be, occupied. The Treaty on the Non-Proliferation of Nuclear Weapons is the most important step in this global exploitation. For it bans any country *acquiring* nuclear weaponry but does nothing to restrain or limit the Big Two, who alone can proliferate at will, and continue to expand their nuclear arsenal. The danger of nuclear war is still present, it is not lessened, but what is really aimed at is a monopoly of atomic energy by the Big Two, both for war and for industrial development, holding the rest of the world in fear. India, the other potential emerging power of Asia, has understood this very well and resists with all her might the signing of the treaty. But will she be able to resist the relentless pressures for its acceptance?

During the whole period of the establishment of socialism, the Chinese say, the struggle goes on between two lines, the capitalist and the socialist, two possibilities of the economy; two mental superstructures, two world outlooks. Even when socialist power has been consolidated, there is always the danger, through bureaucracy, through the apparatus of power becoming corrupted, of reversal, and this can happen through *peaceful* transition, without violent overthrow or military coup, through "a handful in high places," as this is termed, wresting power and bringing about a restoration.

The class struggle therefore persists and must persist and *in new forms*. And since there is no ostensible bourgeois class, no visible capitalist or businessman, no big monopoly, the fight is against the bureaucrat, the occupiers of power who use it for their own interests, against the new class which can, and does, emerge out of the communist party apparatus itself, in alliance with remnants of the old bourgeoisie. How right are the Chinese? And how far will their example influence the rest of Asia?

Peter Ritchie-Calder. *Used with permission of the National Portrait Gallery, London.*

3

How Long Have We Got?
23 November 1971

Peter Ritchie-Calder

INTRODUCTION

The 1970s was a time of optimism for environmental action with great scientific advances accompanied by policy action and growing public engagement. The first world Climate Change Conference was held in Geneva in the final year of the decade just as Margaret Thatcher, a scientist by trade, became the United Kingdom's prime minister and the first world leader to put climate on the political map. A year later, in 1980, her ideological soul mate, Ronald Reagan, took office in the White House. Together, they were a formidable team, spreading neoliberalism across the West. By the time they were both out of office, climate change was no longer championed by Thatcher as a question of science, it had become one of ideology. In the decades that followed, climate was de-prioritized as economic growth continued to be pursued more ruthlessly than ever before.

This lecture, written in 1971, is chilling to anyone who has been following the public debate around climate change in recent times. Written and delivered by the Scottish-born academic and science journalist, Peter Ritchie-Calder, it would be difficult to find a more eloquent and captivating analysis of humanity's relationship with the planet and the devastating outcomes of it. If even up until very recently science communicators believed that volume and clarity of information would engage the public, Ritchie-Calder clearly understood something I have learned through my years as a researcher of climate communications – that engagement lies in story, in tapping into the emotions and values of readers and listeners. The earth as a "space capsule" and "mountains reduced to wrinkles," expressions which stop the reader in their tracks as they rework the visual landscape in their heads. Facts alone do not do it.

The lecture also betrays Ritchie-Calder's roots – born in Forfar, he later worked in Scotland's biggest city of Glasgow, my hometown. It is a city with a rich history of socialism, perhaps most known for the Red Clydeside, a period of radical political action in the early twentieth century, which took place on the banks of the city's central river. Ritchie-Calder was steeped in this socialist tradition and known for it in his native land. In his telling of the story of humanity, he centres the social, the interactive web of human co-operation and alliance that pooled intelligence and resources to bring about civilization. His critique similarly is founded on these values. If the social should work towards a common good, something that benefits all, the relentless pursuit of profit was the wrong path. As he sums up: "Growth to meet growth in terms of human essentials, yes. Growth for the sake of growth itself, no." This statement, and the lecture, leaves us with the biggest of questions; did we get it wrong?

And are we still getting it wrong? Because if the alarm bell was being ignored in 1971, it is still in many ways being ignored now in 2021. Decades of political inaction have left us far closer to climate catastrophe than ever. The young are still calling it out – with Greta Thunberg and her school strikers currently sticking Ritchie-Calder's metaphorical finger in the ear of the adults. This lecture is as important today as it was then. But will we listen now? If not, when?

*

Dr Catherine Happer is Senior Lecturer in Sociology and Deputy Director of the Glasgow University Media Group. She is an expert in climate communications and media, is co-author of *Communicating Climate Change and Energy Security: New Methods in Understanding Audiences*, and has given evidence at the House of Commons Select Committee on Climate, Policy, and Public Understanding.

LECTURE

McGill-Queen's University Press published Peter Ritchie-Calder's three Beatty Lectures in 1972 in a book titled *How Long Have We Got?* The following is an excerpt from the third lecture presented on 23 November 1971.

How long have we got? Is *Homo sapiens*' lease of this Planet Earth really running out? In his bleaker moments, Bertrand Russell said that it was a fifty-fifty chance that the human race would not survive this century. That was when he was convinced that a nuclear war was inevitable and that devastation and radiation would destroy life and leave this planet a radioactive desert. That was what Brock Chisholm meant by man's capacity to "veto the evolution of his species." If we avoid a total nuclear war, there is the other grim alternative that the species may multiply so much and so fast that it will starve or stifle itself to extinction. This includes the prospect that Space Capsule Earth will become a Black Hole of

Calcutta in which too numerous and too congested human beings will die from the heat generated by their own bodies.

We have to remember that Planet Earth is indeed a space capsule which is travelling at nineteen miles a second in its orbit round the sun. It is enclosed in an envelope, the atmosphere, strapped to it by the forces of gravity. While astronauts have demonstrated that it is possible to breach the gravitational fence and escape to the moon, for all but the very few, we earthlings are confined to the surface of this planet and our living space is definitely limited.

An eye, human or electronic, looking eastwards from the moon or from a space vehicle sees a globe round which a man-made satellite can travel sixteen times a day and of which only three-tenths is land and seven-tenths is covered with water. That eye, human or electronic, sees mountains reduced to wrinkles; evidence of surviving forests; tawny expanses of hot deserts which cover a fifth of the earth's surface and cold deserts which cover another fifth. It can distinguish the pattern of cultivation, the arable or cropped lands which account for only one-tenth of the land surface. That is the extent of man's family estate of which we are, at present, the improvident stewards.

In those terms, earth is not, like the moon, the inert geological relic of a cosmic incident; it provides the biosphere, the living space, for the evolutionary process which, we like to think, had its consummation in man.

A quarter of a million years ago, or thereabouts, *Homo sapiens* took a lease on Planet Earth. He shared occupancy with his fellow lodgers: the beasts, the birds, the fishes, the micro-organisms, and all the forms of plant life. His, however, was a special contract with nature, because he was now Thinking Man, whose conditions for survival depended on the use of his intelligence, his imagination, his foresight, and his finger-skills.

Let us be clear about this when we speak about man "interfering with his environment." The only reason we are still here is that *Homo sapiens* managed the hostile and inhospitable environment. The odds were decidedly against him because, without fang or claw, beak or talon, fur or feather, scale or carapace, naked to his enemies and to the elements, he had been, of all the creatures of the earth, the least likely to survive. He could not outwrestle or outrun his natural predators but he could outreach them with clubs and spears and slings. He made fleshing-tools to strip them of their pelts and clothe his nakedness. He tamed fire, which terrified all other creatures, and used it to heat his caves and cook his food. To that extent, he mastered his environment because with clothes and heat he could escape climatic restraints. In this way he had leased the whole planet since he could choose to migrate and settle anywhere from the Tropics to the Arctic.

Later, from being a hunter, he became the domesticator of animals – decoying, taming, and breeding them. With such flocks and herds, pastoral man moved to seasonal pastures synchronizing with nature. Then from being a food gatherer, he became a food grower. He discovered that seeds and certain grasses were nourishing but he also discovered that, if those seeds were scattered, they would take root and grow, and that they would grow better if the soil were delved to receive them and better still if they were properly watered. So he became a tiller and irrigator, settling in the alluvial plains of the rivers and creating a self-sufficiency of food for his family and for his domesticated animals. He presently found that there was efficiency in the division of labour and that some of his kind were more proficient than he or others in contriving tools, making pots, building houses, weaving baskets from rushes or clothes from finer fibers, or, a great advance, making wheels to lighten his haulage. From the produce of his land, the tiller obtained the produce of the craftsmen.

As a husbandman, he was still in communion with nature, nursing the soil, but he provided for the priesthood which had to intermediate between him and the gods who were the embodiment of elemental nature, sending thunder and lightning, floods and droughts, pestilence, and earth convulsions as reminders to Thinking Man that, no matter how ingenious he might be in modifying his environment, there were two parties to the lease and nature was still the landlord.

The temple tithe-barns of the farmers' tributes to the gods became entrepôts. The traffic in those farm goods produced trade with other communities and, when direct barter became too cumbersome, tokens of exchange had to be created; so money was invented. The money became a commodity in itself to be traded by the money-lenders, the money-changers, and the merchant bankers. Tangible wealth became attractive to marauders. So protection was necessary and warrior kings and conquering dynasties came into being. Settlements became walled cities.

This, the growth of cities, we call civilization but the whole superstructure, the craftsmen and their auxiliaries such as miners, the priesthood, the tax gatherers, the bazaar traders, the import-export merchants, the financiers, the soldiers, and the feudal systems and imperial adventuring of kings all depended on the labour of the tillers and on the soil which they husbanded.

Cities brought their own hazards. Thousands of years ago there were problems of overpopulation; congestion within the city walls; slum conditions; infections and contagions; sewage and trash accumulations, so that the archaeologists find the miniaturized version of our present pollution problems in the succession of cities built on the midden heaps of their predecessors.

And there were conservation problems. For irrigation, dams had to be built. The greatest king of the First Dynasty of Babylon was Hammurabi (circa 1800 BC), who promulgated a legal code regulating the management of dams and canals. For instance, Section 55 reads: "If anyone be too lazy to keep his dam in proper order and if the dam breaks and all the fields be flooded, then he in whose dam the break occurred shall be sold for money and the money shall replace the crops he has caused to be ruined."

In the excavation of the Indus civilization of five thousand years ago, the ruins of Mohenjo-Daro revealed the existence of booths where drinking water was sold. Alongside were huge spoil-heaps of broken cups, far in excess of the ravages of the most careless dishwashers and evidence of a sanitary code: When someone bought a cup of water, the crock was broken. This is what we would applaud as "hygiene." Today, and every day, hundreds of millions of plastic containers, cans, and non-returnable bottles are discarded. In the cities we call this "refuse"; in the countryside we call it "litter"; and, in general, we call it "solid pollution." The *once-onlies* of the Indus civilization have thus become a threat to ours. The largest kitchen middens of neolithic man, accumulated over centuries, measure no more than a few thousand cubic metres. Any township deserving a mayor will produce that much in a week.

Four thousand years ago the Minoan civilization was advanced in sanitation. Clean water was brought to the capital, Knossos, in pressure pipes; cemented stone drains provided the sewerage system; dry refuse was collected and deposited in large pits outside the city, earth silos in which wastes fermented into compost for manuring the fields. In AD 100, nine great aqueducts, with a total length of 424 kilometres, brought water to Rome and lead pipes carried it to houses and to one thousand public baths. The Aedile (the nearest approach to our borough engineer) could ride in his state barge along the main drain, the Cloaca Maxima, under the city to the Tiber. His scavengers, slaves, or prison convicts, shoveled the city's refuse, domestic and animal, through manholes into the sewer to be flushed into the Tiber and thence to the sea. This was commendable public health engineering. Today, grave concern is expressed with justification about the pollution of the Mediterranean by untreated domestic and industrial sewage. The sea itself has become the Cloaca Maxima.

In 1229, Henry III granted the first charter to the town of Newcastle-upon-Tyne to dig for coal for the comfort and warmth of its citizens. Seven hundred years later citizens of London, by the thousand, were dying of lethal effects of coal-burning. Today, by imposition of smokeless zones, London's public buildings are being restored to their pristine state.

In 1859, Drake's Well was drilled at Titusville, Pennsylvania, and the internal combustion engine was on its way to unleash ill-combusted hydrocarbons from automobile exhausts into the atmosphere. Today 6,000 million tons of carbon dioxide ransacked from the geological vaults of coal, oil, and natural gas, which were locked up tens of millions of years ago, are being vented into the atmosphere as an annual increment to the 360,000,000,000 tons of carbon already released in the industrialization processes of the past century. The concentration of carbon dioxide in the air we breathe has increased by approximately 13 per cent above the equilibrium of a century ago, and if all the known reserves of coal, oil, and natural gas were to be used similarly, the concentration would be ten times greater. In other words, the amount of carbon dioxide would have been doubled.

This increase is something more than a public health concern about damaged lungs and smarting eyes; it can materially affect the climate and conditions of the biosphere, on which all things, including humans, depend for survival. The climatic changes involve the "greenhouse effect." This is not a new scientific discovery. It was first suggested by John Tyndall in 1863.

The atmosphere is semi-transparent for solar radiation but is fairly opaque for terrestrial radiation – that is, for the heat radiated by the earth itself. For instance, in clear atmosphere (containing an average amount of water vapour, carbon dioxide, ozone, and dust) about 65 per cent of the incoming solar radiation reaches and is absorbed by the earth's surface. For the same atmospheric conditions, however, only about 10 per cent of the total radiation leaving the earth's surface is directly released into space. The rest is reflected back to the surface. As you can see this is similar to a greenhouse which lets in the sun's rays but confines the heat under glass.

In this mechanism, carbon dioxide is important because of its strong absorption (and subsequent emission) of infra-red radiation. In the atmosphere it would absorb the earth's heat, re-radiate it back to the surface of the earth, and further inhibit radiative cooling of the ground.

Fifteen years ago, when I was in the Canadian North and before the International Geophysical Year surveys began to quantify the carbon dioxide effects, the process was recognizable. It was beginning to impinge on the permafrost system. The Old Hands in the Subarctic were commenting on the extension of the black earth northwards. Areas which had been permanently frozen were beginning to thaw. In the Barrens the snows had reflected the sunlight but the seasons seemed to be changing. The black earth of the thaw was left longer exposed and black earth absorbs and retains the heat of the rays which the white snows would reflect. Thus the warmer soil remained longer exposed. In Norway they began to find in the black earth of the erstwhile snowlands the arrowheads of the time of Eric the Red, a thousand years ago, when in the natural cycle the soil had been last exposed.

You have probably heard the people who say that the scientists cannot make up their minds; they say that carbon dioxide will heat up the surface of the earth while at the same time it will cut off the sun's rays. "Make up your minds," they say. "Are we going to die of heat or die of cold?" Of course, it is not like that. We are talking about a system in which the greenhouse effect can operate at ground level, as it were, while upstairs in the stratosphere, at twenty-five kilometres and beyond, a different process is at work. The ozone (oxygen) absorbs solar radiation, raising the temperature at such altitudes, but carbon dioxide cools it by borrowing part of it so that a drop of temperature results in the stratosphere. The nature of those relationships, the heat exchange between ground heating and a stratospheric cooling, changes the transport system and the role of evaporation and condensation and the role of the ocean in providing a heat reservoir. The climatic forces are, therefore, altered and the lows and highs of the weatherman's chart become childish doodles by comparison. A doubling of the carbon dioxide concentration over the present level, which is possible if we accept the estimates of demands and use of fossil fuel by a doubled population, would result in an increase in mean surface temperature of about two degrees centigrade and possibly a decrease in the stratosphere temperature of four degrees centigrade.

This result will radically change the weather system. Areas now fertile will become arid; arid areas will become pluvial. But where? If the man-made glasshouse effect at the surface of the earth operates on this doubling principle, ice will begin to melt. The polar ice packs are not going to raise the sea level because, as good old Archimedes assured us, the weight of water displaced is equal to the volume of the solid. So floating ice does not count but land-locked ice does. The Greenland and Antarctic ice caps in thaw would be supplemental in volume and would raise the levels of the oceans, altering the fretwork of our coastal land masses. (I have been advising my friends not to take ninety-nine-year leases on sea level properties.) Moreover, there are the ice dams. Those in the Himalayas and elsewhere are holding back stored waters and, if melted, would wreak havoc in the lower levels. However skeptical one may be about the estimates and calculations, the excesses of carbon dioxide, man-produced, cannot be ignored. In greater or less degree it has much to do with man's real-estate options. The International Geophysical Year of 1957–58 alerted us. Far more scientific research is needed to inform us.

And now we have become aware of the ocean. (We talk about the seven seas but actually the ocean is one.) Seven-tenths of the earth's surface is drowned beneath the waters, an area so vast that it seemed that puny man could not possibly threaten it. We have sailed over it. We have hunted fish and sea creatures, including whales, to the risk of extinction. We have dumped, as far away from our own backyards as possible, deadly materials: high explosives, poison gases, radioactive materials, dangerous industrial chemicals, trash of all kinds, and domestic and industrial effluents.

We might, if we thought about it to that extent, console ourselves that nature has been pretty extravagant in the way it has discarded stuff into the oceans. For countless millions of years, the oceans have been receiving substances which we nowadays categorize as pollutants: radioactive nucleotides as a result of cosmic ray bombardment from outer space, and the erosion of rocks containing radioactive elements; the erupted products of volcanoes and chemically charged effluvia from seismic vents; hydrocarbons such as those found in oil, coming from natural submarine seepages, due to earthquake ruptures or evolving from the natural decay of marine plant and animal life; the accumulated effects of hydraulic mining;

the natural erosion by rivers and coastal waves and (always underestimated) the wind-transported particles from the continental hinterlands.

For example, for thousands of years, around the Mediterranean, man's "civilized" activities spilled pollutants. In the samplings of the sea bottom of the Mediterranean one finds the discards of the earliest copper-miners in Cyprus, of the ferrous metal-workers of Asia Minor, of the Phoenician tin-workers, of the Hibernian mercury-workers, and so on. And, of course, there was always domestic sewage but that encouraged, rather than threatened, marine growth.

The difference between now and the past, remote and more recent, is that human activity, multiplied by numbers, the needs and the ingenuity of an enormously increased population, is adding substantially to the amounts of those materials and particularly of man-contrived substances such as chlorinated hydrocarbons and radioactive materials which did not exist in nature and with which the marine ecology cannot cope. Such activities, divorced from nature, are doubling the natural concentrations of marine chemicals and introducing new chemicals – innovations – in quantities approaching those of naturally occurring chemicals. Those concentrations may be localized in terms of the vast expanses of the oceans but the effects may not be localized.

The direct effect of surplus and novel chemicals on the marine environment, particularly within enclosed systems such as the Mediterranean, is on marine biology. Marine life is a fine web of interrelated food chains which depend upon the chemical constituents of the sea. Diversity of species is essential to the stability of the ecological system. Crucial to the food chain is the phytoplankton which are responsible for 90 per cent of the living material of the sea and, moreover, for about 70 per cent of the oxygen of the earth. That is, our breath of life depends upon them. They provide the "pastures" for the rising scale of sea creatures. Their function and their profusion reside in the sea's surface layers to depths penetrated by the sun's rays. Those rays are responsible for photosynthesis, a process which, apart from producing food, liberates oxygen.

The ecological balance of the complex chain of life can be upset in a variety of ways. Some pollutants simply poison the plants and animals with which they come in contact. Others make such demands on the oxygen dissolved in the seawater that other living things competing for that oxygen suffocate for lack of it. Some pollutants encourage the excessive growth of a single species of plant or animal so that it prevails over others. Other pollutants are concentrated in species which have an affinity for them, without deleterious effects on themselves, but which pass them on up the chain in increasing doses until they become dangerous or lethal to other species, including humans.

An example of the first – direct poisoning – was the consequences of the spilling of two hundred pounds of endosulphan into the Rhine, with the massacre of the fish life. An example of the second – oxygen deprivation – is oil pollution. Apart from killing sea birds and so on, the natural decomposition of an oil slick requires its oxidization by the action of bacteria in a process which depletes the dissolved oxygen supply on which marine life depends. (One litre of oil depletes four hundred thousand litres of water of its oxygen.) An example of the third – excessive growth – is eutrophication arising from both domestic and industrial discharge which provides an excess of nutrients such as nitrates in fertilizers or phosphates in detergents. The excess produces a "bloom," a rapid growth of responsive marine species, usually phytoplankton, which multiply at the expense of other species. This is familiar in the coarse, slimy, blue algae associated with the outfalls of untreated sewage or the "red tides" of the Florida and California coasts and elsewhere. Obnoxious smells are usually associated with such "blooms," which in their proliferation kill other forms of life, and the blooms themselves, when they die, cause the deoxygenation of the water and the production of a sea desert. An example of the fourth – the "addiction" of certain forms of life for certain chemicals – is the now familiar story of DDT. This chemical can directly kill insects by paralysis. One of its virtues in the prevention of insect borne diseases is its persistence, lasting decades. It has been estimated that about 1,000 million pounds of DDT have already been introduced into the biosphere, and what with the wind-borne aerosols of spraying, and the run-off from agricultural activities, and DDT's long-life, most of that amount has, or will, finish up in the oceans. DDT, like other chlorinated hydrocarbons, is not readily metabolized but is stored in fat. Even when it is metabolized (changed by physiological chemistry in the body itself) the end result is another form of chlorinated hydrocarbon. Thus DDT (and the other chlorinated hydrocarbons) accumulates in marine life and is concentrated, in increasing proportions, in the food chain. Oysters have been found to amplify small concentrations of DDT seventy thousand times in one month. DDT has been found in penguins in the Antarctic, where DDT has never been used and thousands of miles from any sprayed areas. It has been found in the flesh of whales off Greenland.

Although we have seen what has happened to the streams, the rivers, and the Great Lakes, we still tend to think of the oceans as so vast that they can cope with all the waste we like to put in them. We forget that the ocean is a living system, not just in terms of the plants and creatures which it sustains within it but in terms of its circulation. This fact was powerfully brought home to me in the study which I did on the pollution of the Mediterranean.

The circulation of water, and with it of oxygen, in the Mediterranean is regulated by two "lungs" located in the Provençal Basin and the Upper Adriatic. The currents of Atlantic water, coming into the Mediterranean through the straits of Gibraltar, sweep into those two localities where the "healthy," oxygenated, surface waters are chilled by the cold winds spilling down from the Alps. They become dense and sink. The water thus transferred to the depths off the south coast of France goes into circulation in the western Mediterranean; that from the Adriatic goes over the sill of the straits of Otranto and travels eastwards to the Levant. With urbanization, industrialization, oil shipments, and the run-off from "medicated" soil of the inland farms, it is just in those "lungs" that the major pollution of the Mediterranean is taking place. If the transfer of oxygen between the atmosphere and the surface of the sea is impaired by thermal pollution, or chemical layers, or if the oxygen released by photosynthesis in the upper layers is reduced by interference with the micro-organic life, the respiration of the Mediterranean is affected and ultimately it will become a stagnant sea, like the Black Sea, depleted of oxygen. This possibility, in terms of posterity, is something more serious than the inconvenience to present day tourists of filthy beaches. By our irresponsibility today we are reducing the options. We are mortgaging man's family estate and nature may foreclose.

I have said, in the House of Lords, "Pollution is a crime compounded of avarice and ignorance." Avarice because of the reckless use of resources and destruction of amenities and the environment for the sake of quick profits. Ignorance because industrialists do not bother to find out and anticipate the effects of their activities. But we who protest against such things are also accessories to the crime. If more and more people want more and more goods and want them cheap, then the abuses become more and more exaggerated. It is a question of cost. Pollution can be prevented by industrial precautions, which are costly. When we insist upon them, industrialists tell us, "But you will price us out of business because our foreign competitors are not under those restrictions." Or the community picks up the social costs. But I also try to remind businessmen that pollution is gross mismanagement, incompetence, and the squandering of real wealth. What we call fumes, or effluent, or slagheaps contain valuable materials. Even eutrophication, which we hear so much about, is too much nutrient (from domestic or industrial sewage) in the wrong places.

How long have we got? Well, it is later than most people think. The alarm clock has gone off but, as parents of young children know, the child climbing up on your chest or poking a finger in your ear can rouse you more effectively than the bell. The youth of today and the protesting students are doing the Dennis the Menace job of clambering over our somnolent forms and sticking their fingers in our ears. We can make it if we rouse and run, but we have to run because we are on a down escalator and must move fast just to stand still, let alone mount. Our difficulty is how to arouse many of our institutions, including our academic institutions; how to arouse our political institutions and our institutions of moral evaluation, including the churches. The churches have the Sodom and Gommorah syndrome: if disaster is coming it is because we deserve it. Instead of standing back and disapproving, with pious horror, the self-assertiveness and irreverence of the young, we should be listening to their concern and their recognition of the unpleasant truths of the human predicament, which we, not they, created.

In the 1950s, young people marched to the dirges of despair because, like Bertrand Russell, they believed there was no future; the Bomb was to take care of that. Then, in the 1960s, when they began to realize that they might have a future, they did not like the look of the future they foresaw. Now young people are beginning to identify the nature of that future. Their concern about pollution, their concern about the environment, and their recognition that non-renewable resources are being squandered have brought them to their point of modern heresy. They are daring not only to question but to deny that growth, either for profit or for gross national product, is a paramount necessity. They recognize that prosperity bought at the price of pollution, of built-in obsolescence, of non-returnables, is no betterment of the human condition and is ominous for their future. Growth to meet growth in terms of human essentials, yes. Growth for the sake of growth itself, no.

In my experience the younger generation is asking the right questions. They are setting a timetable by the very urgency of their protest. That protest may sometimes sound discordant. It may be in an idiom that their elders find distasteful. Their methods may be brash and often repellent. But they are sticking their fingers in the ears of those who did not rouse to the alarm clock. Their priorities seem to me to be right and even unselfish – because it is very easy to conform and become Organization Man, especially when professional jobs are scarce and becoming scarcer.

After all, it is their world we are talking about. It is their responsibility from now on and the least, indeed, the most, my generation can say to theirs is: "We shall do everything possible to ensure that we do not do anything more to reduce your options to make your own mistakes." Time is of the essence. If we convert our awareness and our concern into institutionalized efforts to change the trends, we can postpone perhaps indefinitely the forbidding prospects on which these lectures have dwelt. I am an optimist. I believe we can beat the clock because I sit at the feet of my own children and listen with profit and encouragement.

One last word. I have given up predicting; I now prognose. There is a difference; if you predict, people plan for the prediction and in so doing confirm the trend. In prognosing, one is saying, like the wise physician, "I do not like the symptoms, and if you and I do not do something about it your prospects are pretty grim." But the operative phrase is: "if you and I do not do something about it." Here is the option and the commitment and the challenge which removes the sense of inevitability and increases the time span.

Robert Sinsheimer. *Used with permission of Caltech Archives.*

4

Genetic Engineering: Ambush or Opportunity?
7 November 1972

Robert Sinsheimer

INTRODUCTION

The acclaimed molecular biologist Robert Sinsheimer well understood that advances in human genetics would not only have major implications for human health and human evolution but would also have profound ethical and social consequences. These issues are explored in his 1972 Beatty Lectures. The first of these lectures "Genetic Engineering: Ambush or Opportunity?" focuses on genetic variation, human inheritance, and the prospect of taking over the human evolutionary story.

It is widely held that the Human Genome Project was the brainchild of Sinsheimer,[1] though Rene Dulbecco and Charles DeLisi are also credited with advancing this project.[2] Sinsheimer, a humble man, described his contribution in modest terms: "I merely provided the push to start the snowball rolling."[3]

In 1985, while chancellor of the University of California, Santa Cruz, Sinsheimer hosted a workshop to discuss an ambitious "Big Science" project for biology – to map and sequence the entire human genome. He saw this as a unique opportunity to "illuminate the ancient human quest to know what we are and where we come from."[4] The proposal initially met with considerable skepticism (first regarding its feasibility and then regarding its desirability). But clearly this was an idea whose time had come. The Human Genome Project was officially launched in October 1990 and completed in April 2003.

Since then, genetic and genomic research and applications have exploded. And, with the advent of CRISPR technology in 2012 and the birth of the first humans from genome-edited embryos in 2018, we are clearly on the cusp of taking over the human evolutionary story. As foretold by Sinsheimer:

> We are at that fateful moment when at last the species understands its origin, and thereby acquires the mastery of its future … As a species, we hold now in our hands the key to all the future of evolution.[5]

But do we have, in Sinsheimer's words, that "delicate balance between humility and hubris that will determine how far we shall trust our intelligence to displace that chance, which has brought our species to this point"?[6]

As we contemplate the possibility of altering our inheritance, it behooves us to ask and answer the question, "What kind of world do we want to live in?" We cannot know how Sinsheimer might answer that question today, but in 1972 he warned of "a growing profound disaffection with the swift moving course of Western culture."[7] He anticipated that this would "grow rather than diminish, for too many find it too difficult to obtain elemental human satisfactions in the modern world."[8]

Indeed, this basic stress has grown in the intervening nearly fifty years. This fact of our world informs my answer to the pivotal question. As I wrote in *Altered Inheritance*, I want to live in a world that "promotes equity and justice, and celebrates difference; a world that embraces neighborliness, reciprocity, social solidarity, and community; and a world that values collegial as opposed to competitive relations."[9]

I would like to think that were Sinsheimer alive today, he too would want to live in such a world. Is this wishful thinking? I hope not.

In his 1994 memoir *The Strands of a Life,* Sinsheimer wrote of duty, self-reliance, and responsibility. He acknowledged that it is "the capacity for voluntary action, that makes us human"[10] and that with choice come responsibilities. He also expressed gratitude to his forbearers for making possible the life he had enjoyed. These insights suggest that Sinsheimer would be inclined to carefully consider the interests of future generations in decision-making about efforts to control our biological evolution.

*

Françoise Baylis, CM, ONS, PhD, FRSC, FCAHS is University Research Professor at Dalhousie University. She is a member of the Order of Canada and the Order of Nova Scotia, as well as a fellow of the Royal Society of Canada and of the Canadian Academy of Health Sciences. She is the author of *Altered Inheritance: CRISPR and the Ethics of Human Genome Editing.*

LECTURE

The following is an excerpt from the full Beatty Lecture delivered on 7 November 1972.

In this evening's lecture I hope to develop the thesis that our inheritance has something to do with the fact that we are human beings, and indeed that our inheritance determines very considerably just what manner of human being each one of us is.

Now, this concept that we are each of us, through our inheritance, intimately linked to our past, our collective past, is not exactly new, although it is often received somewhat less than graciously. In my second lecture, I will hope to discuss some of the means by which our newer knowledge of genetics might be used to modify our inheritance, and the social and ethical problems into which this potential may lead us. But this evening I wish primarily to document this proposition to a detail that was really not possible until a few years ago.

In Shakespeare's great play, *Hamlet*, while conversing with Horatio after the wrenching funeral of Ophelia, Hamlet declares somberly, "There is a divinity that shapes our ends, rough-hew them how we will." In this and elsewhere in this enduring play, Shakespeare incisively comments on the human scene, and on the paradox of man, free and yet not free, whose most noble purposes are all too often confounded and confused by the inherent inequities of a chance-driven world. As Hamlet says, "So, oft it chances in particular men, that for some vicious mole of nature in them. As, in their birth – wherein they are not guilty, since nature cannot choose his origin." To paraphrase Shakespeare, I think one might also say that there is a pendulum in time that periodically shifts our human perspective, rough-hew that how we will.

In history, man's sense of his own destiny has oscillated between an exuberant freedom and a resigned fatalism, between the mood of the endless frontier and the mood of the limits to growth. And thus a century after *Hamlet*, John Locke wrote in a more hopeful vein of the tabula rasa of the human mind as a blank slate on which any message might be inscribed. And the pendulum has continued to swing between these poles, between seeming imperatives of nature and the apparently unbounded horizons, or the evolving human culture.

Now in our time we rely more upon science to sharpen our vision and do a larger understanding of the natural universe, and now increasingly of man's place therein to provide a fresh perspective in which to view the ancient dichotomies. And sometimes this enterprise provides a pure and a more profound comprehension of more familiar matters from our everyday world. A clarifying insight into truths which genius may have already included within, in poetry and theatre. And there was emerging in our time a new perspective on this old dilemma of human nature, and it derives from one of the major intellectual achievements of our species, from the discovery of the nature of heredity, and the understanding of the genetic process as a molecular map, comprehensible to man, explicable in the terms and laws of natural science.

In the past century, science has woven a faithful and brilliant synthesis of the concept implicit in the disparate discoveries of Darwin and Mendel in nature. The synthesis provides a biochemical understanding of the nature and transmission of life, and of the origin of those variations in transmission, which, as they provide the substrate for the sifting of natural selection, become the numberless steps of evolution. In the light of this new comprehension, we can now begin to glimpse our origins individually and as a species. We know that in the evolutionary sense, man is but the latest development in the whole continuous chain of life. The genetic endowment has derived by chance and selection from that of his immediate ancestors, and theirs from their ancestors, and he is ultimately surely defined and limited by his endowment, as they by theirs, with just perhaps one astonishing deliverance.

We can now see inscribed in our very molecules the traces of our ancestors of a billion years ago, and we can read the record of evolution's course. We can see also that our human civilization is not just a veneer, but is embedded in the genetic grain of man. And we are coming slowly, hesitantly, and perhaps prayerfully, to realize that we stand at the turning point of all evolution. That we are at that fateful moment when at last the species understands its origin, and thereby acquires the mastery of its future.

What truly have we learned? We have learned of the existence of the DNA memory, the molecular memory of life. We use chemical code as written, the successful designs evolved and accumulated over the billions of years. We have learned of the hierarchies of molecular design through which the sculptured molecules form a self-reproducing cell, and through which the clustered cells form an organism, and through which the interlaced neurons form a brain. We have learned of the interactive chemical machinery of each cell in which the DNA memory finds its expression and of the cellular organization in which arises the potential for DNA's self-reproduction. We are learning of the nuances of the control of DNA expression that permit the specialized diversity of cell types, so to compose the brain, and the muscle, and tissue. We are learning of the faithful human consequence of inevitable error in the DNA memory and therein we begin to glimpse the meaning for each individual man of his particular genetic endowment.

There are the twenty-three pairs of chromosomes that comprise the human genetic endowment, and these twenty-three pairs of chromosomes is the blueprint for a human being, a complete album of the genetic background. If we could read the DNA chains of these chromosomes alright, we would know the potential height of this particular individual, his colouring, his skeletal frame, his likely lifespan, the chance he will develop schizophrenia, become diabetic, suffer from hypertension, or fall victim to certain forms of cancer. We could surmise his IQ and foretell his likely personality. Now I do not wish to imply that this blueprint rigidly defines the end product. Rather it defines a potential, or especially in man, a set of potentials for with his enlarged cerebral cortex, man is both more plastic and less specialized than most species. Man is peculiarly the social animal, designed both to need and to take advantage of the society of his fellows to achieve his potentials. Thus, we all know that the children of this generation are taller and reach puberty earlier than those of earlier generations, presumably as a result of better nutrition. What uses can be made of that cerebral cortex undoubtedly depend upon what knowledge and experiences are stored in them, and what skills in the manipulation of experience are inculcated. But always within the building limits.

As Noam Chomsky has deduced from his studies of linguistics, the language children learn to speak clearly depends upon what they hear, but their ability to learn a language and the deep rules of syntax underlying all known language are inborn and not learned. But the blueprint is truly individual, is insured by the remarkable diversity of the human gene pool. Spaced along these twenty-three human chromosome pairs are the individual genes, the determinants of specific traits of the structure of a protein such as hemoglobin, or the level of thyroid hormone circulating in your blood, or your ability to develop an immune defense to a specific invading organism. At this time, we do not yet know the true number of genes in the human organism and the human chromosome set. Five hundred thousand is a plausible number. In general, each gene is carried in a defined location in a particular chromosome. Thus, the gene which specifies the structure of the enzyme glucose-6-phosphate dehydrogenase is known to lie on the X chromosome, that which specifies the enzyme thymidine kinase on chromosome number seventeen, and so on.

Now such a gene may exist in more than one form. The two or more forms of the same gene are called alleles. Since we each have twenty-three chromosome pairs, which originated as twenty-three chromosomes from our father and twenty-three from our mother, we have in general two copies of each gene. These may or may not be alike. The diversity of the human pool of genes is such that it is a reasonable estimate that some 15 per cent of your pairs of genes are unlike. With such heterogeneity, then we are indeed each unique and never to be repeated.

Much of our knowledge of the human inheritance is derived from studies of the consequence of its occasional imperfection. Thus occasionally, in approximately one birth in two hundred, a human is born with an altered chromosome set. Such a defect is most often, but not always, fatal. Indeed, many more are so conceived, but perish before birth. Sometimes it happens that an X chromosome is missing to produce the XO genotype, where there is one X chromosome, but not another X nor a Y. It is estimated that over 90 per cent of conceptions with but one X chromosome will die and abort before birth, but a few per cent survive. They will have what is known as Turner's syndrome. They will be females, sterile due to ovarian agenesis, short in stature, but predominantly normal, but with what is of particular interest, an unusual cognitive defect. The mean IQ of a person with Turner's syndrome is not significantly different from normal. However, it is observed that this mean is a consequence of an enhanced verbal IQ combined with a distinctly sub-normal performance IQ. The mean difference between these two scores approximates twenty points. Further analysis has indicated that the poor performance IQ is a consequence in these individuals of a major deficit in spatial perception.

A group of XO individuals from thirteen to twenty-six years of age was given a simple direction task. To follow visually a test route with forty-two turns and asked to specify visually the direction of turn, left or right. A controlled group of student nurses with the same average age given the same test made an average of 1.9 errors. The Turner syndrome group averaged 9.5 errors. No nurse made more than seven errors, while three quarters of the Turner group made seven or more errors. The ability of such persons simply to reproduce a geometrical design after a ten second exposure is markedly impaired. They were exposed to this design for ten seconds, and then asked to draw it. Similar difficulties were encountered in the direct copying of visual design. Again, these subjects ranged from ten to twenty-four years of age.

It is very tempting to associate this observation upon the XO people with the remarkable observations made in the past few years in professor Roger Sperry's laboratory at Caltech upon the lateral localization of cognitive abilities in the human brain. In these studies performed with human patients in whom the nerve connections between the two cerebral hemispheres had been severed as a therapy for epilepsy, Professor Sperry has shown conclusively that the left or a major hemisphere is the one normally employed for verbal and analytical cognition, while the right or minor hemisphere is the one normally employed for spatial or visual perception. In a formal sense, it would appear as though the XO condition resulted in a relatively enhanced development of the major hemisphere at the expense of the minor.

Now this is an exceptionally clear example of an unusual and specific cognitive defect associated with a chromosomal abnormality, and serves pointedly to emphasize that each of us feels in our very potential to perceive the world, to analyze and reconstruct it, to operate upon it, each of us is a product of a fabulous blueprint, and each of us is the product of our individual blueprint with its own constraints, and its own potentials, rough-hew them how we will. There are other syndromes associated with other chromosomal abnormalities such as the presence of extra chromosomes. Thus, the presence of an extra twenty-first chromosome, a karyotype with three number twenty-one chromosomes results in Down's syndrome.

The presence in males of an extra Y chromosome, the so-called XYY condition is known to be associated statistically, although by no means invariably, with increased tendency to unusual height and to difficulty in adapting to our social norms. Now, I should point out that it is only within the past three years that it has been possible to identify uniquely each of the twenty-three chromosome pairs. Newer methods of staining, particularly with fluorescent dyes as shown here, have enabled cytologists to recognize a specific banding pattern along the individual chromosomes. The examples of chromosomes six, seven, and so on, demonstrate the consistency of the banding patterns along the individual chromosomes. And these now permit an unambiguous identification of which particular chromosome one is looking at, by analysis of the unique banding patterns.

However, new technology has also resulted in a very unexpected finding. While there are characteristic banding patterns, they are not the same throughout the human population, and the banding pattern of a particular chromosome is a constant, and it is inherited. For example, in one case, the band pattern of one of the number three chromosomes of the father is different from the other, and from that of the number three chromosomes of the mother. The banding parent of both number thirteen chromosomes of the father differs from the mother in this instance. Likewise, the banding pattern of the X chromosome of the father differs from those of the mother. As yet, we have no idea of the significance of these individual variations. Because they are inherited, they have already found a somewhat ironic use in the resolution of cases of disputed parenthood.

Because they are less likely to be so devastating and fatal, we more often observed the consequences of modifications in single genes. The individual genes are segments of the DNA, tracts of several hundreds or thousands of nucleotide pairs, along the double helix of Watson and Crick. That is, a single gene is a track of some several hundred or thousands of these nucleotide pairs.

The whole genome of man comprises about six billion nucleotide pairs distributed among the forty-six chromosomes. We of course cannot yet begin to see the variations among the different alleles of a gene, but we can increasingly detect the variations in the gene products coded by the diverse alleles. And as a consequence of the increased recognition of the role of inheritance in human affairs, it has been increasingly possible to associate such variations with medical and behavioural syndromes. Some two thousand human ailments are now recognized to be the consequence of genetic variation or genetic defect.

A classic instance is that of sickle cell anemia. In this crippling disease under reduced oxygen tension, the red blood cell is deformed from its usual biconcave disc shape into a sickle shape, which in turn occludes small capillaries, and becomes increasingly fragile. We now know the cause of this disease to be the presence in the affected person of an altered form of hemoglobin, a mutant form due to the presence of a mutant allele of the normal gene for one of the two protein chains of the hemoglobin molecule. This mutation, which is probably a change of only one nucleotide pair in the DNA, affects only one of the 146 amino acids of the protein chain, but that is sufficient. Take for instance the amino acid sequence for the beta chain of hemoglobin. It starts in a shorthand. This is a code. These are code words for the various amino acids, as this chain is composed of 146 amino acids. In this specific sequence it starts with valine, histidine, leucine, threonine, proline, glutamine, glutamine, et cetera, and this chain, when properly folded, comprises what is known as the beta chain of human hemoglobin. The amino acid sixth from the beginning, is glutamic. This is in normal hemoglobin. In the beta chain of the human who has sickle cell anemia, there is one change. In this chain, the glutamic is replaced by the amino acid valine, and that is the only difference, and that one chain results in this crippling disease. All the rest is the same.

An instance in which a single gene alteration has an altered behavioural characteristic is that of the Lesch Nyhan syndrome. Among the characteristics of this syndrome is a periodic compulsive self-mutilation. Biochemically, this gene, which is known to be located on the X chromosome, determines the structure of an enzyme, which is known as guanine hypoxanthine ribosyltransferase (the name just proves that we know what to call it). And this enzyme is defective in the afflicted children. The connection between the enzyme defect and the behavioural trait is as yet, however, obscure.

In other instances it is clear that a complex of genes generally unknown in number, but certainly more than one, may determine an important characteristic. Detailed studies of twins, of siblings, of families of natural and foster children have all substantiated the conclusion that at least within our Western culture, performance on IQ test is principally determined by inherited qualities. But the number and nature of the genes involved therein is quite unknown. Similarly, the tendencies to schizophrenia or to manic depression, again, have major genetic components. The results of twin studies done on the American veteran twin registry show the concordance rates, that is what is the likelihood in this set of data that if one member of a twin is manic depressive, the other will be, is 38.5 per cent from monozygotic twins. There is no concordance for dizygotic twins. Monozygotic means what we call identical. For schizoaffective cases, it is 50 per cent. For schizophrenic, 23.5 per cent. Since the normal incidents of any of these in the population is of the order of 1 per cent or less, this type of concordance between identical twins is far outside the bounds of ordinary probability, and clearly indicates a genetic component.

With our increasing ability to cope with diseases of external origin, these complex ailments of internal malfunction, such as hypertension, diabetes, various forms of mental illness, sickle cell anemia, cystic fibrosis, and so on, have come to comprise a major source of human woe. It is estimated that 25 per cent of the hospital beds in the United States are occupied by persons suffering from diseases with major genetic components. Thus, our health, our norms of behaviour, our abilities to cope in a complex world depend very directly upon the inheritance we have for so long taken for granted – on this genome, this fabulous complex of chromosomes and genes, of which we so often only become aware when the machinery fails in its intricate task.

Now, this remarkable genome of course did not arise fully developed from simpler atoms and molecules. It evolved over the tens of hundreds of millions of years through innumerable trials and innumerable selections, resolving in a progressively more complex organism, better suited to adapt and to survive. And because evolution proceeds step-wise by small modifications to existing patterns rather than by scrapping the whole design and starting all over, the traces of our ancestral forms are still to be seen in our genes and our molecules.

Consider the other chain, the alpha chain, of the hemoglobin molecule that I referred to previously. Now all the vertebrates have red blood cells with hemoglobin, and one may compare their molecular structures, the molecular structures of their hemoglobin, with that of man. This gives the alpha chain in the same shorthand of normal human hemoglobin. And we find that we can retrace the course of vertebrate evolution in these molecular relationships. The alpha chain of the hemoglobin of the chimpanzee is identical. In the alpha chain of the hemoglobin of the gorilla there is one change in an amino acid. All the rest is the same.

Looking at considerably more different species, the hemoglobin of the horse differs in its alpha chain from that of man in eighteen of the 150 some-odd amino acids, all the rest, again, are the same. Still more remote are the lines which lead to the fish, such as the carp, which differs in sixty-six amino acids of the 141, and actually has two insertions and one deletion relative to that of man. But conversely, seventy-five of the 141 amino acids are identical in the identical positions. Now the evolutionary lines that lead to carp and to man are thought to have diverged some 400 million years ago, and yet we can still read the evidences of our relationship. With other molecules more basic to every cell it is possible to trace our ancestry further yet. In the cytochrome molecules, which are part of the respiratory chain in every cell, one can find evident progressively divergent molecular relationships going back through the vertebrates into the invertebrates, even into the fungi and the yeasts. The lines leading to the yeast cell and to man diverged perhaps a billion years ago, but both show the molecular imprint of our common ancestor.

These relationships can also be shown, as yet less adequately, in the nucleic acids themselves. Our relationship to the other primates has long been evident morphologically. It can now be documented as I showed in terms of hemoglobin structure, and also at the level of DNA. The DNA of man and the DNA of the chimpanzee differ in terms of nucleotide composition by less than 2 per cent. An important 2 per cent. Now, what is important, of course, in our relationship to the primates is the fact of our differences, and we are slowly gaining anthropological and ethological insight into the evolutionary changes that accompanied that critical development. And it has become clear in retrospect that the development of culture itself acted as a new and powerful selective agent, once the species undertook to rely for its survival upon the cultural transmission of acquired knowledge instead of relying solely upon the slow accretion of genetically transmissible behaviour patterns.

Once the species crossed that Rubicon, then selection favoured those variants that were best able to acquire, and utilize, and transmit the accumulating culture.

From that time on the behavioural qualities of man, his abilities to remember, to communicate, to reason, to anticipate, were shaped by his culture through genetic selection. And these qualities in turn shaped his culture in a synergistic, progressive positive feedback, which must have led to an extraordinarily rapid evolutionary process. In the course of this, man became the social animal, adapted to and dependent upon his culture for his full development, with a brain adapted to acquire a language, and to use tools if given examples, and with cerebral feedback processes dependent upon outside response for their closure.

In recent millennia, the development of culture has proceeded rapidly with, as far as we know, very little change in human inheritance over the past thirty thousand years. And we are perhaps beginning to be aware that the evolution of culture itself has its own laws, that just as the external culture is an element in the feedback cycle that has led to the evolutionary development of modern man, so also man can be thought of as an element in the feedback cycle that governs the evolution of culture. And we may also perceive that the direction of the evolution of culture is not necessarily such as to remain in harmony with the unchanging human inheritance. Indeed, today we see a growing profound disaffection with the swift moving course of Western culture, and I expect this basic stress will grow rather than diminish, for too many find it too difficult to obtain elemental human satisfactions in the modern world.

Now we know, as yet, all too little of the changes in the cerebral organization that accompanied the transition from primate to man, and correspondingly, we know all too little then of the genetic basis of man's most distinctive characteristics. It is plausible that there must have been an increase in cerebral plasticity to accommodate to the acquisition of cultural information. Originally plasticity may have been introduced as a means of developing through experience more accurate perceptual and motor mechanisms than could readily be built in with imprecise parts. In the development of man, this modest device has perhaps been exploited into a whole new dimension of learning, but its mechanism remains obscure.

But that this evolutionary invention of a culture-using species with an expanded but inevitably limited cerebral plasticity should have been so extraordinarily successful could hardly have been anticipated. That this species should also thereby have invented science and demonstrated a capacity to comprehend the basic laws of nature seems even more extraordinary. And that this species, building upon the profound knowledge of the nature of matter acquired by the advances in physics and chemistry in the first half of this century, has now been able to elucidate its origins and comprehend at least an outline of its intricate inheritance can only be considered a miracle. But there is yet more, for we can now see that such a species stands at a unique point in the whole panorama of evolution.

These remarkable discoveries do more than simply add to our store of knowledge. They add an entirely new dimension to the realm of human choice. And in so doing these discoveries must inevitably change man's outlook and his relation to his universe. I think they have already made certain the final acceptance of the concept of human evolution, and with this also the acknowledgment of the very significant role of genetic determination in our individual human destinies. But such acknowledgment can now be more palatable, for it need not be coupled to a despairing fatalism. If we can comprehend our inheritance, we can by the same token conceive its deliberate modification, and we are already hearing such proposals for the relief of genetic defect, and beyond that for the transformation of man.

As a species, we hold now in our hands the key to all the future of evolution. The issues and responsibilities posed by these new possibilities are strange and they are unfamiliar. They arose apprehension and nervous concern, but they also impel us to probe most searchingly into the basic questions of the meaning of humanity. To probe into the definition of man, and the acceptable range of human genetic variation, into the responsibility of man, the first informed species, for this planet and all of the life upon it. To look into that delicate balance between humility and hubris that will determine how far we shall trust our intelligence to displace that chance, which has brought our species to this point.

The issues posed by the potential for human genetic change are indeed profound. They may transform philosophy into an experimental science, but they cannot be avoided ever again, for in fact, here we are at this point in our evolution. We will need new guidelines. Indeed, I believe in new perspective with which to view this new challenge. But perhaps we can find a new stance for man in a lucid understanding of our roots in nature, and the clear demonstration that man is complex and often erratic in behaviour, which is in fact the logical outcome of his evolutionary origins. We are in nature and of nature, an extraordinary product of unfulfilled and probably undreamed potential, but we are not alien. We belong here. As we climb arduously out of ignorance, out of the shadow depths, to look back from time to time may help us to understand where we are, and to see how far we have come, and help us to sense how very far we may yet advance.

Alfred North Whitehead, the British mathematician and philosopher, wrote, "It is the business of the university to create the future, and let us work at it."

NOTES

1. L. Roberts, R.J. Davenport, E. Pennisi, E. Marshall, "A History of the Human Genome Project," *Science* 291(5507) (2001): 1195, DOI: 10.1126/science.291.5507.1195.
2. Lisa Gannett, "The Human Genome Project," *The Stanford Encyclopedia of Philosophy* (Winter 2019 Edition), ed. Edward N. Zalta, https://plato.stanford.edu/archives/win2019/entries/human-genome.

3 Robert Sinsheimer, *The Strands of a Life: The Science of DNA and the Art of Education* (Berkeley, University of California Press, 1994), 270.
4 Robert Sinsheimer, "To Reveal the Genomes," *American Journal of Human Genetics* 79(2) (2006): 194–6, DOI: 10.1086/505887.
5 Robert Sinsheimer, "Genetic Engineering: Ambush or Opportunity?" 7 November 1972, McGill University, Montreal, Canada, https://www.mcgill.ca/beatty/digital-archive/past-lectures/robert-sinsheimer-1972.
6 Ibid.
7 Ibid.
8 Ibid.
9 Françoise Baylis, *Altered Inheritance: CRISPR and the Ethics of Human Genome Editing* (Harvard: Harvard University Press, 2019), 220–1.
10 Sinsheimer, *The Strands of a Life*, 291.

5

The Emergence of Intelligent Life in the Universe

20 March 1975

Fred Hoyle

INTRODUCTION

Sir Fred Hoyle FRS is an iconic figure in astrophysics, known for his demonstration that stars produce the bulk of the elements out of which practically all matter is composed – including that in our own bodies. When Carl Sagan famously said, "we are star stuff," he was referring to Hoyle's work, now the bedrock of our understanding of stellar structure and evolution. But Hoyle is also infamous for coining the term "Big Bang" on live BBC radio in 1949, while ridiculing the now established expansion theory of the Universe and its implied initial explosion. Even long after the data incontrovertibly proved the Universe is expanding, Hoyle persisted in trying to prove it wrong, working to demonstrate a "steady-state" Universe that remains the same for eternity.

But one could argue that if a great scientist is not wrong some of the time, she is not thinking "big" enough. In considering the origins of life in the Universe, as discussed in his Beatty Lecture in 1975, Hoyle was clearly thinking about big topics. Driven by the then-recent discovery of molecular gas throughout our Milky Way galaxy, Hoyle surmised that planets bearing life in some form must be ubiquitous, since life's constituent building blocks were everywhere.

Today, we know of over four thousand planetary bodies outside our Solar System, with over a dozen confirmed to be rocky, like our own Earth, and at a distance from their own host Sun that suggests they could be life-bearing, and even habitable by human-like creatures.

However at the time of Hoyle's Beatty Lecture, the discovery of the first "extrasolar planet" was still two decades into the future. Today, detailed studies of the atmospheres of planets around distant stars can be done, including searches for "biosignatures": chemical signs in atmospheric composition of the likely existence of life on the planet below. But in 1975, such studies would have seemed more like science fiction.

Fred Hoyle. *Used with permission of the University of Waterloo Library, Special Collections & Archives, Central Photographic Negative Collection.*

This is what makes Hoyle's Beatty Lecture all the more astounding for its prescience; he was "bang-on" a topic that has today, nearly a half-century later, undergone a technological revolution. The search for extraterrestrial life has been embraced by mainstream astrophysicists, atmospheric scientists, geologists, and biologists, including at McGill, in the McGill Space Institute, in a search that some think could yield first fruits within the lifetime of people on Earth today.

One of Hoyle's other major contributions to science is apparent in his Beatty Lecture transcript – his gift for explaining science to the public. Hoyle's ability – and interest – in making the public understand complex but fundamental scientific concepts was ahead of its time and is as relevant today as it was in 1975, perhaps more so. Today's world could use more Hoyles – controversy and all – both to drive forward the frontiers of science through vision, knowledge, and creativity, as well as to engage non-scientists in these era-defining endeavours, while promoting reason, logic, and evidence-based thinking.

*

Victoria Kaspi CC FRS FRSC is Professor of Physics at McGill University, and holds the Lorne Trottier Chair in Astrophysics and Cosmology as well as a Distinguished James McGill Chair. She is the inaugural Director of the McGill Space Institute, and specializes in observational studies of neutron stars and fast radio bursts.

LECTURE

The following is an excerpt from the full Beatty Lecture delivered on 20 March 1975. Unfortunately, the source recording of Fred Hoyle's Beatty Lecture was incomplete and therefore this excerpt ends abruptly.

There may be many forms of life of which we are totally unaware, and which we can only barely conceive. For example, you might speculate on the possibility of life being based on the properties of what we call nuclear matter, the centres of atoms, rather than on the electrons which surround the centres of atoms, life in an exceedingly dense state.

At our present level of understanding, this would be more a matter for certain kinds of science fiction stories than for a talk such as this tonight. What I propose to do now is to bypass all the strange things which might possibly exist in the Universe, in favour of an attempt to argue in terms that we can be fairly certain that we can grapple with in a tolerable amount of detail. This implies that in discussing the emergence of life, I will be meaning chemical life based on the properties of the carbon atom.

In contrast to the situation a few decades ago, we believe today that we know quite a bit about the nature of this kind of life. We know that this kind of life is based on a complex of chemical atoms, of chemical reactions, with substances called proteins playing a dominant role. Although in terms of the food that we eat every day, we know that we are required to have a certain intake of proteins in our food, it is important to notice that we do this not for the sake of those particular proteins that we eat but, rather, for the substances out of which the proteins are made. These are called amino acids. What happens is that these amino acids, which are contained in the proteins that we eat, are built up within our own bodies into our kind of proteins, the proteins required specifically by our kind of creature, the human being. A dog proceeds similarly, using the same basic amino acids that we do, but building them into proteins structures suited to itself, and so for all the animals. We all use the same basic amino acids, but we arrange them individually according to our separate needs.

How is this done, you might ask? How does each animal manage to build just what is right for itself? Nowadays, we even understand the answer to this crucial question. Each of us contains within ourselves a kind of vast chemical blueprint, which is simply copied time and time again as our kinds of proteins are made, enough to serve our bodily functions.

It is not my purpose, however, today to develop the chemical basis of life, such as I have been hinting at now, in any real detail. What I am concerned with, just in these introductory remarks to my talk, is to emphasize that life is now seen to be based on a complex, but well-ordered, form of chemistry, which is to say, on the relation between various kinds of atoms. The relations between atoms are described by physics, by methods that are well understood.

Indeed, no very deep knowledge of physics, such as one would require in order to grapple with modern problems on the inner structures of individual particles, is needed in order to calculate how an atom of sodium and an atom of chlorine combine together to form the molecule of sodium chloride, the molecule of common salt. The relevant basis for this kind of understanding was discovered nearly fifty years ago in the work of Heisenberg and Schrödinger. It came already at the beginning of that revolution of physical thinking, which became known as quantum mechanics.

Yet, although we believe we understand the basic principles on which molecules and atoms joined together, are constructed, it is beyond our ability to calculate, starting from the basic principles, the detailed behaviour of any but the simplest molecules. It would be possible to calculate the properties of a very simple molecule like sodium chloride, common salt, with reasonable precision, but it would be quite beyond our powers to calculate the properties of a protein containing a thousand or more of these amino acids. The intricate maze of detail involved in such a calculation goes beyond our capacity, even when we are aided by the most powerful of modern computers. In other words, the world possesses a level of intricacy which we cannot remotely approach, even though we believe, with some justice, that we understand the principles on which the intricacy is based.

All this is very odd and very interesting. By restricting ourselves to the study of very simple systems, we seem to be able to discover rules, according to which the world is constructed, on a much more complex scale. Perhaps, you might ask, could it be that our ability to follow through to an understanding of the more complex scale is a temporary handicap? Could that be? Could one suppose that, eventually, all these complex matters will be calculable as science advances? Many scientists believe yes, but I must say for myself, I doubt that this will turn out to be so. I doubt that there is any simpler description of the Universe, taken as a whole, than the Universe itself.

The usual concept of the scientist, that eventually he will be able to build a so-called model of the Universe, which will serve to describe with complete accuracy the behaviour of the actual Universe is, I personally believe, an illusion. What we can do, however, is to build models which give a satisfactory description of limited aspects of the Universe. It is when we come to demand full detail that the trouble arises. As I just said, we can manage to deal with the molecule of sodium chloride perfectly well and, in doing so, we gain insight into the general properties of proteins, and of even larger biochemical structures than the proteins, but we fail in our endeavour to describe full detail.

To put it very briefly, I think our brains permit us a perceptive view of the Universe, but not a complete view. It is subject to this inherent limitation that I am going to consider what can be said, first, about the emergence of life in the Universe and, second, about the emergence of intelligence. Then, by combining what we learn about these two things, I wish to go on to give some thought to what the outcome for life here on the Earth may turn out to be in the centuries and millennia that lie ahead of us.

Although I spoke of amino acids as being much less complex in their structure than proteins and, although the proteins themselves are much less complex than the remarkable long-chain molecules which carry our genetic heritage, it is important to realize that even the amino acids are complex compared with the substances that life evolved from in the first place. These must have been quite simple molecules, such as a molecule of water, hydrogen cyanide, carbon dioxide, and possibly ammonia, in fact, just the kind of molecule which astronomers have recently discovered to exist in vast numbers within the gas clouds of our own Milky Way. Take for instance the Rosette Nebula. Within this nebula are lots of places where there are just dense blobs of gas. It is inside those blobs that systems like our Sun and planets are supposed to be formed. There is another one, the so-called Trifid Nebula, where you can see the gas is lit up by the stars which lie inside it and also great bands, which are the clouds of dust and the gases being made to glow by the stars.

I would like to stress that the people who are interested in the origin of life had already specified the sort of molecules that they thought life would be formed out of, long before these astronomical discoveries were made. It is not that these molecules have been found and then chemists have said, we could make something out of those. By thinking about the problem of how you might make amino acids, chemists had decided that these were the sort of molecules they would like to have. Then, what has happened is that astronomers have found them, not on a planetary scale, such as our planetary system, but in gas clouds that contain, on a simply fantastic scale, tens of thousands of times the amount of material that there is in the Sun.

There is absolutely no shortage at all of the basic life-forming materials. In view of this widespread diffusion of the basic life-forming molecules, as we have been seeing everywhere in the galaxy, and almost certainly in all the other galaxies, too, one would naturally suppose that life is likely to be widespread throughout the Universe. The beginnings are there, the right beginnings from a chemical point of view, and the basic physical laws which permit the chemistry of life, are also the same everywhere in other places.

Similar structures to ourselves can be expected, simply because of the vast profusion of planets and stars. There is something like a hundred thousand million stars in our galaxy alone. Astronomers nowadays believe that quite a large fraction of the stars probably possess planets of a similar kind to those which move around our own Sun. In other words, there are strong reasons for thinking that a considerable fraction of the stars in our galaxy, perhaps 50 per cent of them, possess planets moving around in them. In considering the emergence of life on a galactic scale, we have to think of something of the order of a hundred thousand million possible sites of a planetary type.

Life might also arise, of course, in other ways than on planets – I am not excluding that – in ways that we can scarcely conceive of. We do not really need to worry about that, to speculate about it, because we have got such a rich number of possibilities that it is quite adequate if we simply keep to a hundred thousand million possibilities.

Of course, you can say, well, even granted you have this enormous number of planetary systems, not all of them will be suited for the emergence of life. Among the planets of our own system, the Earth is very special, as we shall see. If we look at Jupiter, it has a very large number of possibilities of places where there are great disturbances. Some people have speculated that Jupiter is a possibility for life, particularly the kind of polar regions which seem to have considerable convective up-drafts of material in the atmosphere, where some form of kind of living cells might be suspended there. This has been speculated as a possibility, but this planet is very, very different from the Earth.

Saturn also is very, very different. If there is any form of life, it is kind of not our kind in these places. What I should say, is that the basic chemicals are very much the same. One has to take it perhaps with a fairly large pinch of salt, that there is the possibility. It would not be outrageous if somebody did find living cells in a planet like this. The chance, I think, of those living cells having aggregated to form any complex creature, multi-celled creature with the sort of complexity that we find in the plants and animals on the Earth, will be rather slight. One might expect something like the single-celled bacteria or single-celled algae to be possible here.

If you see a picture of Mars from close by, it looks less inviting than Saturn. This is why it is called the Red Planet. It does not look awfully good at the moment, although again, it has to be regarded as a possibility that cannot be dismissed. The moon too is not an inviting place at all. There are people who say that we are going to get rid of excess population here on the Earth by going to places like this, well, not me.

The Earth however is so manifestly different from the others as to bring home to us that if the Earth had not been present in our system, if a Sun, a place, possessed eight planets without the Earth, then it is quite reasonably probable that the solar system would be sterile. Among other systems of planets, we must appreciate that, indeed, some of them, perhaps many of them, will be sterile in the same way. There will not be life there.

You could ask the question, what fraction would you expect of other planets to show life? In one sense, this is a very critical question and we would certainly like to have a definitive answer to it. Actually, it is a question that we can bypass because it is less important, important as it may be in itself, than a second question. For all the astronomically and chemically unfavourable cases, does a large number of suitable sites for the emergence of life still remain? That is the more important question to consider tonight. After all, of the something like a hundred thousand million possibilities to start with, and if only 10 per cent of them are astronomically suitable, and if only a further 10 per cent have the right kind of chemistry, you still have as many as a thousand million favourable sites left. It seems rather unlikely, from the kind of estimates that we can make, that the favoured fraction would be much less than this, less than, and I will repeat it, a thousand million favoured sites for the origin of life.

The first step toward the origin of life is comparatively well understood, and this is the first step where these molecules get together into more complex structures like amino acids, structures not complex like the proteins at all, or like the still bigger biochemical molecules, but a sort of intermediate stage of molecules contain something like thirty to a hundred atoms.

The central feature of this first step is that it supplies a store of energy, which can then be used to drive the more complex systems. This source of energy comes from a central star, in our case, from the Sun. This first step is simpler than the later steps, and it has been studied in quite a lot of detail. I think it is right to say that, essentially, all the workers who have been involved in this matter, seem to have little doubt that it would take place in almost all cases. It is not difficult to produce a door, the situation where, if you are given a source of radiation like the Sun, the radiation is able to feed into the building of molecules, molecules like the amino acids or like the sugars, that have got an in-built source of energy within them.

So far, so good; yet, given this energy store, while obviously still a long way from a synthesis of the exceedingly complex molecules on which life is based, this is now a very interesting step. It is a first lift in a hierarchy, the hierarchy of life, in which work is going on today, the gap between the amino acid and the protein, trying to investigate the further steps which must take place before the first self-replicating biological cell can happen. Until more is known about this big first step in the hierarchy of life, it is still too early to make a quantitative estimate of the probability of life emerging in a particular case.

There could be barriers, requiring highly improbable circumstances, which could eat into a thousand million cases-plus, even to quite a substantial degree. On the other hand, one must say that it has been the experience so far that estimates of probabilities always seem to rise, not to fall, as more becomes known about the problems that are involved. This has certainly been the case on the astronomical side. Concerning these molecular clouds that have been discovered recently, the same thing is demonstrated on the chemical side. A few years ago, people would have thought one was crazy if you had said yes to whether the whole galaxy is actually chock-full of things like hydrocyanic acid.

My guess is that the same situation will again occur as more becomes known about the biological details in regards to this first step in the hierarchy, where you go from molecules containing, say thirty to a hundred atoms, up to the proteins. One could really say that what at first sight seems incredible and unobtainable, becomes credible and obtainable as our knowledge increases. For this reason, I do not think it is an unreasonable speculation to suppose that life has arisen in many millions of cases, perhaps in tens or even hundreds of millions of cases. That is in our own galaxy alone. If this were so, it would set the nearest planetary system to our own, on which life has arisen, at a distance of about a hundred light years, meaning that if we could exchange messages with intelligent creatures in such a system, the message would take a few centuries to pass between us. This is to run quite a bit ahead of what I want to say about intelligence. We are still back at supposing this first step in the hierarchy has been achieved and we have the first living cell. Much still remains before life, as we know it, can happen, particularly before intelligent life can emerge.

Even on the Earth, complex life forms, creatures aggregated from very many cells, were a long time in coming. To show what happened to life on the Earth, you have got to think of a clock, where a hand goes from the twelve o'clock position and makes one circuit in clockwise sense. It takes the full age of the Earth to make that circuit, four and a half billion years, or thereabouts.

Consider the Earth four and a half billion years ago, and then four billion years ago, three, two, and one billion years, a thousand million years, and so on. The emerging life forms started off as bacteria. They have existed an awful long time. I was a bit surprised about this. I thought for a time that bacteria would not get along unless they had animals to deal with. Yet, animals only arrived right at the end of the business. They really have a great ancestry, running right back about three and a half billion years, at least.

Then the next thing emerges, the green and the blue-green algae that run back something like three billion years. It is only in this last sector, spanning five or six hundred million years, that all the kind of complex evolution, which has produced the life that we normally think about, the plants, animals, and so on, has happened. This evidence seems to indicate that, until comparatively recently, a barrier of some kind existed on the Earth, a barrier which prevented complex multi-cell creatures from existing and which only permitted the single-cell. The bacteria and the algae are single-celled. It is interesting to speculate that this barrier, which seems to have been present on the Earth, might have arisen from a temperature effect. It is interesting that there is a very clear correlation, with respect to temperature, of these early life forms.

The oldest life form, the bacteria, can exist up to the boiling point of water. The next highest form of life, the next form of life existing up to a high temperature, the green and the blue-green algae, will go up to about seventy-five degrees centigrade. Fungi will go to about sixty degrees and then, of course as you come to the multi-celled creatures, they can only exist at a lower temperature. It seems an attractive idea that what happens if you have a high temperature is you still have life, but the cells have got to be so protective in their outer regions. They have got to have such a low conductivity to heat that this inhibits the properties of the cell walls. Cells are very constrained in their abilities to join. You have got far fewer chemical possibilities for allowing one cell to join with another.

It was only as the temperature came up on the Earth and this inhibition was removed that the cells needed far less in the way of protection against temperature and that they developed the ability to join. That is what it seems to have been. The interesting thing is, this evidence that the Earth was hot at one time, that leads, often, to very different directions, very interesting astronomically, but I do not want to get into it in this lecture.

Yehudi Menuhin. *Used with permission of Getty Images.*

6

Interpretation in Music and in Life
7 December 1975

Yehudi Menuhin

INTRODUCTION

I was eleven years old when I had my first personal encounter with Yehudi Menuhin. An aspiring violinist, I was allowed to go to the dress rehearsal of his performance with the Oakland Symphony (my mother deemed it too late to attend the evening concert on a school night). Afterwards I waited at the stage door hoping for an autograph. He appeared at the door, his parents in tow, both of them old and hunched over, she all in black and him in a too large trench coat, both worrying over their son as if he were still a young boy. It seemed exotic to me, a scene from a picture of the old world.

I have never forgotten that image. Nine years later I played for him for the first time at the International Menuhin Music Academy in Gstaad, Switzerland. I remember playing the third movement of the Bartok Concerto No. 2, and being not at all sure if it was good or not. His extremely kind and empathic words relaxed me immediately. He spoke as if to a colleague, complimenting me on things, correcting others, and commiserating as a fellow violinist in general on the difficulty of the piece. He spoke with great respect of Bartok's love for structure and the perfectionism evident in all his works, speaking to my young but eager understanding of those things.

In the many encounters over the years – lessons, rehearsals, concerts, recordings – I learned a tremendous amount from this great artist. Menuhin's desire to communicate the deep import of music, the foundations of creativity, indeed creation itself, and what the understanding of that means to us as individual artists and the world at large made me curious at the time and has reverberated throughout my life. Even as a young child, Menuhin seemed to already have access to this knowledge, and to be able to tap into it from somewhere deep inside himself. He spent his life trying to understand it and to share it with the public at large and with students who were ready and able to hear it. His teaching included instructions about education in general: philosophy, physical wellness, form. He was far ahead of the times in his holistic attitudes.

One can feel in this lecture two recurring passions from Menuhin's life. In the first part, his fascination with the universal themes of mankind. He speaks about the nature of creation as well as some quite spiritual concepts, for instance he refers to the "wedding of the personal with the universal" and describes in detail his theory about the advancement of humanity through three principles: empathy, the transformation of coarser matter to finer, and finally humankind's ability to actualize through inner vision. In the second part, the listener cannot help feeling Menuhin's sense of urgency as he translates his knowledge and observations into practical solutions for mankind. He then moves on to a rather prophetic analysis of the dangers of reducing what we consume to the lowest common denominator; that which sells, or of people losing their individual ability to discern what is good and healthy, the loss of humanitarian values, the exclusion of minorities, the necessity of the rejection of "isms," or the importance of self-imposed discipline and renunciation. In 1975 he sees the world at a turning point and appeals to the younger generation to take heed.

As with Menuhin's artistry, there is a timelessness about this wonderful lecture. It is not affected by trends, fashions, or popular opinions, instead it comes from a deeper level that runs underneath all the noise.

We are left with the feeling that one understands completely as he speaks to us, but the minute he stops, we cannot quite reconstruct it on our own. As so often when a master speaks, we realize that he has touched on something true and that there is a kernel and a seed of that knowledge in all of us. His words are as water, encouraging it to grow.

*

Nora Chastain, granddaughter of composer Roy Harris is a well-known soloist and chamber musician who is at home on the world's concert stages. She is a professor of violin at the University of the Arts in Berlin and gives regular master classes internationally where she combines the traditions of the American and European styles of the past fifty years. Her main influences were Dorothy DeLay, Sándor Végh, Ana Chumachenco, and Yehudi Menuhin. She is a founding member of the Menuhin Festival Piano Quartet.

LECTURE

The following is the full Beatty Lecture delivered on 7 December 1975.

I know I gave myself a very wide latitude in the title of the lecture. It is always safer that way. And I intend to use it in the sense of drawing the broadest possible parallels between the very specific, and certainly, judged by the area, very limited experience of a violinist, confined to a few square inches, not quite the full length of his arm. Although, in my case, my arms are short, so it is nearly the full length of the right arm. And otherwise, all the rest of the experience, the intangible part, being in fact, very wide, very deep, and covering centuries and encircling the globe. But, if there are later on, or if you have come with the hope of hearing specific comments on violin technique or violin interpretation, which you have the right to hope for, owing to the title of the lecture, perhaps you might then bring whatever you have missed in my words up in your questions.

I have prepared a few notes – one never really knows in writing them the day before, whether they are appropriate to the actual moment because one writes what one feels or imagines, but we will judge that later.

The violinist, perhaps more than anyone, is aware of the overriding importance of dreams, visions, ideals, of illusions, aspirations, and delusions and how very much we become and we are what we intend to be. The violinist must divine the composer's oral intention, the oral equivalent of a vision, extended and pulsating in time, a living entity, as it were, consisting of textures, speeds, volumes, and note pitches which must magically conjure the composer's private world – his ethos, period, and his message – and recreate this vibrating continuum for all to share.

The violinist is playing upon an instrument which embodies that specific quality and dimension of sound—another vision, which the great violin maker dreamt of as he chose in fashion, the wood. Finally, the violinist is himself an individual being possessed of his own dream and sound world, modeled on his personal experiences of life.

Now add to this trinity of – if we may call the idea oral visions, which is in fact a contradiction in terms, but I hesitate to use the expression "hearing voices" because that implies an abnormal condition – the living atmosphere of the occasion to which associated musicians may contribute, but above all the more or less enlightened expectation of an audience, and you have a typical human situation, consisting of our various indifferent dream worlds which we are trying to join – as far removed apparently from an assembly of nations, or businessmen, or from a marketplace as it is possible to be.

The difference is of course that in listening to music we all collectively submit to and accept one general vision, whereas when left to our own devices, we pursue narrower, often conflicting objectives no less illusory or visionary, which may or may not include an extended group of people.

The violinist is a solitary phenomenon. He carries his violin and bow. In my case, he rarely even uses a chair. He finds his own notes, he draws his own sound, he and his vision totally occupy his place in space and his instant in time. As a laser beam focuses light through space and time, so does the violinist tune in on his fraction of infinity and eternity. In saying this, I feel that I am in fact describing a typical act of creation. That single unique act, which partakes as much of infinite past as of infinite future. That sublime and ecstatic instant, sublime for being at the same time the assertion and the immolation of I, of the ego upon the altar of unknown, ultimate purpose. Prolonged and extended is this instant in music, poetry, in meditation, and in the creation and contemplation of great works of art, and repeated countless billions, trillions of times, in the eons of time, by almost every living creature, so that gradually and painfully, we have created our living earth, with all our fellow life with which we share it.

Thus, are we individually and collectively driven and beckoned, inhabited and possessed, by that greater purpose, greater than our own life. The human being, far exceeding any other animal objectifies this purpose. Art, symbol, ritual, music, and finally, every human activity, dress, food, manners, conventions, games, war. They all describe and express, they all pay tribute to this alter ego, the conscious self which sees itself. The fundamental duality of a nature which is and is aware. Is it any wonder that man's first created object, no doubt fashioned in all modesty – a clay human figure – became an object of worship, an idol, and that God himself was assumed likewise to have created man in his own image?

However elusive and mysterious the vision of ultimate purpose may remain, I do believe it is possible to discern a very definite general direction in the evolution of our own minds and bodies, and this process is not unlike a composer's or an author's gestation and bringing forth. Nor even the more humble violinist in his effort to shape a phrase, to convey the very maximum in meaning, inflection, universality, and subtlety to the music, to the sounds he is making. It is a process, and I am continually speaking of the creative process, of simultaneous identification and communication, the wedding of the personal with the universal. The reconciliation of the instant with eternity. The inspiration and excitement of the newborn of that which has never been before with the immutable, repetitive rhythms of timeless continuity. Our technique provides the well-trodden, carefully cleared path. But our message comes on the wings of the moment, and it comes from somewhere within, behind, and above us.

I have a theory and it is that humanity advances, or that a work advances, or that a thought is shaped according to three criteria that are related to each other. The one of increasing resonance, the other, the second, decreasing density, and finally, evermore pronounced definition. By resonance, I mean that which enables us to vibrate in sympathy with everything else. Humankind, above all other forms of life, has the ability to increase its own sympathetic vibrations, and to stir in compassionate resonance with the most diverse manifestations of life. Regarding decreasing density, humankind, by taking thought and opening its heart, can leaven that impenetrable dark density of coarser matter. Finally, humankind can define and can become its vision.

I think that the vision of what lies before our fantasy is in fact always that which comes before the formation, the reality, which gives it shape and form. But alas, we know from bitter experience that human visions can be appropriated and even conceived for both good and evil. In fact, good-evil, as one word, is the potential of all our knowledge, of all our talents. When we try to find what there may be, which is only good, it is almost impossible to grasp it because the human mind can turn everything to both ends. Nor can we always distinguish ourselves between the good and the bad.

But there is one injunction, which to my mind, does tip the scales of good and evil towards the good side. It is quite simply, that injunction: "Love thine enemy." This does not imply sacrifice your own life to his, but rather to help him to dissolve his hate, his fear, and it is in harmony with, "Do onto others." By the way, when I say man, I would like every lady here to know that I mean woman, and every child that I mean child, and it is simply the shortest possible, no, it is even less than a four-letter word, it is only a three-letter word. But in many of your minds, it may be equal to a four-letter word.

Man is essentially a religious animal. A superstitious animal. For our duality, our consciousness imposes a constant presence, a witness to all our acts. We call it conscience. And we play games with it. We are continually trying to please that mirror of ourselves. To placate him, deceive him, reason with or lie to him, deal and bargain with him, thus making a sacrifice to win the favour. Sometimes arranging to pay ahead of time or on delivery, or by installments, or never.

But the measure of our conscience is surely that degree of resonance we share with the living. Often, in hotel rooms, I have opened the inevitable Bible at Solomon's proverbs, when considering the behaviour of nations, great and small. Inevitably those qualities: love, mercy, truth, trust, humility, readiness to learn, the illusory quality of wealth, the blessedness of understanding and knowledge, these are always referred to and that is why I feel that there is, inevitably and intuitively, an understanding of the good and the bad. We are wont, in our own day, to use our new literacy and our very cleverness to try to give everything an equal hearing, which is right and proper, and we are privileged to learn the degrees of good and bad, or the degrees of anything. Whereas in previous ages, we only knew certain things as definite, irreconcilables which had no relation to each other, today we are beginning to understand that there are degrees between everything. Degrees of speed is perhaps what distinguishes light from black holes in the universe. It is always the degree of speed.

But we are going too far in that we are suppressing also our innate sense of what is right and wrong, what is good, what is clean, what is wholesome, what is sensible. For instance, to quote from a few of these proverbs, "If thine enemy be hungry, give him bread, and if he be thirsty, give him water to drink." And then, the inevitable suicidal quality of pride and anger and that very wise admonition, which would really bankrupt our advertising agencies, "Let another man praise thee and not thine own mouth; a stranger, and not thine own lips." Now another quotation which would have something in common with my theory of density, "He that hardeneth his heart shall fall into mischief."

I believe we are meeting today at a turning point of history, for we have all reached certain limits which are obliging us to discover unknown denominators. We are, and you particularly, are now preparing to formulate a new and common set of values. They must be firm, but yet flexible enough to admit adjustment in accordance with a wide variety of human conditions and backgrounds. I believe the young people of the world have much in common. For one thing, we all share the effects of our technology and of pollution, off mental nervousness and physical strain. We have all come to admit our mutual interdependence, and the interdependence of all life on earth.

For the first time, young people are creating their own culture, and it is a universal one. Hitherto the elders had a strong hand in determining the direction and the conviction of the younger generation, and stability was provided by this admixture of the older generation's presence and authority. However, the young were exploited in the sense that they had to follow established, unquestioned tenants. Today, peer groups, largely autonomous, are formulating their own codes. The great question is, what permanent values will the young people of the world embrace? They are reacting against everything that is so propagandized or advertised. That is good and proper. Yet, they lack those permanent values which would enable them effectively to resist exploitation. Youth is still reactive and perhaps not as informed as it will shortly be.

On the other hand, the crystallization of permanent values is taking shape. Again, it is the realization of the interdependence of all life, the need to live within our means, the requirements of continuity in terms of recycling raw materials and energies. The essential requirement of reconciling discipline with spontaneity as artists must do every day. The rejection of the hypocrisy associated with the perpetuation of power, whether money or political, and the responsibility associated with free choice. Youth must now take upon their shoulders the responsibilities of the new power and independence.

If the young people do not serve society, serve the sick and the helpless and the old people, and defend their humanitarian values, recognizing their own interdependence with other generations, they will find themselves again regimented into Hitler-Jugend or any other jugend. I would urge them to choose not the transient idols but values of greater permanence. I would urge them to spell out their positive convictions. To reject all isms, to keep the good of each, to learn from each, but to become the slaves of none. I would urge them not to reject their parents or their teachers, because they are deeply concerned and love them, and wish them well and need them to learn from the children, as much as the children may have learned from them.

For just as the human young must have a longer period of preparation and education at the beginning of their lives than do other species, so too when emerging from their teens should the children provide their parents with a longer period of support and devotion. Youth too need places of worship and refuges for peace. These can be anywhere, in churches, in the mountains, and within ourselves.

We are in fact in a totally new age. For the first time in history, humanity is expected to be adult. We are no longer protected by a paternal God, nor are we any longer playing with toys. The distinction between toys and their adult equivalent, is of course, that the toy is not intended to injure or kill. Humanity is now able to destroy itself along with all other life. Pockets might well survive in China and in remoter corners. What is so tragically depressing is that total absence of adulthood in the deliberations, decisions, and goals of nations, their spokesmen, and their peoples. Mentally, psychologically, they are playing the old game as if nothing happened, bereft of vision. We know from the proverbs again that, quote, "Where there is no vision, the people perisheth," bereft of our objectives to our new broad responsibilities, unable to define worthy purposes.

Man has always been a creature prone to madness. Not only will he sacrifice himself and his beloved for a community or a principle, and this is one of humanity's titles to greatness, but also blinded by his ignoble passions, he will sacrifice himself, his country, and his world to inflict a lesser penalty on his enemy. Especially if he is sufficiently shortsighted to ensure, or so he thinks, today and tomorrow with no thought or responsibility for the day after.

We know in our heart of hearts that mankind does not control the bomb. We also know that mankind does not control the computer. For the computer is unable to provide guidance with undefined criteria, with matters containing imponderables, and cannot define goals. As an example, man has collected all the criteria required to go to and to survive on the moon. Speeds, distances, environmental situations, communication, et cetera. Perhaps hundreds of thousands of elements, assembled by teams working together to one clear aim. But in the total absence of true vision, what criteria do we feed into the computer for the survival of human beings? Have we defined or can we define the quality of that survival? Can we even speak of survival when our means are by definition suicidal?

And if we did decide to supply our computers with qualitative data, the basic animal and spiritual requirements of life, and if we did decide to explore the meeting points of Christian, democratic and communist, and Buddhist ideologies, including the humble study of smaller so-called primitive societies, the world over. And then if we did decide that the military defense of a nation is no longer consonant with that interdependent resonance binding humanity across national boundaries. And if we fed our computers with the essential criteria defining a creative peace with dignity between opponents – instead of supplying these computers with criteria for war, or for saving the status quo in terms of economics and power (which is, in fact, a nonsense, a non-assignment for we cannot save the status quo – it is in constant flux and shift) – and even if we defined humane goals, realistic ones, not mad or unreal ones, would we then abide by the computer oracles, the pronouncements?

We must be sensitive not only to the will of the majority, but to the needs and the ideas of the minorities. Just as we have recognized the principle of the equality of cultures, we have also thereby recognized the principle of equality for the smallest and the least. This principle was very well acknowledged in the principle of two houses of parliament. The one, according to numbers and the other, according to units of culture or states. I think that we must go back to that in any assembly. We cannot forget that we are dealing with human beings and the suffering or the aspirations of a single unit are no more or less than the sufferings and aspirations of any single unit anywhere. This is a healthy principle and will trim the arrogance of dominant cultures.

We also as musicians must not allow our democratically elected majorities to ride roughshod over minorities. I make an unashamed plea for active choice and for variety as against passive choice, and for that fierce and universal demon in all societies today, the minority or independent tastes. We all taunt the totalitarian countries when we question the choice there exists between candidates of a one-party system.

Yet, there is in fact greater choice between at least the personalities of two people, living people, than between the choice of identical mass-produced music and other events on our communications media and TV channels today. This kind of choice does not represent the organic variety and diversity of tastes of a population. It merely represents the choice of the purveyor governed by the calculated and the arbitrary, the largest and lowest common denominator of the saleable, producible, and the tolerable. We criticize our fellow men submitting to a numbing state propaganda. Yet, twist the dial of your radio and TV – and I admit that in my country, a few miles south, it is much worse than here – what do you find? A relentless onslaught, a battering, which if submitted to, reduces our living faculties, our expression of the verb to be. For one can be more or less. The index of creativity can be higher or lower.

For instance, when Ravi Shankar plays, or your wonderful Maureen Forester sings, the index of creativity is high. We are in fact remade as we listen to her, the compassion that our image of the world around us becomes a little more complete as we listen. We are revealed to ourselves. We know more, we feel more, we share and participate more. Therefore, we are more. The index of creativity is very low among the listeners who devour hour after hour of triteness, of overworked formula, of fodder for what I call the battery consumer, stuffed like those wretched battery hens. What choice is theirs indeed? Just as a drug addiction induces that pathological state in which the victim is no longer able alone to recapture health and independence, so too are the purveyors of our media responsible for abusing our freedoms.

I believe a very great deal would improve in our societies with self-imposed restraints or simply imposed restraints on our media. Several months without cheap sensation, without the teaching of the example of the incitement to crime and violence, without debased vulgarity (for there is a healthy and a wholesome vulgarity), without the driving us to the twin reactions of apathy and violence. Several months of real variety, not engineered choice. Several months of creative effort with programs of good music, not necessarily classical, popular as well. On TV and radio. Good illuminating plays of good and illuminating information – education, lectures – of insights into the many cultures represented in our great world. Every kind of art and folk art.

Am I speaking of utopia or is it really something within our reach? I believe in cross-fertilization. Not everyone likes Beethoven for instance and people should have great choice, but choices of quality. Minority tastes are my plea. We pretend to believe in equality but what is provided to us is rather the leveling of the bulldozer. Equality presupposes variety for there is no need of equality when uniformity prevails. Real equality is the mutual respect which the different accord each other. Real equality is the recognition that majorities and minorities have equal rights.

For instance, nobody in Canada would propose that an English or a French majority dominate the country, nor would they propose in Switzerland that an Italian, or German, or French, or a large majority or minority have the last word. It is of course easier when a separate language, region, culture, creates an easily recognizable entity and each has its separate means of expression. But in the mixed, urban population, where children, adults, students, people of every race, colour, creed, musicians, architects – they are all together – must they all gape at trash, at one kind of trash?

We should be quite clear about the universal evils in the free societies. We suffer in a different way, but with an equal assault on our minds and bodies. We are paying with cancer for the economic luxurance of our industries, and our commerce, and our economy; for the pollution of our minds with trash by which I mean anything that is saleable, the only criterion being that it be bought. These are the evils to which we will succumb. These are society's abominations. We have already discovered that we breathe, we drink, and we eat cancer. I personally do not feel that wealth created at this expense of shame is any more justified than the wealth created on the backs of slaves.

We are becoming sick societies and music is one avenue to compassion, discipline, and a new set of values. But even musically, we much impose restrictions. Our ears are assaulted when we shop and when we fly. We are not allowed one moment of peace or silence, but every opening is exploited as a commercial challenge.

You see, the violinist – as any artist or craftsman – knows the dimensions of the areas of the possible and the impossible, feels much about resonance and sympathy, and the mysterious realm of emotional and spiritual communication. And he knows that the creation, the forging of a new vision, and a new symbol is a solitary process.

The violinist also knows the uses of limits and restraints. We must begin to recognize the need for self-imposed limits. Our present limits do not stem from restraint, self-discipline, courtesy, or good taste. The limits we recognize belatedly are the crude ones of the marketplace or the disaster, saturation, dust bowls, economic crisis, manmade and natural disasters. The harm man can now do, even a modest, humble man with an electric saw, a bulldozer, a bomb, even a soft drink salesman peddling cancer, a peddler of drugs, or pornographic books. The damage these good, honest, simple people can do is appalling and frightening.

Our civilization does not teach restraint of appetites or self-discipline nor does it hold up high aims of service. Our education is in large measure one for career and for the making of money. In certain socialist countries, it is of a high order albeit somewhat old fashioned and rigid. But apart from the countries of eastern Europe, we have much to learn from the most primitive savage, who has his music not supplied by third parties, and has his tribal taboos. But we, without either primitive taboos or civilized restraints, what stands between us and chaos?

To understand how contagious is our present illness, we need only read certain papers from totalitarian countries. From those countries – which build the walls which separate certain peoples, north from south, east from west – in which they overlook their own glaring lack of experiment, innovation, they overlook the suppression of originality, and the challenge of individuals with authority. Their argument is like ours, that a culture must be a majority expression. But this is hypocritical because it never is and it carries the same false morality as our own argument that the majority public choice is final. It conveys the same arrogance of approach which refers to, quote, "Achitects of a new social order." Or, quote, "People as a whole."

One cannot think only of people as a whole any more than governments can think of people as a whole. We must think of all the people, and all the variety, and all the individuals, and all their needs. Nor in the final analysis can we expect our music or our art to save us. We must save ourselves.

I believe that we are on the eve of a new moral formulation. One which you will help to establish. This formulation must be consonant with our knowledge, the interchangeability of matter and energy, the equation, which I think is a parallel one, of flesh and spirit, to matter and energy. Respect for all forms of life, encouragement of individual, independent, creative voices. Yet, this new morality must be willing to accept restraints of every kind, of every kind of abuse, and must further and enhance that quality of life; the reduction of waste, the extravagance; the living within our means which is so important; the further control of the poisons which affect us physically and mentally, and which we breathe and drink. We must move away, I believe, a little bit away, but not all the way, from a moneyed, quantitative, and competitive society to a flexible, subtle, and qualitative one.

We should try to learn economy along with economics. We should try to study health along with medicine and disease. We should try to understand the human requirements for an inspiring and livable environment rather than study only engineering.

The violinist also knows that progress and achievement are not citadels to be stormed, not the achievement of demigods, nor within reach of mobs, but the result of a constant and gentle but unyielding faith in perseverance in the service of a loving vision, the one we carry in our hearts and minds so we may become that vision and thus be worthy of you and your children.

Ralf Dahrendorf. *Used with permission of J.H. Darchinger, Creative Commons License 3.0 Unported.*

7

A Swing to the Right? Socio-political Changes in the Western World

23 March 1981

Ralf Dahrendorf

INTRODUCTION

When Ralf Dahrendorf (1929–2009) at the age of fifty-two presented the Beatty Lecture in 1981, he had already become a towering figure. As director of the London School of Economics and Political Science, he saw this institution through a time of great changes; as a leading sociologist of his generation, his books on class society and role theory had become required reading in Europe and North America alike; and as public intellectual, his commentaries were omnipresent, convinced of "the duty to doubt everything that is obvious, to make relative all authority, to ask all those questions that no one else dares to ask."[1]

Dahrendorf's Beatty Lecture was no exception. He probes deeply into the great questions and policy debates of the early 1980s. Today´s readers will be surprised by how much of his diagnosis remains valid and impressed at how astutely he anticipated changes to come. He pointed to the dangers ahead including the crisis of democracy, populist politics and, as he would later call it, the "authoritarian temptations" of those left behind. The ligatures, that is, bonds that hold societies together by grounding individuals in value systems, had begun to weaken, creating opportunities for political entrepreneurs of many kinds.

By the early 1980s, the shift from an industrial to a service economy gained momentum, the welfare state entered a profound crisis, class systems began to change, and for many, a new confusing disorder and confusion ("neue Unübersichtlichkeit," in Dahrendorf´s words) seemed to take hold. He argues in his lecture that, "in a strange way, we are faced in many OECD societies today with a conflict between yesterday's world and the world of the day before yesterday."

What was this conflict about? Those from yesterday´s world kept fighting for more citizen rights and entitlements, and for more redistribution to achieve greater equality; those from the day before yesterday wanted to return to old values, and, in the name of individual liberty, "to take back from government what was once ours," to paraphrase Ronald Reagan. And here we see the direct link to major political events that had taken place just within two years prior to his 1981 lecture, namely the rise of Margaret Thatcher in the United Kingdom in 1979, with her bitter fights with the miners and the unions; and the election of Ronald Reagan as US President in 1980, carried by a surge of conservative values. For Dahrendorf, both events were carried by discontent and signaled profound shifts: changing loyalties, declining political participation, and realignments among voters.

For Dahrendorf, what the new conservatives and the established social democrats represented seemed not only outdated but also dangerous. Would a return to old values not also invite many of the past conflicts back in? And would greater entitlements and more equality not amplify rigidities and lead to inert societies? Without using the term civil society, Dahrendorf then suggests an alternative and envisions "a society in which decentralized units, and participation in decentralized units are the crucial social force, and in which governments appear increasingly irrelevant, whether they pretend to be benevolent, or whether they want to reverse course." This vision is a strong political statement, and Dahrendorf may well have been emboldened by the changes that swept through Central and Eastern Europe less than a decade later and helped elevate the importance of vibrant civil societies to centre stage.

Dahrendorf would return to his vision of the relationship between civil society, market, and government – outlined in the Beatty Lecture – in his later writings, especially in his sociology of conflict.[2] Yet he would also continue to struggle with that relationship, when at the height of the globalization spurt he argued that a growing and globalizing world economy would create "perverse choices" for liberal democracies: over time, staying competitive required either adopting measures detrimental to the cohesion of civil society or restricting civil liberties and political participation. For the West, the task ahead for the early twenty-first century, he wrote, "is to square the circle between growth, social cohesion and political freedom."[3] This challenge became known as the Dahrendorf Quandary,[4] and we are still trying to solve it a quarter century later.

*

Helmut K. Anheier is past President and Professor of Sociology at the Hertie School, and member of the Luskin School of Public Affairs, UCLA. From 2010 to 2020, he co-directed the Dahrendorf Forum, a joint project of the Hertie School and the London School of Economics.

A Swing to the Right? Socio-political Changes in the Western World

LECTURE

The following is the full Beatty Lecture delivered on 23 March 1981.

Mr Chancellor, thank you very much indeed for your kind and almost extravagant words of welcome. Nothing pleased me as much among them – if I may say so without being misunderstood – as to learn that I am indeed a sociologist on leave, who has been on leave from his discipline now for at least twelve years, which I am sure many of you in the audience will notice.

When I came, Chancellor, I thought I had reason to envy you presiding over a university which I learned was private, but received 80 per cent of its funds from a state government, since I am coming from an institution which is part of a university that is public, but now that overseas student fees have been raised to outrageous heights, only receives about 45 per cent of its income from government.

Since I have come here, I am afraid I have learned that our problems are very similar indeed, and that it is not the difference between public and private that is crucial; there are many other things which we have to worry about, and do worry about. I also learned, of course, ladies and gentlemen, that I have come into the middle of an election campaign and had I known that, I might have been a little more cautious with the subject which I have chosen.

But just to be sure that I am not misunderstood in what I am trying to say tonight, let me begin my story where it should begin, and that is, in Sweden. Sweden, as you undoubtedly know, is a country in which the Social Democratic Party has been the strongest party in parliamentary terms since 1917, and for much of the period starting in the 1930s, the Swedish Social Democratic Party, sometimes together with others, formed the government of the country. It was therefore a very considerable surprise to many people outside, if not inside Sweden, when in the early 1970s, in 1973 to be precise, the majority dwindled away, and the country for the first time had a shaky minority government, with an exact balance of political forces, and then in the next two elections, a majority of shaky coalitions of the centre-right rather than the centre-left. Indeed, there were many all over the world who took this to be a signal of changes in the political mood of countries which had traditionally looked to the centre-left for policies which would lead them into a better future.

Since these changes in Sweden, there have been a whole series of other developments which are worth mentioning as one takes a first glance at the Western world, the OECD [Organisation for Economic Co-operation and Development] world, with which I shall be concerned in these remarks. In the OECD countries, election results have been uncertain in their drift, but there have been changes which might be interpreted superficially as changes to the right. In Japan, the forever governing Liberal Democratic Party – "Liberal" means conservative in Japan – has strengthened its position after a phase in which its strength was doubted by many, indeed in which it might after all have fallen apart. In Italy, it is probably true to say that there is much less talk today about Euro-Communism than there was a few years ago, and it is probably true to say that the Democratia Christiana, which has also governed the country since the war, is once again firmly in power. Then, of course, there are the two events which are most often quoted in the context of the subject that I am talking about, that is the election of Mrs Thatcher in Britain in 1979, and the election of President Reagan in the United States in 1980. All this, even apart from what happened outside the OECD world, say in Jamaica, or in a totally different part of the world, in Poland, all this is often interpreted as a significant change in the underlying political mood of the developed countries of the world.

However, if we take a second look at the picture, even the figures to which I have referred by implication, look a little different. I already mentioned that in Sweden there was a period in which the two sides had 175 seats each in the Swedish Parliament. In the absence of a Social Democratic majority, the government coalitions of the centre-right have been exceedingly shaky. There are other examples, to be sure, there is Germany, although it has sometimes been said that Helmut Schmidt is the best conservative leader Germans could hope for. There are the examples of a number of OECD countries.

Who knows what the example of France is going to tell us when the French elections have taken place later this spring? But above all, there are certain significant, if frequently overlooked facts. Mrs Thatcher in Britain had in her sweeping "landslide victory," 33 per cent of the electorate on her side. President Reagan in the United States, in his own sweeping "landslide victory," had 25 per cent of the electorate on his side. Mrs Thatcher had fewer votes than Mr Heath had had in 1970.

This takes me to my first major, rather simple, but nevertheless perhaps not totally unimportant point. Not only did Mrs Thatcher have fewer votes than Mr Heath had in 1970, but the Labour Party in 1979 had fewer votes than the Labour Party in Britain had had at any time since 1931. As one takes a second look at the apparent changes in electoral preferences in the Western world and analyzes the figures that are now available more closely, it becomes increasingly apparent that what has happened in these recent years is not so much a truly significant shift from one side of the political spectrum to the other, as a turning away of a growing number of people from the traditional parties to which they had strong allegiances throughout the 1950s and well into, if not throughout, the 1960s.

There are analyses of electoral allegiances in a number of countries, and it is quite clear from these analyses that the proportion of the electorate which would vote for a particular party come what may has declined in every single country of the OECD world. Britain is perhaps an extreme illustration of this particular development. Figures seem to indicate that in 1951, the heyday of the two-party system in that country, 80 per cent of the electorate said that they would vote for one particular party and that party only. Today, the proportion of the electorate which is as firmly committed to one particular party has shrunk to nearer 20 per cent. In other words, in these last thirty years there has not only been a significant growth in the number of floating voters, but there has been a significant decline in the intensity of commitment to the major political parties. A second look at the electoral figures of recent years shows above all the enormous uncertainty which there is in people's minds as far as their political orientation is concerned.

However, as we look more closely into the situation we come to another point. This point is that there are without doubt in these recent years changes in the prevailing mood, not only of voters, but of those who are responsible for political debate in journalism, but also in the world of political theory. It is quite amusing to remember that when Ken Galbraith's programs on economic theory had barely disappeared from television screens, Milton Friedman appeared on these same screens; and today there are probably as many people, if not more, who remember Friedman's as there are people who remember Galbraith's.

Similar changes have occurred at other levels of debate. This may be a European view, but it seems to me that as one is still discussing John Rawls' *A Theory of Justice*, and is trying to work out some of the implications of that particular sophisticated notion of justice, Robert Nozick's *Anarchy, State and Utopia* has already conquered the minds of many and has introduced a rather different set of approaches to the social contract. Then there is the revival of F. A. Hayek. It is not without interest that this great economic, social and political theorist, who had one of the climaxes of his career in 1944 to 1945, when his *The Road to Serfdom* seemed to define the mood of a generation that was looking for liberty above all, then had, I am almost tempted to say decades, in which he was more of interest to specialists than to a general public. Now he has come back, has had a new revival, and is very much on people's minds as an author who represents the point of view that is characteristic of the time in which we are living.

I wish I could translate the German phrase, although it is perhaps no accident that it is difficult to translate, but in some strange way it is true today that *der geist weht rechts* – that is to say, while since 1848 one has said that intellectual life, intellectual development, intellectual originality, new ideas, the prospectus of a new world come from those who would define themselves as being on the left, we are now going through a period in which it appears that whereas the left keeps on repeating things, perhaps elaborating things, but does not come up with new ideas, quite a few original and interesting ideas come from what in traditional terms would be described as the other side of the political spectrum.

Now this is no more than a superficial introduction to the subject to which I really want to devote my attention, and that is: is there perhaps a change in the prevailing themes of Western social and political systems? This is the question which seems to me of major importance, above and beyond what happens in any election this year or next year. And, are there perhaps developments which turn us onto directions unfamiliar to those who are accustomed to the traditional terminology of right and left? Have things happened perhaps both in our economies and in our politics which lead us to a new kind of orientation into the future? What I want to do in trying to discuss this issue which will take me straight back to the basic question of attitudes to the future is take up two topical and contentious issues, and turn them around a bit to try and find aspects of them which may be relevant to these questions. One of these issues is the future of, what one might call, social policy, and the other is that complex issue which one can hardly call by its name, the issue of law and order.

Let me start with the social policy question. No doubt one of the great and important developments of these last decades, indeed one of the developments which marks the progress of these decades, is the extension of the rights of citizenship from purely formal rights to substantive social rights. I need not in this connection go into the details of a history which began with guarantees of equality before the law, which then went through guarantees of participation in the political process; but I do need to remind you that neither equality before the law, nor universal suffrage are as such full and satisfactory guarantees of citizenship rights. What was, and what perhaps in many cases still is necessary, is that these political and legal rights are filled with economic and social substance. What was, and to some extent still is necessary, in other words, is that people are actually put in a position to exercise the rights which they were given by our constitutions whether written or unwritten. This is the background for that great development which led to the welfare state or the social state, to the net of social security which has come to be characteristic of many, though unfortunately not all, countries of the OECD world.

I would argue – and I want to make this point very forcefully in order not to be misunderstood in my later remarks – that a net of social security which makes sure that no individual finds himself or herself in a state in which they cannot enjoy participation in the life of civilized society, marks enormous progress, and that this is progress which should not and must not be undone. This concerns old age as much as sickness, this concerns education, this concerns unemployment, and many other needs for which the community as a community has taken a responsibility.

Let me add one other point. I am entirely aware of the fact that the net of social security is by no means as tight as it would have to be in order to guarantee that as few individuals as possible can fall through it and suffer the indignities of sickness without help, old age without help, and the same is true for the other aspects of social security. In other words, it is true that we still have poverty, and what is worse, it is true that in many OECD societies, we have new forms of poverty, and perhaps we have not even got the categories to deal with them adequately. The notion of a new underclass is one which must be worrying to many. Thus the job of social policy is not completed.

And yet I would argue that there is, in fact, a set of new problems concerning the net of social security, which are real, whichever political view one may wish to take. This set of problems can be classified under at least three main headings. First, there are problems on the income side of the net of social security or social policy. It is quite clear today that it will be difficult to finance the systems of social security which have been created in Europe, perhaps to a lesser extent in this country, and certainly to an even lesser extent in the United States of America.

This will be difficult partly because we are all faced with demographic developments which are likely to lead, even bound to lead, to an increasing number of people who are entitled to benefits, and a decreasing number of people who contribute. These demographic developments are compounded by developments in relation to the years of life spent in employment. As working lives get shorter, there is naturally an increasing mismatch between social policy entitlements and tax income. At any rate – if I make this perhaps almost momentous remark in parenthesis without taking it up again – this is true as long as the system of social security is based on people's jobs, and on people's work position. Let me assume for purposes of this lecture as it is, for it is a fact of life. It is true in other words that as people's working lives get shorter, there is an increasing mismatch between contributing to the system and entitlements.

Moreover, it is true that all our systems of social security in the Western world depend on a fair, probably 3 or 4 or 5 per cent annual rate of growth – an aspect of the growth debate which is often overlooked, but an aspect of the growth debate which must surely mean that if it is difficult to achieve such growth, the system of social security will suffer on the income side.

Secondly, on the expenditure side there are problems in a similar order of magnitude. More and more people are entitled to social services – and who is to say that they should not be? There is the important issue of the entitlement of women in all systems of social services – and who is to say that these entitlements should not exist? There is no doubt either that the expenditure required in order to implement what is promised will lead to an increase in cost which is badly matched with decreasing income from taxation. There is, moreover, still on the expenditure side, the difficult issue of the bottomlessness of many social services. This is particularly true in the field of health.

In other words, it is very hard to tell when enough has been given in this system of redistribution. If one adds to the problems of income and expenditure a third set of issues, that of the organization of social services, one can see the full magnitude of the problem. What the social state has meant is that in order to enable people to make full use of their citizenship rights, systems of organization, bureaucracies had to be set up which in turn must appear to take away rights as much as they give them. In other words, it was quite inevitable, if one wanted to have a system of health insurance, indeed a system of unemployment insurance, or a system of old age pensions which is fair and acceptable, that one had to set up organizations, which as organizations, had to appear to many individuals as gigantic monsters, indeed as what Max Weber called them, an "iron cage of bondage." There is a sense in which these bureaucracies make people as dependent as they were in the world from which they tried to escape by becoming beneficiaries of the social services.

Bureaucracy is both necessary and ineffective. This leads to one comment which takes me right back to the main point, the political point. When I say that bureaucracies were necessary, but are ineffective, that they were needed and are regarded as new threats, I have made a point about developments of class, and the relations between development of class and political action. It seems to me that it is at least conceivable that there has been one quite significant change in these recent decades in all OECD countries, and that is that a considerable number of people, conceivably even the majority, have left the situation in which there was an antagonism of clearly delineated social classes, membership of which led to unambiguous political expression. Today, we must at least consider the possibility that what has happened in our societies is something very strange, namely, that more and more people find themselves personally and individually in an ambiguous class position.

They are in some ways not only dependent on a system of social security which involves bureaucratic organization, but they like it, because that is precisely what they need in order to have their citizenship rights guaranteed. However, the same individuals also resent the bureaucracies which boss them about, which force them to queue at counters, which turn them into numbers on a computer. In other words, the same individuals throughout these Western societies are both delighted beneficiaries of the system and resentful opponents of the system. And because it is the same individuals, so many of the reactions of people which we can see today, especially in politics, seem confusing and are hard to understand. It is still simple to draw the lines of class in theoretical terms, but it is no longer simple to draw these lines with respect to individual human beings and their social position. Much of the uncertainty of contemporary politics arises from this ambiguity of positions of class in individual lives rather than in society as a whole. I shall return to this point in a few moments.

With respect to the subject of social policy and the citizenship rights of individuals, it is bound to be difficult if not impossible for all OECD societies in the decades to come to keep the promises built into the system of social security. This is bound to be difficult for the reasons which I have given, which you might call economic. It is bound to be difficult also because there are reactions of people to the position in which they find themselves. So what do we do about it? What are the replies to this difficulty on the income and expenditure sides, in terms of organization and in terms of people's attitudes?

Here we begin to see characteristic reactions, in part hysterical, but nevertheless characteristic in the political world in which we are living. There are those who say that all this may well be so, but that nevertheless we have to stick to traditional policies; we have got to make them work by hook or by crook. Some want to do so by moderate means, by adjustments, by minor improvements; others argue that we have not gone far enough at all, and that there has to be a much more radical redistribution. I rather suspect that if they have their way – and this is true for both categories – and if we try to do more of the same thing, we will simply encounter more of the problems of income, expenditure, and organization, rather than less.

Then there are those who are usually meant when one talks about a swing to the right, who say that it is now obvious that we have gone far too far in this direction; people have been pampered, there has been an exaggerated redistribution, there has not been enough healthy inequality, or whatever the argument may be. What we need therefore is, simply and plainly, cuts in public expenditure never mind how they fall or where they fall; and these cuts in public expenditure have to apply to the system of social security above all. There are now examples of that kind of approach. These examples show that anybody who approaches the system of social security in this particular way is quite likely to reproduce yesterday's social problems, made worse by some of the obvious implications of a thoughtless and mechanical cut of public expenditure. I hope therefore that it is possible to think of another, more thoughtful approach.

There is a case for rethinking our system of social security, making sure that there remains a basic security, a floor on which everybody stands, a net, if you wish, through which nobody should be allowed to fall, but making the system more flexible beyond this. There is a need above all for two main developments; one is the decentralization of organization, and the other is individual participation and choice. There is nothing unrealistic about these suggestions; yet whether they will be adopted, or whether the more facile alternatives at which I have hinted, will prevail, is a large, open question.

At this point, let me turn to the other of my two illustrations of socio-political change, that is, the complicated and difficult issue of law and order. Law and order are not terms which a liberal happily uses these days, because they have acquired a specific political meaning in the discourse of our day. This is strange, because while every liberal may have a slight hankering after anarchy somewhere in him, or within her, I rather think that at the end of the day they would come up with a social contract which has a little more substance than the social contract discussed by Nozick in his *Anarchy, State and Utopia*. It is worrying that modern societies seem to have developed in such a way that the fundamental social contract, the agreement to protect one's own life by protecting the lives of others, is at risk.

This is a strange portent and a worrying development, and one which cannot simply be laughed away. I do not want to make too much of familiar figures about crime and increases in crime, but they too are facts which cannot be laughed away. It may be argued that the statement that every citizen of New York City has six chances in ten of being mugged in the course of his or her life is a statement about New York City only; yet something like this is true for cities in general. It may be argued that the statement that in England twelve times as many crimes were reported in 1974 than in 1900 is in part a comment on the expertise of bureaucracy in recording crime, and that in any case London was not exactly a non-violent place at the time of Dickens; but none of this argues away the fact that, taking British figures again, one in ten young people have been found to have committed what are called serious offences. It is very hard to argue away the fact, in other words – and this is the only fact on which I want to base my argument in connection with law and order – that somewhere in the lives of young people our society seems to fail in a curious way to provide any kind of plausible structure, any kind of meaning. It depends on specific circumstances, whether this is somewhere between fourteen and twenty years of age, or sixteen and twenty, or twelve and eighteen, or what have you. But it seems to me one of the most telling characteristics when one is discussing the social contract, one of the most telling characteristics of our societies, that there is the strange social gap in which there are no plausible social institutions, and no immediately plausible values, in which parents have failed, in which schools have failed, in which the world of employment is not open to young people, and in which there are no sensible alternatives. It seems to me that this strange gap in the lives of young people is one of the most disturbing characteristics of all modern societies.

When I say "disturbing," I do not want to be misunderstood. In my view, the choices which modern societies have offered to young people as to others are, like the advances of social policy, one of the great steps forward in the world in which we are living. The fact that there is mobility, not only in terms of stratification but also geographically, the fact that there are economic choices, the fact that there are political choices, the fact in other words, that people are not tied to the social place to which they were born, is a reason for rejoicing for anyone who is concerned about human life chances. But if one looks at the lives of young people – the same is true for others, but I have deliberately picked young people whose predicament illustrates the problem so clearly – it becomes evident that life chances are not merely choices.

If choices do not have meaning, if they are not placed in a set of coordinates which are plausible to the individual, they make very little sense. It becomes evident, in other words, that merely creating a society of infinite options does not by itself mean creating a society of liberty. It becomes evident that liberty is a very complicated fact, or value. Liberty requires not only the choices which an individual has in the economic, political, and social world, but also some categories of orientation which give the individual a chance to attach meaning to doing one thing rather than the other. It is for this reason that I have argued in my last book, called *Life Chances*, that life chances are not just options but require ligatures as well – ties, ligatures in the sense of obligations, ligatures in the sense of linkages – which somehow make human relations, whether relations of authority or of solidarity, plausible.

This again, put here in very abridged terms, is a set of problems like that of social policy with which modern societies are faced whether they like it or not. But once again, as in the case of social policy, it is easy to see how people can react to this set of problems in hysterical rather than sensible ways (to avoid the word "rational" which has so many meanings that one hesitates to use it). Once again, it is easy to see how some can wonder what all this talk about linkages, about ties, about the need for people to have meaning is about. There are so many people left who have not got the choices everybody should have – they would argue – so let us concentrate on choices, let us give them all the same horizon of options. And once again, I would argue that if we followed this particular path we would get ourselves even more deeply into that difficult mess of not quite knowing how societies of extended options can actually be held together, how they can be sustained without jeopardizing people's options. It is also easy to see how many people might come to the conclusion that all that is needed is the revival of traditional values. Let us make the family strong, they argue, let us revive religion, and so on and so forth. I suspect that anyone who follows this particular path is going to find that it is not only impossible to pursue it successfully, but worse than that, the attempt to re-establish a past that is gone is quite likely to lead to a multiplication of the problems of the past, and is therefore the least advisable way, if one is concerned about human welfare and about human life chances.

So far as re-constituting ligatures are concerned, let me just mention the names of two authors who are quite seriously concerned about this particular issue, and are trying to defend whatever the modern world has brought by way of knowledge, progress, and at the same time insist on the need for having ties and linkages as well as options. They may have failed, but I regard them as the kind of authors who are likely to help us more than those who give fairly cheap and hysterical advice one way or the other. One of them is Hans Küng, the progressive Catholic theologian. I am not a Catholic, so I speak as one who reads Küng with a view to finding authors who are trying to make sense of the world in which we live and add an element of ligatures. What he is trying to do is to point out that there may be a way of combining the knowledge acquired in this world in which we are living, as well as the options and choices with a new kind of Christian faith. I am not sure that Küng has entirely succeeded, but I am quite sure that reading his two books, *On Being a Christian*, and *Does God Exist?*, belongs to the more helpful experiences if one is concerned about this particular issue.

The other name which I want to mention, familiar to some of you, though perhaps not to all, is that of the German social philosopher, Jürgen Habermas. Once again, he may not have succeeded in his numerous essays in defining the ways in which new linkages can be created which are different from traditional ones. But when Habermas talks about communication – "unconstrained communication," as he prefers to call it – he is concerned with ways in which people may be able to find meaning through the company of others. In a sense, Habermas too seeks a new social contract, without being carried away by the obvious, though, as I have now put it several times, hysterical reactions of others. What Habermas and Küng prove is that there are ways forward without the rigidities of the past, or a swing to the right.

So much for the examples of social policy, and of law and order. I could have chosen a number of other examples to illustrate the main point which I want to make. I could have talked about economic policy, and about the strange alternatives which seem to arise in the economic policy debate today. I could have talked about international relations, and again, the curious alternative which seems to arise in the intellectual and public debate today. All this only serves to underline the main point which I have tried to make here, and that is that underneath essentially superficial, and in themselves rather unimportant political phenomena, we may find traces of the fact that a great historical force which has taken us a long way forward in these decades has exhausted its strength. One might almost argue that forces of production have turned into relations of production. The great historical force which has led to more life chances for more people has now become part of the rigidity of the societies in which we are living. It is no longer possible simply to go along the path of increasing human options if one wants to increase life chances. It is no longer possible to go along the path of simply tightening the net of social security, extending social policy, if one wants to give citizens in our society the full extent of the life chances which these societies have to offer. And since this is no longer possible, we find ourselves in a sort of quandary. The quandary is made worse by the fact that there are so many people who on the one hand benefit from the advantages of the processes of the last decade, and who on the other hand resent some of the implications of these processes. Bureaucracy is perhaps the clearest possible example of this ambiguity. In the face of this, and returning to the political aspect with which I have begun, one must understand the prevailing political reactions to the problems of today.

There are three such reactions. I have talked about them before, but in conclusion, I want to describe them once again. First, there are those who insist that the problems which we face today, such as those which I have mentioned, are ultimately due to the fact that we have not done enough of the right thing. They think that we have to go further in the direction of extending citizenship rights, or perhaps of creating equality, though that is one of those imprecise terms which are easily used in polemics and have often not got a very good place in analysis. There are those in other words who say that we need more of the measures which redistribute the wealth of societies in order to benefit those in need. Some of them are of a moderate temperament, and want to do so in democratic ways, perhaps social-democratic ways; some of them would prefer more radical solutions and are not that worried about democracy. All defenders of this particular line of political argument are convinced that there can be a benevolent state which can somehow deal with the problems which have arisen. However, it is one of the implications of my attempt to spread out before you the political issues and their underlying social forces as I see them today, that this benevolent state will turn out to be very malevolent indeed. It is my view that this allegedly benevolent state will increase the problems which I have talked about.

Then, secondly, there are those who would like to reverse trends, and they of course are the ones who are usually meant when one talks about a swing to the right. There are those who would like to see a return of old values. They are a very strange group, if one looks at them in practice. I do not propose to engage in a political polemic, but I do want to say that if one looks at what can so far be seen of the practice of this particular attitude, it oscillates between a kind of announcement politics which cannot deliver because the world is recalcitrant and more complicated than is assumed, and simple-minded solutions which lead to the return of old problems in an aggravated way.

Neither of these approaches seems to come even close to the problems which are real enough and which have given rise to them in the first place. In a strange way, we are faced in many OECD societies today with a conflict between yesterday's world and the world of the day before yesterday, and nothing could be more unfortunate for those who are concerned about the extension of human life chances than this particular fact.

Here and there, I have tried to hint at possibilities of another and different solution. I myself am increasingly convinced that it is not the state, not government which will answer the questions which I have discussed. I am increasingly convinced that a better future will come by action which is taken in what you might call unofficial ways, by action which is taken by people where they live, where they work. I am increasingly convinced that what will govern the future is what I like to call a market society: a society in which decentralized units – and participation in decentralized units – are the crucial social force, and in which governments appear increasingly irrelevant, whether they pretend to be benevolent or whether they want to reverse course. I think if one looks closely at the societies in which we are living, one can find many illustrations of the thesis that people are usually better than the governments which they have elected. People usually find more sensible solutions to problems than those who sit in their government houses. In any case, it would seem to me that there are possibilities of which some aspects are real already, possibilities of progress by initiative from below, which are the really significant forces of the future.

However, such developments towards greater individual participation, including participation in safeguarding one's social security, or the creation of new ligatures, will take a long time. In the meantime, the OECD societies are going to be faced by threats, not only from without, but also from within. What I have called hysterical reactions will not disappear. It is quite possible that mistakes may be made. Governments are always better at making mistakes than at constructing a better world. Mistakes may be made for which many of us pay dearly. It is also possible that the price of progress, the absence of plausibility, of meaning, of ligatures, and the presence of gigantic bureaucracies will lead to a fairly lengthy phase of situational politics in which it is quite unpredictable from one election to another, indeed from one year to the other, where people's preferences lie. More than that, not only politics, but action will be situational; it will be blind action, including blind protest. Building new social structures from below is a process which takes more time than most people have these days, and I am afraid it is quite possible that we will not have that time. Yet I have always believed that this kind of overriding pessimism, whether it is about the nuclear threat, or whether it is about internal social threats, must not prevent one from trying as hard as one can to extend and improve human life chances where one lives.

NOTES

1 Ralf Dahrendorf, "Der Intellektuelle und die Gesellschaft," *Die Zeit*, 20 March 1963, translated and reprinted in "The Intellectual and Society," in *On Intellectuals*, ed. Philip Rieff (New York: Garden City, 1969).

2 Ralf Dahrendorf, *Der moderne soziale Konflikt. Essay zur Politik der Freiheit* (Stuttgart: Klett, 1994).

3   Ralf Dahrendorf, "Economic Opportunity, Civil Society and Political Liberty," United Nations Research Institute for Social Development (UNRISD) Discussion Paper 58: 4 (March 1995), http://www.unrisd.org/80256B3C005BCCF9/(httpAuxPages)/AF2130DF646281DD80256B67005B66F9/$file/DP58.pdf
4   Helmut K. Anheier and Alexandru Filip, "The Rodrik Trilemma and the Dahrendorf Quandary: An Empirical Assessment," *Global Perspectives*. Forthcoming. 2021.

Gwendolen Carter. *Used with permission of Smith College Archives, Gwendolen Margaret Carter Papers*, CA-MS-00341.

8

Apartheid: Dying or Resurgent?
9 March 1982

Gwendolen Carter

INTRODUCTION

In 1948, Gwendolen Carter made a trip to South Africa. It was a fateful year for the country, as the white electorate brought into power the Nationalist Party with its agenda of strict racial separation under the system of apartheid. That visit would define Gwendolen Carter's career as well, setting her on course as a political scientist specializing in southern Africa, and as an archivist who would make an immeasurable contribution to historical studies of South Africa.

Carter's opposition to apartheid and its multiple injustices forms an unbreakable line in her work. Her response was scholarly: she embarked on the work of studying a country that she described in her Beatty Lecture as an "affront" to the world. Her reading of apartheid aimed to understand the ways in which the state sought to elaborate forms of control over black people, and the multiplicity of forms of resistance to those efforts.

Over several research visits to the country and the region, she interviewed countless political actors, and formed friendships with many in the leadership of the resistance movements. Among them was Nelson Mandela. She attended the Rivonia Trial in 1963, initially welcomed into the foreign visitors' gallery by the Nationalist Party government who assumed that she (and other foreign guests) would be impressed by the application of the rule of law. However, Carter and her colleague Thomas Karis[1] made apparent that what they saw was a grave miscarriage of justice and signaled their sympathy with Mandela and his co-accused; so incensed was the government that the following day they shut down the foreign visitors' gallery completely.

Gwendolen Carter would go on to become a founder and later the doyenne of African Studies in North America, for a long time the only woman in a male-dominated field. Her research, teaching, and her leadership in the African Studies Association are stellar in themselves. Her public lectures (such as the Beatty

Lectures) brought awareness of the nature of apartheid to an international audience and offered a framework for understanding its particularities.

Carter's most long-lasting contribution, however, was the creation of an archive of documents of resistance. Her work with Thomas Karis was a painstaking scholarly labour involving several fieldtrips to southern Africa and careful accretion of pamphlets, policy statements, and biographies of leaders across the various anti-apartheid political organizations. Four volumes of the archive entitled *From Protest to Challenge* were produced between 1972 and 1977 covering the period between 1882 and 1964, and they extended this with the help of other colleagues in the project in subsequent years.

It is impossible to overstate the value of the Karis-Carter collections, as they came to be known. Karis and Carter offered an influential periodization of resistance in the manner in which they grouped materials and classified events. Many of the profiles were of banned persons inside South Africa, and the documents they collected were not widely available to scholars abroad, let alone within the country. The act of archiving made visible resistance, and preserved valuable materials for generations of scholars who followed.

*

Shireen Hassim is the Canada150 Research Chair in Gender and African Politics at Carleton University and a visiting professor at the University of the Witwatersrand. Dr Hassim researches women's history and feminist politics and is the author of the award-winning *Contesting Authority: Women's Organizations and Democracy in South Africa* (University of Wisconsin Press, 2006).

LECTURE

The editors acknowledge that the sense of appropriateness of language, particularly when referring to ethnic minorities has, rightly, been challenged over time. This speech uses language that was deemed appropriate within its context of production. Please know that it is not our intent to be provocative or offensive to those who now receive this text; rather, this speech is a historical document and should be read as such. To this end, we have also chosen not to capitalize the use of race-based terms in this text. The following is the full Beatty Lecture delivered on 9 March 1982.

As the borders of the majority ruled states of southern Africa have moved to the very edge of South Africa's territory, except on the West and the disputed territory of Namibia, the answer to the question asked in the title of this lecture becomes ever more important. The majority ruled states are seeking to separate themselves to the degree possible from the pervasive economic and financial tentacles of the apartheid system that are undergirded by its massive transport and communication system. But what is crucial for South Africa, and by extension for all of southern Africa, is what happens within that country.

There seemed a moment after Prime Minister P.W. Botha assumed office when the watchword was adapt or die. Botha told the 1979 Natal Congress of the Nationalist Party that apartheid was a recipe for permanent conflict, and that the only alternative towards a revolution was change. In the background was the obvious restiveness of black labour, and of generations of black youth, who had never known anything but apartheid restrictions. The black consciousness philosophy had gone deep into their beings, despite the banning of its organizations in 1977, and also, the black nationalism, so long espoused by the African National Congress (ANC), whose influence is still pervasive despite its own banning in 1960, and indeed is steadily growing.

What has been most influential, however, in regard to change, has been the demand of South African commerce and industry for more regularized labour relations for its booming economy, and in particular, for skilled workers for whom the major pool is necessarily black labour. Some six million Africans are already in the country's labour force, and a further quarter of a million enter the labour market annually. At the same time, the shortage of skilled workers grows by five thousand annually, while it is estimated that the country will need 700,000 trained professional and skilled workers by 1987. Handicapped by the low standards of the discriminatory separate African educational system, few African workers are skilled and all are restive.

Between January and March 1973, African workers had struck some 150 firms in Natal, and the virtual absence of negotiating machinery had vastly complicated efforts to resolve the stoppages. The government then insisted companies establish either works or liaison committees, but neither proved satisfactory, and spasmodic strikes continued: 119 in 1975, 109 the next year. Most startling to officialdom, was when Soweto workers staged a three-day strike in September 1976 in response to student appeals to demonstrate support for their demands for change in apartheid restrictions on the aftermath of their June protests that had been so brutally put-down by the police. A direct outcome of the workers' protest strike was that the government established a commission in 1977 under Dr Nicholas V. Wiehahn to reconsider labour legislation affecting Africans.

Up to that point, African trade unions, although not illegal, had never been permitted to register under the Industrial Conciliation Act of 1956, which only provided for bargaining machinery between employers and white, or white and coloured work unions. The Act was amended in 1979 to include African trade unions and in accordance with the Wiehahn Commission recommendation, but limits that were placed on their membership destroyed much of the resulting goodwill, and later had to be removed. In response to another recommendation, Africans were henceforth admitted to apprenticeship training. But by January 1981, only eighty-one Africans had enrolled, a mere pittance compared to the need.

Well before the Wiehahn recommendations, however, African trade unions had been expanding rapidly, in an atmosphere of growing African assertiveness. Some unions, notably Lucy Mvubelo's long established National Union of Clothing Workers Unions with twenty thousand members, had taken the moderate step in 1974, of accepting association with the Trade Union Council of South Africa (TUCSA), which was directed by white officials, and included white and mixed unions.

Other African unions rejected parallelism, charging that it was a device by TUCSA's white administration to protect their white workers from African competition. The so-called independent unions developed two federations: the non-racial Federation of South African Trade Unions (FOSATU) centred originally in Natal, which had some ninety thousand members by 1982, almost all African or coloured, and the other Council of Unions of South Africa (CUSA) originating from the Consultative Committee on African Trade Unions, based mainly in the Transvaal, with approximately fifty thousand members in 1981, in nine all-African unions. Both of them follow the trade union tradition of working two shops stewards, but the latter are only gradually developing the requisite skills and structure.

Yet a third strand, the unaffiliated African membership unions, of which there were twenty-one by 1981 totaling over 87,000 members, were more militant, adopting a less structured and more aggressive style, bordering on confrontation. They sought their support through local communities. The long-established African Food and Canning Workers' Union in the Western Cape – and by the way, that young white who was found hanged in his cell the other day of whom I will speak later, was the secretary of the Transvaal branch of the Food and Canning Workers' Union – they organized a widespread and relatively successful consumer boycott of red meat in 1980, to back up its demands.

When five hundred of its workers were dismissed, the South African Allied Workers' Union (SAAWU) organized a countrywide boycott campaign against Wilson-Rowntree's products, mainly candies, which was particularly effective in the townships around Pretoria and in Soweto. That same union with over twenty thousand members, organized workers in the wide range of industries in the heavily industrialized East London area. They secured agreements with a number of automobile and tire factories like Ford, General Motors, and Firestone, American multinationals including Johnson & Johnson and the British company, South African Chloride.

Startling and effective was South Africa's first sympathy strikes in May 1981, when workers at Ford and General Motors downed their tools in support of their colleagues at Firestone, leading ultimately to reopened negotiations, and reinstatement of dismissed workers as vacancies occurred, and subsequently over a wage dispute at a nearby components firm in Uitenhage. Concerning itself with the interests of the local communities and also migrant workers and commuters, South African Municipal Workers' Union (SAMWU) refuses to accept government registration as threatening its independence of action. It faces increasing harassment as a consequence of its wide-ranging activities. Sixty of its members were detained during June and July 1981, during what was at that time the most severe and widespread crackdown on labour and political activists since 1977. It proved, however, to be only the first of a series of arrests and bannings. These have intensified since Ciskei, whose leaders are particularly hostile to labour, accepted so-called independence in December 1981, for its sprawling fingers of land that include many holding urban jobs.

While South African trade union leaders were testing the limits of their possibilities in regard both to organization, and to exerting pressures on their employers, the government in response to another 1979 report, this time by Dr Piet Riekert, was tightening the restrictions on influx control, to drastically limit the often illegal flow of migrant labour from the impoverished homelands into the towns and cities where work, and thus support for their families, could only be found. Dr Riekert proposed, and the government agreed, requiring the possession of housing for legal employment, and also that instead of the employee as before, it is the employer who must pay the penalty, a fine of about $600 for employing illegal labour.

These prohibitions created an immediate crisis in Johannesburg, particularly among housewives, few of whose servants could qualify (and there were few houses without servants). A temporary moratorium was granted, but thereafter, the enforced interrelation of controlled employment and controlled accommodation, created what *The Guardian*'s headline on the Riekert Report in its 3 June 1979 edition called, "Laagers Around the Towns." Behind the use of the simile of the wing of wagons used by the Voortrekkers to repel attacks, lies the government's insistence on its own virtual monopoly of African urban construction, and the ever-growing and unsatisfied demand for township accommodation.

The year 1980 had been South Africa's most turbulent industrial year up to that date, with strikes and work stoppages doubling to over two hundred. They were far overshadowed, however, by the tumultuous events of 1981, with countrywide strikes and work stoppages, arrest of workers, court appearances, and mass dismissals. As the size of black and predominantly black unions increased, employers found that they had to learn new ways of negotiation, outside the regular industrial council framework. Where wages had been the key complaint in the earlier years, pensions and their transferability from one firm to another became the most controversial issue as the government considered new draft legislation on the subject.

The year 1981 also witnessed, however, one of the very few improvements in the position of migrant workers, when the Supreme Court ruled in September that a migrant from Gazankulu, who like all other migrants had had to go annually to his so-called homeland to renew his contract, but returned always, for ten consecutive years, to the same job, could reside at long last, legally, in the township, which would mean he could bring his wife and children if he could find housing. This judgment might affect the urban rights of thousands of migrant contract workers and their families, and is therefore still being challenged by the administration.

Testifying on 22 October 1981 before the subcommittee on Africa of the House of Representatives on the Solarz Bill to strengthen the position of African trade unions and American companies, Dr William B. Gould, Professor of Law at Stanford University, called the black trade union movement the one free institution remaining in South Africa, and the principal source of any potential to modify or dismantle apartheid. He warned that new trade union controls were already being fashioned by the government. They cut the links that SAMWU had forged for itself and community groups, and above all with migrant workers from the homelands. For once, this seems a place where foreign owned companies could provide specific safeguards for their own unions, and thereby take a lead of genuine significance.

What the South African government is particularly anxious about is the potential spread of union organization into the homelands, either through the recruitment, or at least association of authorized migrant workers with urban based labour organizations as is now legal, or of commuters linked by long rail lines to their daily jobs. Numbers of the latter had once been urban dwellers before being ejected to homeland areas, through re-districting their areas, sometimes as in Pretoria, to benefit whites.

One notable example of such redrawing of boundaries was to shift the township Mdantsane, where many of SAMWU's workers lived, into the Ciskei, with the consequences already mentioned. Another example of the government's fearsome power was over the 1980 strike by Johannesburg municipal workers, whose union had been organized in Soweto, its African township. When they struck, instead of considering their demands, they were attacked by the police. Many were then thrust into an abandoned mineshaft at the edge of town. After separating those still supporting the union from those who retracted, the former were loaded on trucks, driven out of town, and beaten unmercifully, before being dumped inside Bophuthatswana, a so-called independent homeland north of Pretoria.

Such actions are part of the government's calculated efforts to restrict African trade unions to settled urban dwellers who meet the rigidly specified qualifications for residents, and to provide them with differential treatment in the interest of turning them into so-called system blacks. But the example of Zimbabwe suggests the discontented insiders cannot easily be forced to limit their struggle to the urban areas where controls are strictest, and that the concept of worker's solidarity is contagious. Sooner or later, residents in the urban townships will use their links to the rural areas to politicize and radicalize their rural kinsmen. It has even been suggested that the ferment against apartheid restrictions is already well established within them.

In the end, the heart of apartheid in both its ideal and its present form, is the homelands. In a 1981 article entitled "The God that Failed Afrikanerdom," Colin Legum, formerly of *The Observer*, widely acknowledged to be one of the most perceptive journalists covering the African scene, though generally excluded from his native South Africa, argues that P.W. Botha's manipulations are undermining the foundation of the apartheid system, and that the ruling group in Afrikanerdom has now learned the shattering fact, that the apartheid ideology, and this is, I quote, "Creating a multinational state based on separate development, which would offer racial harmony, a secure future for the white minority under Afrikaner dominance, and justice for blacks, cannot be translated into effective practice."

Legum points out that on the contrary, there is more racial bitterness than there was before, which suggests perhaps that Afrikaner domination and even white survival are threatened. There are also more than twice as many settled Africans in the urban areas than existed there in 1948, when the long process of ejecting them began. Moreover, all urban Africans are bitterly opposed to becoming citizens of their ethnic homelands, as the government maintains they do when these segments of South Africa accept the "independence," and I always put it in quotes, that Transkei, Bophuthatswana, Venda and now Ciskei have, and which of course, only South Africa itself recognizes.

All of these facts add up in Legum's view to the conclusion that apartheid as previously envisaged has been proved unworkable. He believes that Botha is similarly convinced and is working step-by-step to develop a new and more palatable system which can lead gradually to more racial harmony. He points out that Owen Horwood, Minister of Finance, acknowledges the homeland system is not economically viable, and that there must be larger economic units than those provided for the homelands by government fiat. The possibility is thus held out that the government will gradually reduce the barriers between the homelands and the developed white areas, in the interest of overall economic integration.

But even if this should happen, and it is far from sure, does it mean that the homeland system will be discarded? There is much evidence of its continuing utility to the South African government. A basic fact is that the very existence of the homelands relieves the government of immediate responsibility for a large and growing proportion of the African population. The most recent population projections, which are those of the Bureau of Economic Research for 1978, and subsequently they have left out the independent homelands, indicate that the de facto African homeland population is approximately nine million, nearly half the official African population figure of 19,630,000 in 1978.

But African population estimates are difficult to update because of the continuous resettlement of so-called surplus population. One example is a tiny QwaQwa homeland in the Free State next to Lesotho, which grew from twenty-five thousand to two hundred thousand between 1970 and 1977 and has not stopped yet. More than 337,000 residents of black spots – that is land that had been legally owned by Africans in white designated areas before such ownership was outlawed – first in 1936 and again in 1939, have been relocated in the last three decades.

More recently, with increased mechanization and the abolition in the 1960s of black tenancy on white farms, another 1.3 million Africans have been removed. The borders of Ciskei as we have seen, are being enlarged to take in more land than people, despite their continuing protests, and its already overcrowded conditions. Moreover, the approximately four hundred thousand Africans arrested every year for possible violations are often deported to a rural reserve, just as are the residents of demolished squatter communities. Yet another relocation has affected more than three hundred thousand Africans, said to have been in the wrong ethnic areas as homelands are supposed to each be a separate ethnic area. It is estimated, another million may be relocated in implementing the government's plan.

The impact of this mass forced population movement, surely one of the largest and the harshest in modern times in any country outside the Eastern Bloc hit me forcibly and painfully when I visited KwaNdebele, the last and newest of the ten homelands which stretches over open land north of Pretoria. There, I had talked with women and children from three different former areas, from rezoned sections of Pretoria itself, the administrative capital, from the African-owned area of Winterveld, whose husbands had been forced to move because they were refused labour permits by the government, and from northern Transvaal farms, as they stood beside a dusty road, while a truck roared by, tipping out sheets of tin and pieces of wood for them to build their own shacks. In the distance, as far as one could see, were close-packed dwellings with little space left for even the barest food production, and far out of our sight, the relocation camps where, perhaps, half of KwaNdebele's population still huddles. At least one knows where these people are, whereas many of those relocated are virtually lost in rarely visited areas.

Besides reducing the African population in so-called white areas, there are other features of the homeland system that the government seeks to exploit to its own advantage. It has tried with limited success to build up homeland leaders as focal points of allegiance. In this regard, Chief Gatsha Buthelezi of KwaZulu stands out because of his royal blood, the memory of the martial prowess of the Zulu nation, and the potential power of his Inkatha movement, whose three hundred thousand members, including administrative and educational personnel within KwaZulu, and substantial numbers outside, formed by far the largest organized forts in South Africa's history. Even here, however, there are undercurrents of internal opposition, as well as overt and bitter criticism from young urban blacks.

Where the nationalist government has been successful, however, is in sponsoring local business and commercial interests within the homelands, which depend on outside support for their success and wealth. These interests often combine with those of homeland politicians and administrators to maintain mutually advantageous links with national and international concerns, and frequently operate to the disadvantage of the local inhabitants because of artificially high prices and limited choice.

Another reinforcement of local interest like Sun City in Bophuthatswana, commonly known as Sin City, where Frank Sinatra performed to huge audiences last year, provides a major source of attraction to wealthy South Africans whose own society does not afford such opportunities. Some suggest there may well be a ring of such imitations of Las Vegas, building homelands around the periphery of the country in due course. Moneymaking. The homeland leaders, particularly those who have accepted independence, and the commercial and business interests within those artificially carved out areas, appear to provide allies to the central government in its efforts to neutralize the population pressures of approximately half the African majority.

P.W. Botha would like to encourage a semi-constitutional relationship, particularly with the four independent homelands, and at one time, had hopes of linking them with neighbouring states like Lesotho and Botswana, in a genuine constellation of states. The African majority states had instantly repudiated the concept, however, as potential Bantustanization. And Chief Mangope of Bophuthatswana also insists on a one-to-one relation with Pretoria. The unsavoury reputation of Venda, which is on the borders, where Lutheran congregations suffer an apparent reign of terror with their injured Dean in the hospital and Bishop Tutu ejected out from a compassionate visit very recently, is hardly a desirable associate. Ciskei seems to continue in its independent status, its reputation of a "Papa Doc tyranny," so named by Colin Legum.

Among the homelands that rejects independence, KwaZulu continues to play a distinctive role despite its fragmented state and desperate drought-stricken poverty. There still seems some hope of an agreed arrangement of sorts to link the disparate white and African controlled territories of Natal into at least a functional working relationship. The Buthelezi Commission is reporting almost momentarily – it was set up by the KwaZulu government – and is one of the plans that has been proposed for a relationship between black and white areas in that province.

But even so, the chance of the scattered African homelands playing a constructive role in pressuring the central government to halt the all too constant resettlements that swell their already overpopulated areas, or modify the apartheid stringencies that impinge constantly on their own migrant workers or their urban brothers, seems slight. Just as is a notion of the central or local administrations willingly accepting the desperate squatters from Transkei, who can find no livelihood or family life within it.

There are two other groups: middle-class urban Africans, and the substantial coloured and Asian population, with whom the Botha government hopes to secure some kind of alliance based on common interest. There is a small but growing black middle class, whose members hold positions in business and industry often but not exclusively in the personnel field, as well as professionals in medicine, education, and the Church. As anywhere else, money, and standards of living tend to separate groups each from each other. And this is true in the urban townships, where a limited number of expensive cars and homes and even small gardens are found, like in Soweto.

What continues this sharp cleavage and bitterness, however, of all Africans, is their segregated existence in ghetto-like townships at some distance from the white urban centres where most are employed. Even more arbitrary and hurtful are the frequent police raids into the African townships, and the arbitrary controls which can be and are instituted without apparent reason, on entry and exit from the townships, and the humiliating procedures from which no one is exempt, including search, and even stripping, that may accompany them. If you listen to Julie Fredrickson on the National Public Radio, I do not know whether it comes here very often, but she happened to go on the day when this was taking place and they stripped her too. They did not do it the day I went, thank goodness.

Speaking to the annual Congress of the Afrikaner Student Organization in July 1980, Dr Gerrit Viljoen, former chairman of the powerful Broederbond and now Minister of National Education, took another line. He coupled a rejection of racial integration, which he called "cultural suicide," with the assertion that in the future South Africa, whites, coloured, and Asians in one form or another, would have joint responsibility for matters affecting the three groups. This association of the three South African minority groups, and a tacit alliance to match more evenly the overwhelming numbers of the Africans, that is nearly eight million as compared with these twenty million, is not a new idea, but it had a fresh constitutional character that bears the stamp of Prime Minister Botha.

Prime Minister Vorster and now Botha have in fact both sought through constitutional manipulations, to associate these two minority groups with the white parliamentary system. Vorster tried to do it first at the level of cabinet advisory committees, and then through an elaborate structure of separate white, coloured, and Asian chambers, with their own cabinets to deal with matters only affecting themselves. On a broader issue, surely, the majority of decisions were to be served to a President's Council, where all three would be represented, but the whites hold a majority, and subsequently handed over to the president himself for settlement.

Both plans were repudiated by representative, coloured, and Asian bodies, because they included no role for Africans, which was justified by the government on the grounds that they were represented by the homelands. Botha's government accepted both the notion of combining coloured, Asian, and whites and an advisory body on general issues, and the exclusion of the African from the central parliamentary system. He took a new route, however, by first securing what proved easy parliamentary approval for the abolition of the second chamber, the Senate, which alone played a minor role in decision making. He then replaced it with the nominated President's Council to be advisory to the government. Under urging and the lure of high salaries, a few coloured and Asians accepted membership in the council, although they were labeled sellouts by more representative figures in both communities, who again repudiated the whole plan on the grounds of the exclusion of the Africans.

There has been one particular moment, however, when it seemed that the President's Council might assume a distinctive and promising role, by providing far-sighted recommendations to the government on how to deal with sensitive issues. This moment came with their recommendation that two areas, District Six in Cape Town, and Pageview outside Johannesburg, from which coloured and Asians respectively have been ejected through redrawing boundaries under the Group Areas Act, should be returned to them. Both situations are highly sensitive issues, particularly the one in Cape Town, because the coloured had a historic connection with District Six, and the corrosive bitterness resulting in both communities from their removal has been a major bar to normal relations with the whites.

The government flatly refused to return Pageview, whose middle-class houses were already in the process of being torn down, and offered only minor adjustments on District Six, which is in just a terrible state of disrepute. They have been bulldozing it for years now. This reaction provided a major setback to those who saw promise in the new constitutional device, and several members, both Asian and white, resigned. The Council still continues its planning but in private.

Although the coloured nation were further alienated by the rebuff over redressing their bitterly resented exclusion from two of their formerly established areas, it would be difficult for them to refuse a full parliamentary franchise, though the government seems unlikely to offer so strong a constitutional link with the whites. In the meantime, representative groups within both communities maintain their insistence that blacks, in the sense of those discriminated against, should stand together.

The basic issues of multi-racialism, or black solidarity, or Africans versus the rest of the South African population, is of major importance in affecting the two key issues presently before that country. One is the threat of a serious split in

Afrikanerdom, between those who support Prime Minister Botha's policies, and the bitter opponents of what is called power sharing with coloured and Asians, and the lower class Afrikaner worker of increased economic opportunities for blacks and especially for Africans.

The first is led by the extreme right wing of the Nationalist Party and the second by the Herstigte Nasionale Party, commonly known as the HNP. The other is the resurgence of the ANC which was founded seventy years ago, predating the birth of the Nationalist Party itself, and though banned, seems to be omnipresent within South Africa today, with its pervasive influence, and its apparent ability to bomb targets almost at will. Ejected from the Nationalist Party in 1969 when it openly attacked Prime Minister Vorster's outward policy of establishing relations with some African governments, and in spending too much on African development, the HNP became active in mid-1979, attracting miners and blue-collar workers by its criticism of Botha's black labour policies.

While the HNP has never yet won a seat in parliament, there was an unprecedented backlash against Botha's policies, when right-wing candidates polled one third of the Afrikaner vote in the April 1981 election, which Botha had called two years early, in hope of being confirmed as the accepted leader of Afrikanerdom. The most serious post-election challenges to his policy and leadership have come from Dr Andries Treurnicht, of the conservative right-wing of the Nationalist Party, and its leader in the wealthy and populous Transvaal province. Openly criticizing Botha's black labour policies after the election, Treurnicht who had once headed the Broederbond, late in February 1982, led twenty-two MPs in voting against a motion of confidence in Botha's power-sharing proposal, and was supported by former Prime Minister Vorster in his opposition to any form of parliamentary representation for coloureds and Asians. But confronted, thereafter, – and this is very recent, of course, – in his own Transvaal head committee by Prime Minister Botha, in an unprecedented move, Treurnicht could only muster thirty-six votes in his own head committee, to 172, was stripped of his membership in the party's executive committee, and told to conform or resign from the Nationalist Party in form of parliamentary opposition. Three days later, Treurnicht resigned from the Nationalist Party, but the following day, he and Ferdinand Hartzenberg, Minister of Education, – that is white education and training – and fourteen others were formally expelled from the Nationalist Party.

When parliament reassembled, and this is just ten days ago, the sixteen former nationalists took a place on the opposition bench. It is between the official opposition, the PFP, and the Natal-based NRP. In addition, there has been growing evidence of a widespread underground presence of the ANC.

Long the standard-bearer of African nationalism, the ANC was banned in 1960, after the Sharpeville massacre, but its militant wing uMkhonto we Sizwe continued to make its presence felt through bombing installations, up to the point when its secret headquarters was uncovered in 1963, in a wealthy Johannesburg suburb. There followed a spectacular trial of those leaders who had not already slipped over the border in response to instructions, and who have all since directed the international organization led in exile by Oliver Tambo. Nelson Mandela, who remains the acknowledged leader of the ANC, and several other top figures of that organization are still on Robben Island, under sentence of life imprisonment. But the multiracial, though essentially African ANC, has been surprisingly mobile for the past two years in the underground role of bombing essential installations.

Most striking was the ANC's successful attack on Sasol, South Africa's oil from coal facility, through which it hopes to free itself from dependence on imports of that crucial commodity, the only one that it does not itself possess. The ANC has also bombed with sophisticated explosives, widely separated power plants, railway installations, police stations, and even a major military installation close to Pretoria.

Not surprisingly, this revolutionary black nationalist organization has absorbed much of the Marxist philosophy, which many third-world movements have found so useful. Its aim is to bring together different race and class groups in a common alliance to overthrow the existing South African regime, and to establish a more equalitarian non-racial society under majority rule. Its own alliance with trade unions goes back even earlier than its alliance with the Indian, coloured, and white organizations, with which it adopted the Freedom Charter in 1955 which begins, "South Africa belongs to all its people, black and white."

In the middle of 1981, thirty organizations representing a wide range of interests and activities, black and white, pledged their allegiance to the Freedom Charter, again in protest against the government-sponsored celebration of the twentieth anniversary of the Republic. The breadth of interest and membership in the groups that joined together indicated a surprising degree of common commitment to change, and to the minimum core of faith, on which they could all unite. This willingness of the ANC to continue its own basic commitment to so unifying a principle, at the same time that it is continuing its widespread attacks and sabotage, which do not, by absolute pledge, include the killing of people, is a mark of its sophistication in recognizing the need for the broadest possible base for its ultimate hope for success.

Naturally, the official charge against the ANC is that it is a communist dominated organization that aims to pervert or destroy the existing fabric of South African society. The chief of the South African Defense Force, General Constand Viljoen, in a wide-ranging interview given to the *Financial Mail* in mid-January of this year, declared that he planned to put into operation an area defense system to meet what he termed a growing area war, assault by the Russians and their proxies, which translates into the ANC and black nationalism.

General Viljoen points out the ANC is not conducting a border war, as SWAPO (South African Municipal Workers Union) is in Namibia, but rather one that is aimed at creating an atmosphere of instability within South Africa, both to ensure maximum publicity for their efforts and to spread security forces more widely. He warned it might be necessary, therefore, for the full-time forces to call on sufficient auxiliary power; he has already done so, so that all areas in South Africa will be less vulnerable to attack. He also declared that the commandos' service would be revised to achieve on-the-spot defense, and that industrial enterprises and businesses, including of course those that are foreign-owned, might be called on to take more responsibility for guarding their own premises, none of which will be at all popular.

By General Viljoen's estimate, the ANC has not yet succeeded in politicizing the black community sufficiently to carry out an effective subversive campaign, a deduction he draws from the fact that ANC operations continue to be secret. More and more, however, supporters of the ANC display its colours and slogans and sing its songs at mass meetings and politically significant funerals. Most strikingly, the ANC flag was carried openly in the streets of Johannesburg, at the funeral last month of Dr Neil Aggett, Transvaal Secretary of the African Food and Canning Workers' Union, the forty-sixth, some people say the fifty-sixth, political detainee to meet a violent death in the last two decades, but the first white. Throughout the country, more than fifty thousand and I have even seen the figure, one hundred thousand workers, mostly black, stopped work for thirty minutes in protest against detention without trial.

General Viljoen warned in his interview, that in the absence of concrete reforms to meet black demands, the ANC may well achieve greater success with the black community. Without such reforms, he foresees the security threat intensifying. In the second place, while affirming his confidence in the government's ability to carry through necessary reforms, he makes it clear that the military is holding itself in readiness, to maintain what he calls peace, in case the government encounters major difficulties, presumably from the nationalist right-wing, in instituting the changes it recognizes are needed.

Writing in *The London Economist* in October 1981, editor Simon Jenkins in his second wide-ranging article on South African developments also foresees Prime Minister Botha calling in the army to secure his own position in the face of right-wing hostility to his program. Jenkins' view is that this could mean the end of the South African parliamentary system, and suggests that Botha could govern thereafter with the support of the army, and quite possibly Chief Gatsha Buthelezi's Zulus, which he notes is the only tribe larger than his own, and maybe some middle-class coloured, Asians, and Africans.

If one puts together Legum's and Jenkins' forecasts along with the comments of General Viljoen, there might be a scenario such as follows: Botha, aware of the vital need for change to diffuse the black opposition, and frustrated by right-wing intransigence turns to the army to maintain control. He then institutes whatever new constitutional system is deemed appropriate to satisfy the aspirations of all groups in the country. Jenkins asks rhetorically whether liberalism would fight to save South Africa's primary justification for international respectability, its parliamentary system. But it seems more likely it would not go beyond protests. Would the right fight, as it did in 1922, to protect its privileged economic and political position? If it did so, it might plunge South Africa into turmoil, from which the ANC might have a better chance than any other group of coming out, if not on top, at least in a stronger position than ever.

Alternatively, South Africa might simply adopt army rule, foster commerce, industry, and its superb mineral resources, and, confident in its wealth and strongest military force on the continent, ignore pressure from both the right and the left, the HNP and the ANC, and maintain an armed camp at the foot of the continent, none of which would be particularly promising for its own people and especially not for its neighbours.

How likely are any of these developments? Possible. But so is a continuation of the current situation of relative stalemate, waiting without much anticipation for the next proposals of the President's Council and the government's reaction to them. In one sense, Legum's view and that of many thoughtful Afrikaners is correct. The faith in ideal apartheid as an answer which can bring harmonious race relations no longer exists. In that sense, it may be said that apartheid is dying, or even dead. But in the world of reality, apartheid as a system of control, with almost unlimited grants of power at the disposal of ministers and administrators, is omnipresent within South Africa. Apartheid appears on the surface through imprisonment without trial, harsh methods of interrogation, banning of people, books, newspapers, without possible recourse to the courts.

Starting in November 1981, the latest wave of government actions against leading trade unionists, labour experts, students, black and white, and other activists, brought some of the best known into detention. In January 1982, the government released figures recording 179 people detained under various security laws, up from ninety-two a year before. These detainees are in addition to some 520 security prisoners, tried and convicted under these laws, and approximately 160 restricted under various banning orders.

The West with its wealth of foreign investment and profitable trade links cannot escape some responsibility for what goes on inside South Africa. It is not its responsibility to propose a new constitutional dispensation for the country, but it does have a responsibility to urge its government to reverse its repressive course, and to open channels of communication with recognized leaders of the black communities and other leaders who may emerge, and enter into genuine negotiations with them. To be effective, such urging needs to be reinforced by a policy of step-by-step pressures, including economic measures as advocated by Bishop Desmond Tutu. It might well be the group of five: the United States, Canada, the United Kingdom, France, and West Germany, that have forged a partnership over the Namibian negotiations, that might take the lead. It may well be a long process. It is time that it began.

The Africans have tried for many decades to find ways to capitalize on their numbers and international influence to promote change throughout the continent and within South Africa. As the borders of majority-ruled African states have moved to the frontiers of that state, the urgency becomes greater. South Africa has more to contribute to Africa and the world than any other single state, but it still stands as their greatest affront.

NOTE

1 Thomas G. Karis (1919–2017) was an American Foreign Service officer and critic of US policy on South Africa. He headed the graduate program in Political Science at the City University of New York, and became a leading historian of the South African liberation movement.

9

The New World Order
23 March 1993

Mikhail Gorbachev

INTRODUCTION

Mikhail Gorbachev is, without a doubt, one of the most important political figures of the twentieth century. In the West, he was lauded as a reformer, and in what follows, we witness former Canadian Prime Minister Pierre Trudeau admiringly referring to him as such. He is often credited with ending the Cold War, even as he tried to save the fundamentally flawed political and economic system over which he ruled. In the face of popular protests in the communist satellite countries of Eastern Europe in 1989, Gorbachev opted not to send in Soviet tanks to defend their embattled leaders leading ultimately to the collapse of the Berlin Wall in November of that year. As Soviet leader, Gorbachev signed landmark arms control deals with Ronald Reagan and then George H.W. Bush, ending the nuclear arms race and making the world safer. Domestically, he allowed Soviet citizens to examine the tragedies of the past under Stalin by throwing open archives, enabling public debate and protest and even some degree of electoral competition. His economic reforms were haphazard, however, and led to further hardship for the long-suffering Soviet citizenry.

Despite what in the West were viewed as Gorbachev's unqualified successes, in his own country, he was considered a failure. Worried that his reform efforts would lead to the end of the Soviet Union itself, members of his own Politburo initiated a coup against him in August of 1991. While their attempt to oust him ultimately failed, it was his old rival Boris Yeltsin (who like Gorbachev was a former committed Communist Party regional boss turned accidental democrat) who saw to Gorbachev's ultimate fall from power. As elected president of a newly independent Russian Federation, Yeltsin killed off the Soviet Union by banning the Party on Russian soil and usurping authority over Union institutions in Moscow and beyond. Through the autumn of 1991, Gorbachev tried desperately to save some sort of Union government in the face of successive declarations of independence

Mikhail Gorbachev. *Used with permission of McGill University Archives,* PR050789.

among the remaining republics of the Soviet Union, and we see him in the Beatty Lecture refer to this doomed project. He was finally forced from the Kremlin on 25 December 1991.

By the time of his Beatty Lecture, delivered in March 1993, we find Gorbachev still mourning the failure of his federal plan. He finds a sympathetic ear in former Canadian prime minister, Pierre Trudeau in the conversation below. Federalism and the balancing of national identities within a unified state is obviously a subject of great interest for Trudeau, although his battle with Quebec ended rather differently from Gorbachev's battle to establish a re-federalized Soviet state. Gorbachev, as we see, worries about self-serving politicians who use issues of identity in pursuit of their own enhanced power. This is a not so subtle dig at Yeltsin, his bitter rival. Notable too is Trudeau's clear admiration for Gorbachev – he disparages Western leaders who too quickly, he thinks, recognized the statehood of former Soviet republics, further dooming Gorbachev's federal plan. Trudeau also tries to define Gorbachev as a social democrat rather than as the committed and unabashed Leninist he always was. Indeed, in 1993, we see that Gorbachev remains doubtful that Russia could ever actually have private land ownership.

Again, the timing of this interview is noteworthy in that Yeltsin is in the midst of a battle with his own legislature regarding privatization of property in Russia. Eventually, this leads to Yeltsin disbanding and eventually turning tanks on the legislative building itself in defense of his economic reforms. But he takes the advice that Gorbachev offers in the Beatty Lecture to build a strong executive in a new constitution in order to govern Russia with a firmer presidential hand. It is the powers granted to the Russian president in this new document, ironically, that Vladimir Putin later employs to make short work of the open society and politics that Gorbachev had introduced through his glasnost project. Moreover, only a little more than a decade after Gorbachev visited Montreal for the Beatty Lecture in 1993, under Putin's increasingly authoritarian leadership, any hope for Gorbachev's vision of a more open Russia had all but disappeared.

*

Kathryn Stoner is a political scientist at Stanford University, specializing in Russia and the former Soviet Union. She is also Senior Fellow and Deputy Director at Stanford's Freeman Spogli Institute for International Studies, and holds a BA and MA from the University of Toronto and a PhD from Harvard University. Her most recent book is *Russia Resurrected: Its Power and Purpose in a New Global Order* (Oxford University Press, 2021).

LECTURE

Mikhail Gorbachev's Beatty Lecture took the form of a roundtable discussion with former Canadian Prime Minister Pierre Trudeau and McGill professors Valentin Boss, Reuven Brenner, and Charles Taylor. Gorbachev agreed to participate in the roundtable under the condition that it would not be a public event. A private roundtable was therefore filmed on campus and broadcast with simultaneous translation in Russian, French, and English to audiences in two auditoriums on McGill's downtown campus. More than eight hundred people watched the live event including seventy members of the press. This is the only time in Beatty Lecture history to date when a lecturer shared the podium. The following is the full Beatty Lecture delivered on 23 March 1993.

CHARLES TAYLOR: It is an honour for me to welcome Mikhail Sergeyevich Gorbachev, who was leader of the Soviet Union during a time of truly revolutionary change, one that is especially significant to those of us who are partisan of freedom and democracy in the world. I would also like to welcome Pierre Trudeau, another historic figure from this country as not only a leader of Canada, but also a leader of the democratic world for twenty years. I would like also to introduce our colleagues here from McGill, Valentine Boss, historian, and Reuven Brenner, economist. So let me ask Pierre Trudeau to open the discussion by asking a question.

PIERRE TRUDEAU: Thank you, Mr Chairman. I would like to start with a general question on the world economic order — or the world order, period, which we could also call the world economic disorder. From the Treaty of Westphalia in 1648 until the end of the Cold War, the world order was more or less based on a balance of strengths – between countries, between blocs, between alliances. And with the Cold War, all this took concrete form in two principal blocs, East and West, the Warsaw Pact Bloc and the NATO Bloc. Each with its friends, its client states. You changed all that, dear Mr Gorbachev. You are a great reformer. You revolutionized the political landscape, which until then had essentially been based on military concepts, such as NATO and the Warsaw Pact. Suddenly, with democracy, with access to the free market, you completely changed the composition and the nature of the bloc we call the Eastern Bloc. But it did not change as you wished; for example, you wanted to keep a strong federation. You were on the verge of proclaiming it when the putsch happened. You also wanted the countries that were part of the former Soviet Union to move towards a form of independence, but not total sovereignty. You wanted a federation that would respect their local identities, but would be united in a real federation.

I think that we in the West rather hindered things by rushing to recognize the independence of a certain number of countries that had been part of the Soviet Union.

For example, we were in a hurry to recognize the Baltic states, then Ukraine. Once the example was set, it spread very quickly: Georgia, Azerbaijan, and elsewhere in the so-called Eastern Bloc, the bloc of the Third World, and then it was Yugoslavia's turn.

You also wanted to have a gradual reform, you did not want what we call shock therapy. You wanted real therapy, but without the shock. You wanted to move gradually towards a market economy, but to lift controls slowly, as the Western countries slowly lifted the controls imposed on them in World War II. You were also asking for the Warsaw Pact and the NATO Pact to disappear gradually, but you were told, "No, we will continue with NATO and a reunited Germany will be a member of NATO." You tried, I think rightly, during the Gulf War, to find a solution to this conflict, a negotiated, peaceful solution, that would if necessary impose certain assumptions, but you were seeking a solution that would not involve war. Here again, you were told, "No."

My question, Mr Gorbachev, is how do you envisage the new world order? If you could have acted with the cooperation of countries in the West, would you have? You call yourself a Communist, you are proudly Communist, and if I understand the current jargon of glasnost and perestroika correctly, that means a form of social democracy. My question is precise: is social democracy achievable, do you think it can come back? Or do you take a severe view of the way many Westerners think – that the story is over, now there is one superpower, that is the United States of America, with other countries that compete with it – that it is the end of the story? We have a world that is liberal, based on capitalism and the market economy. You yourself, you are a Communist or social democrat, can we go back to that or is it dead – that beautiful ideology in a sense that was based on a desire for justice and equality, but which failed because of Stalinism?

MIKHAIL GORBACHEV: Yes, I see it is a continuation of our talk yesterday around twelve o'clock in the night, and I think we suggested we would continue today so it is a good chance to do so. I welcome this meeting and I think that if right now we are behind in a few things since the Cold War ended and since we left the confrontational period, we are missing a few things. We have not been able to pool our intellectual forces in time to find ways to act in this new situation. In fact, we were also in a euphoric situation when the Cold War ended – confrontation came to an end, we had new chances, new opportunities to develop. We thought it would all go just as easily as a wink, that it would be automatic. I think that we were a bit careless, all of us. My own experience has shown that when a politician is late in doing something, that it is a very costly thing. When events become chaotic the elements go out of control, as we put it, even with healthy spontaneous factors unfolding. Nevertheless there is much of a destructive nature in that. After all politics, the politicians with a new arsenal of knowledge, we could say, have to know how to deal with this.

So in this form of round table, as the respected Mr Trudeau has said, disorder – I think that this is the correct way to put it – is very typical of transition. But I think that this is a very important point, very beneficial. Right now, we have understood that we need to be more active and to understand the great responsibility that lies on our shoulders because we must arm our politicians in the intellectual sense, our society shows them what is the best and most productive way to act in this situation. Yes, you are right, and I share that opinion that when we ran into these factors, into these events, it was a trial for us to see how we would react to a new situation. There were two situations, the first was, for instance, the situation in Yugoslavia. I spoke with my partners, I said that they should not allow all sorts of ... that they had to give the Yugoslavian people a chance to make their own decisions before they recognized the state. So they recognized Slovenia and Croatia, and as you see the situation has unfolded very rapidly since then. I think that was an important moment, as far as the Soviet Union is concerned.

Pierre, I must tell you that although we saw competition between the Western states – and the prime minister reminded me at one point, it was like a gypsy band that was moving around the Soviet Union trying to explain, put forward, its position – but the most important point for the future of the Union and the unfolding process, I think they were all domestic factors really. Most of all, there were major problems within the country that had to be reformed, major issues. It was called the Federation but it was never really a federation, it was a bureaucratic system, a unitarian, and rigid system. When we started to begin democratization and glasnost, in order to fulfill our natural desires to be a sovereign state, we were not ready for that, when the people wanted to be sovereign. Ambitious politicians saddled this process, made use of it for them for their own interests, they exploited it, they exploited the interests of the different people in preserving their identity. Then there were separatist movements that arose. So as far as we are concerned, we got behind in policy.

The second point, is a very powerful strike, the August 1991 coup. Self-preservation came into play. Within ten or fifteen days, all of the states said that they proclaimed themselves independent and they predetermined the weakening of the state and its dissolution. But there is no way that I could say ... the meeting of the three leaders of the Slavic Republics in the Belorussian situation, the August coup, put an end to the signing of the treaty, that is the Belovezha Agreement.

CHARLES TAYLOR: Perhaps another one of the issues for a new world order in the future, is do you think that the international community is powerless before events like the Civil War in Yugoslavia, like the Quasi Civil War (Armenia, Azerbaijan)? Is there a way that the international community can, in an ordered fashion, intervene? We would very much like to have your opinion on that.

MIKHAIL GORBACHEV: Most of all, I think that we should keep the following in mind. We have to realize the aspiration of the people to preserve their identity is just as objective a process. I mean, it is a natural process, there is nothing artificial about it, it is a natural movement, just as economic integration is, these are the two processes that we are seeing now. The stronger is the economic integration, the more people want to have that integration and, unfortunately, there is a danger that all of the differences between the people will be wiped out, and the people are afraid that their self-preservation is in danger, so we have to understand that these are two important trends right now that are in existence. After all, the Maastricht Treaty, what was the reaction to that? Denmark and France did not want to approve these proposals, that is a difficult process too. After all, so many years passed, so many years of cooperation within the European Economic Community and between different structures.

I think we have to find a way to work within the framework of these two tendencies. We cannot just turn away or negate the people's interest in having their own identity, but we also cannot let it be an unbridled process, we have to show them how essential it is. We know that they have to preserve their culture in the languages of the people, but it is also essential to work together to integrate the people in order for civilization to successfully work together, and to meet challenges of the day, that is the first point. We really need a global understanding of this problem and its significance. Further, we have to return to the principles of federalism and what is the idea at its foundation, and how can they be implemented today in the given situation? I think that here is the key to understanding and to the resolution of this problem, which is implementing the federalism principles in the new context, a new reading of the principles, and I think then these problems can be resolved.

Further, if in the final analysis, a certain ethnic group definitely wants to have their own state entity, state formation, then I think we have to have a procedural code, a code of conduct – how can we carry out this process, what are the stages, what is the timeframe for resolving these issues? It cannot all come at once like a landslide, or like a mudslide, in that case we would have to take emergency action. Here we need a code of conduct. For instance, if there is an election or a part of the country has decided simply to form its own state, then there has to be a certain period for carrying out that change – questions of ownership, human rights, all of this has to be considered, discussed, and then maybe, as a result of that, the decision might be taken back.

VALENTIN BOSS: Unfortunately, Landsbergis and Lithuania were not ready. Brazauskas was in agreement with you on that, in order to set up a federal structure that would be supported by those who had a reasonable approach to minority issues. And I think that what is happening now in Lithuania, is that we are seeing other people following that first wave of nationalism, but that first wave was brutal at times. Is it possible to coordinate or to hold back that form of nationalism? After all, in central Asia we have also seen cruelty.

MIKHAIL GORBACHEV: I think that we have to be unequivocal, very decisive in supporting the natural aspiration to preserve people's identity – a rebirth of the different nations – we have to recognize that and each ethnic group has to understand that it cannot be replaced, that it is irreplaceable, and that the whole world community recognizes that. But also we have to be decisively against nationalism, which is often used as an instrument for carrying out political aims, by elite groups, for instance, that have political ambitions, and it is a method for them to simply exploit this wonderful phenomenon that is national identity. I think in that sense, we should be unanimous that there definitely is a danger in nationalism and we have to say that openly and we should be against those dangerous trends. But never say that it is equal, that the people's aspirations to preserve their independence, their way of life, their traditions, their culture, and to confuse that with indifferent nationalists who care not for those interests, they who have their own goals and their own program. That is what I think.

Now you have touched upon the question of mechanisms – how will this be done? Well, I think in that sense, the United Nations has not fulfilled its complete potential, and it was created to do that after all. It was created to have some order in international relations, to make them manageable. It is not that we want to set up a world government. I mean, I think that would be a misconception for sure. But the UN, which as a result of the Cold War, was in a state of inefficacy, let us say, but I think its time has come. The structure and institutions of this organization during the Cold War were so changed that we really have to modernize it. And at the same time, I think that there have to be regional systems which would allow these issues to be resolved. For instance, I hope very much that within the CSCE [Commission on Security and Cooperation in Europe], these mechanisms will arise and I come up often with an idea of the role for the Security Council. Mitterrand, for instance, has been supportive and said that the Secretary General of the CSCE could fulfill these roles in certain situations when it is needed. It would be a way of taking the punch out of the conflicts before they gather momentum. So we have to see the reality here, and we have to see the danger and create the theoretical preconditions for an understanding – you have to give people understanding, new understanding of the world in order for the ethnic issue to remain non-destructive. We have to have a mechanism.

CHARLES TAYLOR: The crucial issue, the issue of minorities – in a way, world history has been here before – after World War I we had, in Europe anyway, the Declaration of the Principle of Self Determination, and new states were created, and essentially, the world order came apart partly on the issue of the treatment of minorities, which really was never adequate or satisfactory. Now the same thing seems to be happening in certain parts of the world, in Yugoslavia, as is notably the case, and in many parts of many republics of the former Soviet Union, particularly with the population so spread out in different republics. In a sense, what the world needs is a code of minorities, a code whereby any sovereign state has to treat its minorities according to certain principles. But do you envisage that that could actually be enforced by a world order, by let us say the United Nations, or maybe as you suggest, by delegating authority at certain cases to regional bodies, but by some kind of international body that could actually enforce?

PIERRE TRUDEAU: You could say at least that a third party country would not recognize the independence of a state unless the principle of respecting minorities were already enshrined.

MIKHAIL GORBACHEV: I think that we should not turn our backs on this problem. In the first place, I think that we have not exhausted the potential of autonomous entities. That is a status that allows a given entity which does not want to be an independent state, but which has the right to have a certain form of national culture which would allow it to preserve its history and culture, its independence in that sense and to consolidate that minority. But I think that is a problem that can be dealt with. It could be dealt with in the sense that the mechanism for division of powers between the centre and the regions, it will be a compact existence of these entities, let us put it that way. That is a possible resolution: a status that could entail certain rights and that would be stimulated by self-regulation, and it would also combine favourably with the centre, it would not run counter to the interests of the centre.

I think that there are very unexpected ways of resolving this problem, when in essence, after the October Revolution, each province was setting up as its own republic, mine as well by the way, Stavropol province. And not just under the guidance of Lenin, but under the leadership of Morozov of which was the Council of People's Commissars, they wanted to set up these republics. Lenin was a unitarian, he knew that this desire existed but he said, let us try an alliance, and he was very much for that alliance and that is how he preserved Russia from falling apart because they took the route of a federative state. But at the same time during Lenin's era, there were more than five thousand national regions, as they were called, within Russia where these small compact entities, let us call them ethnic entities, were looking after their interests.

When Stalin came to power the Federation was buried, it was called a federation but it was buried, and these national entities were liquidated, they were destroyed as such, and that was a terrible blow to everything that was being done by Lenin, to everything that Lenin had formed and created. So I think that we have to find, and I think it is possible to find, a resolution. But it is not enough to denounce, to say, no that is not good enough, you will do it, the majority will do – that is no way to go. But at the same time we have to make it clear that we cannot make these aspirations an absolute ideology. The right to self-determination has to also play a role along with other factors.

VALENTIN BOSS: For instance, natural political tendencies – in the pre-Baltics, for instance, or Central Asia, it is very hard to deal with that.

MIKHAIL GORBACHEV: Yes, I think the processes in the former Soviet republics are very difficult to follow, they have a different mentality, different culture. In the Central Asian republics, for instance, what we are seeing is in fact the rebirth of traditions that have been forgotten. Yes, that is happening. Also I think the situation will unfold in such a way that the people who are on the crest of the wave of destruction of the Union, I think that they will leave the scene because the tendency right now is centrifugal, the centrifugal tendencies are gaining momentum, they are talking about confederation, maybe it will be several republics and then if others want to join they will. Then there will be differentiated links between other parts of this alliance, some will be economic and some will be political. I think there are many different scenarios here. The important thing is for us to see this in time and to facilitate the process, because as I mentioned the Russian leadership is missing that possibility, they have missed their chance or they are missing it. I think that there has to be initiative on the part of Russia, much depends on that. There is much in what happened between Russia and Ukraine. In the level of the peoples, there is no conflict, there is not that isolation or that alienation.

CHARLES TAYLOR: Do you think that in time there could be a new federation between Russia, Ukraine, Belorussia, Kazakhstan, not necessarily all the republics of the former Soviet Union but a new federation among those in our lifetime? I am not talking about the twenty-first or twenty-second century but soon.

MIKHAIL GORBACHEV: If it happens it is not going to be with the centre in Russia, it will be on an equal basis, it will be voluntary, that has to be the way, that has to be mandatory. Since the August coup, when they saw how the Russian leadership has taken certain steps that look a bit like imperial actions, I think that the republics are putting themselves at a distance from the centre. They want some kind of alliance with a centre but federation in the sense we perceived it before the August coup will not work, not right away anyway. It is not a union, it will be an alliance of states with their own institutions, economy, social defense, institutions. It will be a very long process but that is okay, as long as it is voluntary and it is the people's choice, not that they are going to be forced to enter an alliance.

VALENTIN BOSS: Do you deal with the problem of the constitution right now in Moscow? A real constitution, a permanent one, does not exist in Ukraine, in Belarus, and the other republics, and this constitutional phase is very important. Have we passed that already?

MIKHAIL GORBACHEV: No, I do not think I can agree with that statement. I mean, without a constitution a state cannot exist after all. But you should not forget that a constitution has a certain established form of state formations, division of powers, and all of that is right now at the beginning stage, the stage of a search for solution. So we cannot make a constitution right now that tomorrow will be no good. So on the basis of the older ... the old constitutions, I think we should make modifications in those and then arrive at a certain stage where it is possible to go on and I think we are at that stage right now. Other republics are approaching it. It is possible to set up a new constitution.

VALENTIN BOSS: What do you think, are presidential or parliamentary constitutions best?

MIKHAIL GORBACHEV: I think that Russia should have a strong executive power because Russia cannot be managed if the problem of freedom to the regions has not been resolved, because you cannot run a state like that, a republic like that, from Moscow. And naturally we have to have a strong parliament, but in that event there has to be a balance of power between the centre and the regions, between the legislative and the executive powers. Now I can see that this balance exists in the institution of presidential power, and I see once again both positive and bitter experience in that.

REUVEN BRENNER: Do you see that currently by advancing the Kremlin's enhanced centrifugal powers, that the states will become more independent, and is it a problem that that would imply that Russia would have to give up its status of a military superpower? Is that one of the reasons that there is opposition?

MIKHAIL GORBACHEV: Well, if you have in mind that a superpower is only based on military power – I do not think that suits us as Russians. We need a superpower that is based on a different economy, on reliable stability within the country, and on adequate defence. I think that is what the formation of Russia will be based on as a new superpower. As for the first part of the question, as I understood it, you would like to clarify how the present situation will affect the formation of the Russian Federation and the reform process. I think that if this reform process is drawn out and if it is confrontational between political battalions then that will have an effect on all the processes within Russia, because Russia is now at a critical point in its reforms where many important solutions are being found to approach the market economy, the social orientation of the economy, and I think in that sense, the regions are not satisfied that at the federal level we have got this confrontation. They are looking for agreed upon actions from politicians and a policy that will allow the republics in all of Russia to have a good future. However, those structures that we work with in Russia are not capable of generating an agreed policy that would open the doors to an exit from the crisis situation, so I think we need elections.

REUVEN BRENNER: You mentioned that there are various possible ways and sequence of events that can integrate people, some are political and some are economic. Also there have been many attempts done to integrate – and politically, relatively less was done to integrate them economically, and by this I mean the following. For example, today only 3 per cent of the land is privatized and that 3 per cent supplies about 25 per cent of the food. A few years ago it was already known that China followed the following model, that it privatized land and it also allowed three zones and that was the source of prosperity. I know that you frequently expressed your opinion that you do not think that some countries should emulate other countries' models. As part of the planned referendum, which meanwhile was cancelled, one of the questions that Mr Yeltsin intended to ask was about private ownership of land. Do you think that this is where reform should start in 1993?

MIKHAIL GORBACHEV: Well above all, I would like to insist on the following. In China, reform should be done à la Chinese, and in Russia they should be à la Russian. Because since January 1993, it has been going à la Harvard, and that has led to the culture – the whole social structure has renounced this mentality because they do not understand the whole context of the reforms and that is why they have been defeated. I think in Russia, the reforms have to be revolutionary, and I think that counting on collectivization in the beginning was a mistake and on monopoly of state ownership, same point. I think that denationalization and privatization across the board is not realistic and it is not a proper orientation. I think we have to reaffirm freedom and equality of ownership, all forms of ownership, and also free choice for the people of their form of economy. Let people choose, because I am sure it will be a mixed economy and not just in the transitional period but in the future as well. I think there will be a mixed economy because that is part of the Russian tradition.

So artificially imposing a structure, like Stalin did during the collectivization – that smells of Stalinism. It is not democratic reform when they try to forcefully give people a good life. You have to form the preconditions and people have to make their own decision, they know what is good and what is bad, and so they will voluntarily, independently make their decision. And that is what I am talking about when I talk about preconditions.

The second point is that we have to move most of all towards privatization of small and medium-sized business in trade, service, and in land reform. Here there is great potential, but as far as the land is concerned, the question of land for Russians is not a simple question. It does not just mean that you get a little plot of land where you are going to grow corn, or wheat, or rye, or oats, it is a question for Russians of its own feeling of statehood. The land – for the Russians – is a value that is irreplaceable, extremely important, and not something that should be speculated with.

As you know since serfdom ended, it was not the peasants who received the land, but peasant associations and they gave per capita to each male a certain amount of land, so you gave three tenths of a hectare to each male in the family, as soon as they were born, and the land was used five or seven years later. For instance, the association would decide how to distribute, they say, Well you had a plot over here maybe that is good, maybe that is bad, well, we are going to give you another one here in a different spot. You remember how painful that all that was, and all the more so during the Soviet era. Within the framework of Russia, I think the process of land reform will take different forms in different regions. Then when we were discussing the land reform, and the idea was to hold a referendum on ownership of land, whether to recognize it as a viable solution or not, the Uzbek leadership, and not just the leadership, were against privatizing land, against introducing private ownership. Why? Because they have irrigated land, the whole system is irrigated, all of their system is based on this. It is okay for them to lease it, to be able to inherit lease rights, everything that is involved with that is fine, but not ownership because the whole land, the whole country, for the Uzbeks is built on that system, because for them when water ends everything ends.

In Russia, there will be different features to the land reform. I think there will be big differences, it depends where you are, in the centre of Russia is one thing, if you are closer to Belorussia, or Pskov, or to the south of Russia, it will take different forms. But I want the constitution to fix the right to choice. If the people want that then I welcome that. There should be a master on the land, whether it is through lease rights, which would put the land at a farmer's complete disposal and to allow inheritance, or the resale of leasing rights, that is fine, we can envisage all of that. Or if they want to privatize, then we should ask them if they want to. The urban population wants to have privatization of land, they want to have their own whereas the farmers are against it in the rural areas. We have to use the land properly in Russia. In certain parts of the railway lines along the border there are millions of hectares of land, so this reform will allow those who want to organize the farmer associations to do it.

REUVEN BRENNER: That is exactly the advantage of a federal system in principle – that you allow states to compete with various arrangements. So let us say Uzbekistan does not want to try it, then they do not try it, but another republic which votes for it can try it and then we will see which one succeeds within five years. That is how people learn one from the other.

MIKHAIL GORBACHEV: Yes, I agree with you on that. Pierre, incidentally in his introduction, brought up so many issues and questions that I cannot possibly ignore them although I do not know if I have time to answer them all. Of course, you brought up the theme of how the West has compromised. I think that is a just question because setting up a new world order is something that is right now at the first stages, and we have to work together on the basis of the fact that we are all equal and that we act on one standard and according to the same rules. I think that for building a new world order it is unacceptable to have one country or a group of countries who dictate their conditions, to say this is how it is going to be done, this is the standard, this is the way the world order will be – no, we have to make this new world together and I return to the UN on that. I think the question should be one of setting up regional structures to facilitate the formation of proper interaction and proper relationships on the regional level. But I think there has to be an understanding throughout the world that we all have to change.

I must say that we expected changes from the Soviet Union both domestically, through reform, and in the external policy, foreign policy, through the new thinking, as we called it. Yes, we thought that we had to show the initiative, we had a great responsibility on our shoulders, somebody had to begin. But now the process has to begin only with compromises and mutual understanding. If somebody right now is planning to say that, okay, here I am and I am going to collect these berries that are already well grown and simply make use of the results, ready-made – no, these results are not there, we have to work together, understanding that we are equal subjects involved in creating a new world order, a new civilization. What I would say is when I heard voices saying that communism has been defeated, that the Cold War was won by the Western countries, et cetera, I really must say that that is so superficial, it is either for an election campaign or simply a populist approach because a serious politician could not possibly think that way. We all lost the Cold War, particularly the US and the Soviet Union, and all of us have won by leaving that period. I think that that is a scientific conclusion, that is the first thing.

Secondly, what does it mean to have capitalism victorious and that we must now in this capitalist society – mind you I do not know where there is a capitalist state actually in existence. Who can show me please? Is Canada a capitalist system? Germany, a capitalist state? Oh hardly, this is from our old lexicology, from our old vocabulary. We have to do a scientific – that is all in the level of emotions – we have to do a scientific analysis if we are going to say what was defeated. Socialism? No, socialism was not defeated. The Stalin model, a utopian model imposed upon this whole country and other countries by repressive methods and supported by the totalitarian regime – yes, that was defeated, and domestically, for the most part, because it took away the oxygen from society. But if you tell me that there is no significance in our search, or our considerations, or our thoughts about a future society – I think that all human values have no place there – then I cannot agree with that. I think everything that we have put together, all of our experience and the experience of our society will be a fusion of these cultures and these feats.

VALENTIN BOSS: I think the most important historic victory was over Stalinism and therefore I was very interested in your statement. It was a number of years ago, but despite your attainments, you said that Stalinism is still alive. What did you mean by that?

MIKHAIL GORBACHEV: What I mean when I say that Stalinism is alive is that within the society those forces still exist in the mentality of people, the faith in a leader that he has to decide everything for them, there is all sorts of speculation on the part of the current leadership, and they all think they are all-powerful and that the leadership can decide everything. That is a dead end. That is not the only thing that Stalinism manifests itself in. Democratic transformation to the interests of the people, if they are to be done by breaking people over their knee without paying any attention at all to their material state of being, to make all of them very poor – and that is Stalinism – that is a system that does not care for the people at all. It is a state where you are just a cog in the wheel, you are no one. And there again you have a leader who once again patronizes the people. If you want to call yourself a democrat then you have to be concerned with having reform lead to political, legal, social preconditions, and I would even say ideological preconditions, spiritual preconditions, for raising human beings to a level of freedom, to freedom of choice, that would preserve and uphold its interest, so that it plays a political dictatorship, then we have a dictatorship of law. In that case, that is fine. Otherwise, all you can see in this is Stalinism.

In an interview here in Canada, I was asked, is it possible for the Bolsheviks to come back to power? I said, well they are in power right now. They said, what do you mean? Because what they are doing was done by the Bolsheviks in the same way, without taking into account the interests of the people, as if they were gods who were going to manipulate the people, put them into a labour force, and then left, left, right, left, order them around. That smells of Bolshevism and Stalinism and nothing else. The interviewer did not like that and said, "I think you think that Yeltsin is Stalin?" No, I did not say he was Stalin, I said that he uses Stalinist methods and has blood … definitely.

REUVEN BRENNER: You mentioned two things. One, is the word equal, has to be treated as equal? Do you think that Russia should participate at G7 meetings? And the other question, what can the West or Russia do to prevent arms from being sold to volatile regions?

MIKHAIL GORBACHEV: Yes, okay, of course, but I can answer the first question, very simply. If we want to demonstrate that we are now entering a new world order and that there is no division between the West and East, as there was in the past, and that groupings such as the G7 exist, then to demonstrate changes in the functioning of that institution as a result of the participation of Russia, I think that is a very important factor. Let Russia be for the moment a participant, a beginner, let us put it that way, in the field, but I think that it would be a very big step.

PIERRE TRUDEAU: If you want to participate in the G7, you are becoming capitalist. It is quite simple. You said –

MIKHAIL GORBACHEV: I do not consider that France is capitalist or that Germany is capitalist in their pure forms. I think there is a lot of social democracy in their systems.

REUVEN BRENNER: Private ownership, in that sense, is the tenant of capitalism.

MIKHAIL GORBACHEV: No, I do not think the form of ownership determines the nature of the system. I think it is the state or the condition of the human being within that system, how socially or democratically he is well provided for, or how humane the system is, I think those are the characteristics of a system that determine what type of system it is. I think we should renounce those foundations now. Pierre and I were speaking yesterday about the Caribbean crisis. John Kennedy said one thing when he welcomed representatives of the minorities, the ethnic, the First Nations, and they said, "Look how many people have come from other continents." He listened to them very carefully and he said, "Okay let us begin with making our time right now, and the future, just." So let us not talk about capitalism and socialism and let us not waste our intellect on that. Let us see what the new civilization should be like at the turn of the twenty-first century and take into account the challenges that exist, the global challenges, the problems of achieving freedom, the powerful processes that have taken hold of whole continents. I mean there may be difficulties, there may be possible breakdowns in the process, but it is a fact, let us think about that.

PIERRE TRUDEAU: There is not a single social democratic regime in the countries of the West that can do without the banks. If the banks do not like its politics, then the socialist government falls. I do not think that is the socialism you want to build. But what is it? I asked you in the beginning. When you say "I, Mikhail Sergeyevich, am a Communist," what does that mean? You said, "Well, economy x," you said, "Social reasons, justice." Very good. But if you tell me that you are a social democrat as understood in the Western countries, then that is really the end of the story, because everyone agrees on capital, on a certain justice. But everyone also agrees that the state favours, first of all, capital. That is a philosophy that says capital is required for production, while Marxism, Communism, Stalinism, say no, the workers can take their destiny into their own hands, they can be the owners. They even should be in charge of their destiny. When we ask what your economic ideology is, it really seems to me that it is rather like my liberalism. Liberalism in North America, in Canada, is a form of capitalism tempered by a state's effort to redistribute wealth. Wealth is still produced by capital, not by workers. This may be the only possible way, but it seems to me that there must be theoreticians somewhere in the world who should be trying to develop something that would perhaps be more generous, more egalitarian in its essence than the capitalist system as we know it.

MIKHAIL GORBACHEV: Well above all, I talk about answering the question of myself. People ask me, what are you exactly Mr Gorbachev? Social Democrat, Democrat, Communist, Socialist, Liberal, whatever. I do not think that we will ever get rid of these old concepts. I think it is time to reject them because we are in a different world now. I think we should be talking about new values that we can and should discuss and then transform our theoretical foundations, our politics, and to head for a new civilization. I do not think these are thought up concepts of a new civilization. I think it cannot be said those people who represent the liberal tendencies, that their teachings can resolve everything. No, we know that right now. The thing is that many liberal movements have been more flexible than the socialist movement. Liberals are very quick to adapt to the situation and they were able to make use of the socialist values and they worked together with Lenin to stimulate – they worked in a partnership to stimulate the economy, not to lead to a great differentiation of the strain of society where you have got polarization like a north and south which enter into a confrontation, which is the class struggle.

That is how we had a socially oriented system, economy, a role of the state. So I think that all of that is very important to see and understand and I would like to repeat that I do not see, and I do not consider in the near future for instance, in the twenty-first century, that the choice is socialism or capitalism. I think the choice has to be for a new civilization which would organically incorporate within itself on the basis of everything that we have renounced, and understood, renounced, and tried, and is taken from what is good, those values that we can apply. No, I do not think that the principles of ownership – and as we know, they are the ones that create stimulus – but we in embracing practices, we cannot get along without social democracy, we cannot get along without freedom, we cannot get along without tolerance for other people's opinions.

CHARLES TAYLOR: We have come to the end of our time, I regret it very much, it has been an absolutely fascinating discussion. I want to thank my colleagues, Professors Boss and Brenner, and I want to thank you Pierre Trudeau, and, above all, to thank you very much Mikhail Sergeyevich for being with us today for this marvelous discussion. Thank you very much.

10

Right of Interference: Progress and Failure in Conflict Prevention in an Age of Global Anxiety

4 November 1996

Bernard Kouchner

INTRODUCTION

"Auschwitz was not an internal affair." This pithy sentence in Bernard Kouchner's Beatty Lecture on "Conflict Prevention in an Age of Global Anxiety" captures the essence of his thesis on "the right of interference" against genocide. Born in 1939, his grandparents perished in Auschwitz during his early childhood. The Holocaust profoundly shaped his empathic worldview. "It is our first mission to answer the anguishes of men and women," he told the lecture audience. His life's work would be defined by the basic intuition that confronting evil was a moral duty. By 1996, when he delivered his lecture at McGill, he had already become an iconic figure in humanitarian circles. Beyond his fame as co-founder of Médecins Sans Frontières, he had emerged as a notable public intellectual, soon to become a prominent UN diplomat and French politician. His shift from healing victims as a physician to pre-emptive interference as a policy-maker, was based on the simple premise that we must devise "systems to act before it is too late." Amidst the promise of the post-Cold War era, he helped popularize the obvious yet revolutionary truth that unlike natural disasters, mass-atrocities were political choices that could be prevented through timely intervention.

At the time of this speech in 1996, it was a particularly poignant period to speak about the prevention of genocide. In 1995, the mass-execution of some eight thousand Bosnian Muslims in Srebrenica had starkly demonstrated the catastrophic consequences of the world community's inaction against "ethnic cleansing." The year before, in 1994, the withdrawal of UN peacekeepers amidst the extermination of some one million Tutsi in Rwanda had become an indelible stain on the collective conscience of humankind. It had exposed the vows of "never again" as

Bernard Kouchner. *Used with permission of Getty Images.*

empty words. The UN Security Council had established the International Criminal Tribunals for the former Yugoslavia (ICTY) and Rwanda (ICTR) where I served as a prosecutor at the time. It was difficult during this time not to come across Bernard Kouchner, whether on the conference circuit or in conversations with colleagues, or even by chance on the Amtrak train between New York and Washington DC where I once met him. He was a man on a mission, always on the go, spreading the message of prevention with boundless energy.

While speaking of ideals, however, Bernard Kouchner's prescient questions voiced in his Beatty Lecture were also a warning for the future that we now encounter: "On whom can we rely to avoid genocides, like in Rwanda? How can we avoid the anxiety emerging with the crisis in all the developed countries leading to nationalism, egocentrism, and finally racism?" Today, twenty-five years after those words, we can point to progress: there is a UN Special Adviser on Prevention of Genocide; an International Criminal Court at The Hague; a sizeable community of scholars and think tanks, diplomats and activists, engaged with the prediction and prevention of mass-atrocities. The forces of global integration have accelerated, not least in the Information Age where events in the most remote corners of the earth are instantly brought to our attention. Yet, despite these developments, we are now confronted with the genocide against the Rohingya in Myanmar, just as some years ago we learned about the extermination and sexual enslavement of the Yazidi in Iraq, and before that the horrific atrocities in Sudan's Darfur region. And instead of rising to the occasion with collective vision and volition, we find ourselves in the grip of populist hatred and delusional nationalism; a retreat from multilateralism and failure of political will in the face of global threats, rather than building on the painful lessons learned from Srebrenica and Rwanda.

Bernard Kouchner's words are as relevant today as they were in 1996, except that now we have even fewer excuses to be bystanders in the face of radical evil. This historic Beatty Lecture is a powerful reminder that bearing witness to human suffering, and above all, acting with genuine determination rather than paying lip service to platitudes, remains a central moral challenge of our times.

*

Payam Akhavan is a Senior Fellow at Massey College and a Distinguished Visitor in the Faculty of Law at the University of Toronto. He is a Member of the Permanent Court of Arbitration at The Hague and was a Full Professor in the Faculty of Law at McGill University from 2005 to 2020.

LECTURE

The following is the full Beatty Lecture delivered on 4 November 1996.

Our world is crossed by a fire belt of internal conflicts. We feel, in Europe, as in the United States and Canada, sheltered – concerned – but still sheltered. Of course, public opinions have been emoted by the ex-Yugoslavia conflict, but this emotion occurred after long months of conflict and a lot of death and desolation.

The last "international war" was the Iraqi conflict when a tremendous amount of money was spent to win the Iraqi army and preserve the precious lives of our soldiers. As today, with the dramatic and foreseeable exodus in Zaïre. We knew this terrible issue, but nothing has been done to avoid it. Every time we feel the same emotion, and every time we say that something could be possible to avoid such dramas. We are waiting for the next images on TV screens.

The end of the Cold War, the end of the separation in two big blocs, must provide us an opportunity to revise the means to ensure peace for the people living on the planet, and specially the minorities. What is the international community doing to preserve peace not only between countries but also inside countries to protect minorities? On whom can we rely to avoid genocides, like in Rwanda? How can we avoid the anxiety emerging with the crisis in all the developed countries leading to nationalism, egocentrism, and finally racism? What kind of means can we employ? What are the ways for a better cooperation between all the bodies of the international community – political, NGOs, churches, universities, media and people – one-by-one?

In fact, we are facing the same situation that our parents faced before World War II. The situation is explosive, because of the disorder caused by the economic crisis. We must invent a world and re-equilibrate the relationships and the richness. If we do nothing, if we do not invent equilibrated and civilized systems, a brotherhood and a collective solidarity, if we do not find common values to create collective mechanisms, then we shall have to cure, again and again, wars and desolation, and always too late.

If we wait too long to build some preventative systems, a new economical balance and sustainable development, our world will get more and more dangerous and misbalanced. If we continue on the way of indifference and egoism, we shall for sure continue to pay for disasters until the day we shall lack of cash. Paying and after ... what? On the contrary, nationalism is back, everywhere, mainly in Europe.

BACK TO NATIONALISM?

In fact, people feel threatened. The fear is no longer the fear of an attack by another country, the fears are coming from the weakness of the economic systems, growing unemployment, the difficulties people meet in their daily lives, the privations, the proliferation of the free delivered weapons, repressions, oppressions operated by terrorists or dictators, the violations to elementary human rights.

So what can we do, political bodies, humanitarians, functionaries of great international bodies, money providers? Which answer can we bring before the blood begins to be poured, before poor nutrition and illness do their bad job? It is our first mission to answer the anguishes of men and women, to find and implement systems, to act before it is too late, before the fear turns into hate for the other, the neighbour, the one who is different. Could we let them die? Do we reach to such a selfishness that we become indifferent to the massacre of minorities?

The nature of society has changed, so can we still think that the face of security and world peace is the same? A sustainable peace is acceptable and beneficial only if it is shared by everybody, in spite of its colour, religion, or conviction. This aim can be reached if, at the international level, a cooperation is found based on solidarity, justice, and reciprocity.

Let us come specifically to our subject. Before, massacres of minorities were carried out inside the countries, hidden and considered as a matter of "internal affairs." It was the "war of the others," and nobody felt concerned: it was not known. We began to feel an interest only if it threatened our countries. Democracy and information have changed the world. We need only a few hours to know what is occurring on the other side of our planet. This does not permit us to prevent conflicts. But we cannot say, as we were used to saying before, "Sorry, we did not know about it!" But, from now on, is there a moral advantage to know, if we remain passive?

There are still massacres, genocides, hidden behind frontier walls. We call that, as we did for a long time in Chechnya, an "internal Russian affair." And what about Tibet? Preventive diplomacy – ingérence remains beautiful – and voluntaristic projects are not yet sufficiently efficient to prevent what occurred in Sarajevo, Kigali, Monrovia, and certainly tomorrow in Burundi. We need diplomatic activity, but also political harassment and preventive instruments.

HUMANITARIAN ACTION

Humanitarian action is to be considered as a means not as an aim. Humanitarian action tends to occur once it is too late. It signs and confirms the failure of the body politic. It is necessary to treat the victims, but it is better to avoid exterminations. On the contrary, the more money is used to cure, the more that money is too late for humanitarian activities. There is less for development and prevention.

The current change in mentalities is happening because we feel that we can reach prevention as a result of the growing influence and popularity of humanitarian action, maybe also because we feel we can no longer spoil enormous amounts of money. During the past five years, the global humanitarian action has reached more than four billion dollars. We must deal with war, as we must deal with questions of health: to cure is not enough. We must impose prophylaxy, preventative action. And this notion has to stamp the third step of a process that began in the middle of the nineteenth century. We have to deal with what we are not directly concerned in, but what is concerning the fate of other people.

HUMANITARIAN GENERATIONS

In 1859, Henri Dunant, who was not a doctor, had the new idea to treat those who were wounded on the battlefields, from both sides. This was the beginning of the Red Cross. There were no good or bad victims, just victims, and the desire to care for both sides justified the neutrality and required the authorization of the governments of the states. Today a question is to be raised: are the aggressors to benefit from the same status as the victims? Can those who throw bombs, benefit from the same status as those who are wounded by bombs? These were the limits of this first generation. But it has been a useful generation.

A long time after this, the second generation arrived: that of the French doctors, who besides the members of the Red Cross, worked during the Biafra War, at the end of the sixties. They decided not to remain prisoners of borders, but to treat everyone in need of their care, with or without the clearance of the government. The needs of victims, for the first time, initiated the caring process, not governments. These doctors also decided that they had to bear witness to what they had seen and to protect the victims. According to them, according to me in particular, state sovereignty was one thing, but more important were the wounded men and women. The most important thing was the violation of human rights.

The third generation will be the interference generation. It will prevent massacres. Shall we succeed? We do not know, but we shall have tried. We are accused of "playing politics," as if to prevent massacres of minorities was not simply public *salubrité*, or because we are well informed about urgent situations given that our efforts are taking place within the European area. This area was constituted of countries born of war and massacres, and these European countries have united themselves to avoid a new Auschwitz; this was the first interference: the European Union. Humanitarian action is a right which softens and codifies war within the framework of international rights. It is the idea that, inside war – accepted as an inevitable human activity – there are rules to respect. Excellent, but not sufficient! Let us go further. Extermination of a group of human beings must not remain the domain of the internal policy of a state: over and above the national sovereignty of a state, there must be human rights and even the rights of a single human being. The victims are proclaiming and denying the right to massacre minorities in the name of closed borders, dictators, national sovereignty.

GENOCIDE IN BOSNIA? GENOCIDE IN RWANDA?

Within the European Union, the years 1993 to 1995 have been particularly marked by what has been called the "Yugoslavia drama" and the "Rwandan genocide." The European Parliament where I am elected has reacted by voting in a lot of resolutions. These resolutions are not enough, even if, generously, they were proclaiming the rights of minorities, the recognition of genocide and ethnic cleansing, and rights of the refugees. Sometimes, and it has become more and more frequent in these last two years, the resolutions were insisting on the necessity of humanitarian intervention and on the implementation of a real system of conflict prevention.

We are building the new right: the right of interference. For the moment, the debate on prevention, or preventative diplomacy, remains too theoretical, because we are institutionally limited. But we parliamentarians feel that the European Parliament has a part to play, affirming itself as a moral authority and as a tool that can be used to put pressure on the Union political bodies and on the member states in the matter of conflict prevention and preventative diplomacy.

Our institution, the European Parliament, in a recent resolution on April 1994, on the "right of humanitarian intervention," adopted a text in which it was clearly defined that it is no longer acceptable to refer constantly to the traditional arguments of the sovereignty of the states in permitting any arbitrary acts perpetrated in a country, by a government, or by a group. This text also stated that the situation of human rights in a country is not an internal affair. We, as the expression of the citizens of the member states, have recognized that Auschwitz was not an internal affair. It has taken almost fifty years to reach this statement, as an international body. There is now a favourable trend: the period from 1993 to 1994 has led to the adoption by the Security Council of the United Nations of resolutions upon the right of intervention – in a large sense, for humanitarians and respect of motives of human rights. Among these:

- Resolution 929 of 22 June 1994, to approve a multinational operation with humanitarian purposes in Rwanda.
- Resolution 836 of 4 June 1993, on the protection of six regions of Bosnia Herzegovina described as security areas.

- Resolution 45/100 of 1990 of the UN General Assembly consecrating the humanitarian corridor concept, which will be applied in December 1992 to save Dubrovnik.
- Resolution 43/131 of 8 December 1988, humanitarian assistance for victims of natural disasters, but also political or military consequences. This resolution will be implemented immediately, in Armenia, for the earthquake, by sending more than five hundred rescuers.
- Resolution 688 of 5 April 1991, of the Security Council imponing the international relief for Kurdish refugees from Iraq.
- Resolution 43/131 of 1988, laying down the principle of free access to disaster victims in case of natural disasters and similar emergency situations.

In fact, the definition of the right and duty of intervention leads to two kinds of problems. Firstly, the absolute necessity of an effective system of crime prevention. Secondly, the definition of the means of intervention and procedures to implement: the sending of observers; special envoys; peacemaking or peacekeeping armies; the protection of humanitarian convoys. In fact, there is a great confusion between the judicial, diplomatic, political and, by the way, budgetary initiatives, and this confusion tends to paralyze action. There is confusion between political and humanitarian action. There is no synergy, but rather suspicion and bad will. It is the wrong way to proceed. The two bodies are necessary. The first because it has the instruments to decide, the second because it can act and oblige the others to decide, and the politician to move.

Last year, the whole international community spent more than four billion dollars as I said before, on official humanitarian help. Two thirds of this help came from the European Union. In 1994, ECHO, the humanitarian desk of the Union, provided finance of 764 million euros. Twenty years ago, it financed only five million. It cannot go on like this. This enormous increase cannot go on. Everybody agrees. But who does what? We need prevention, worldwide as well as on the European scale. But what are the best solutions and who can do what?

HUMANITARIAN ACTION IS TOO EXPENSIVE SO WE MUST IMPLEMENT PREVENTIVE DIPLOMACY

The resources, the will, and in some cases the necessary competencies to put this idea of prevention into practice seems to be lacking. There is also a lack of resources. Who has troops? Who has the personnel required for timely preventive diplomacy? Even the United Nations does not have them. Can the Union reach an agreement within the member states and in the context of the next intergovernmental conference, to create such a body? Is there a real political will?

Within the United Nations, various departments and agencies have met regularly since 1993, in order to develop a new early warning mechanism, but the success is not obvious. In fact, there are still not enough agreed upon indicators which could initiate action to prevent conflicts. In the same way, there is still no means by which the Security Council is made aware of a problem, and can then consider what action should be taken.

The starting point for preventative diplomacy, or any conflict prevention, is the means to be properly informed of threats to peace and a good mechanism to galvanize actions in them. To be serious, the United Nations needs a special office for preventive diplomacy that can rely on the Security Council to forward its analysis. The Union, to improve its preventive performance must also create, within its institutions, in the best and the right place, a similar kind of office or centre, able to make concrete recommendations for preventive action to the Commission, Council of Ministers, and to the United Nations. The point is that these recommendations must be pursued politically. It also means that the Union must have a common foreign and security policy. A centre for prevention is helpful and useful only if we can act, and only if we have the means to act. That is why our major efforts must be focused on the intergovernmental conference. We must ask our governments to implement a common foreign security policy.

THE PART EUROPE CAN PLAY

The European Union can play an active part in the promotion of peace and international security — it is no longer enough to ensure the protection of its fundamental interests and of its own security. We are the first commercial power of the planet, the premier provider of humanitarian help, the organism that has two members within the Security Council. We must, with our other partners, USA, Japan, Canada and others, even our partners at the AUO, assume responsibilities in this period following the Cold War, in which new equilibriums must be found at the global level.

We have to implement a more efficient foreign policy that takes account of and integrates commercial policy, cooperation and development policy, and also questions of security, with a permanent strategy with the international organizations. The United Nations has a permanent bureau in Brussels, but we never meet them to exchange information. Why? All of our anachronistic mentalities have to be changed, we must communicate with the world – no one is responsible for this or that, rather we must have a collective responsibility. What is the internet if genocide is still possible?

The present system relies upon a structure and upon intergovernmental modes of functioning, hardly reconcilable with a concept of a "community pillar." Unanimity, the limited role of the executive bodies, the non-existent role given to the impression of the civil society, are preventing the Union from fully participating in international relationships. For instance, too frequently, Council action is paralyzed by veto and antagonism, constraining the efficiency of common action and emptying the common positions of all of their sense, as little more than common denominators, when the tragic events of international actuality are requiring urgent and decisive actions. Remember, Secretary General Boutros-Ghali asked for a preventive action in the Great Lakes border of Zaire more than one year ago. Who refused? France and Belgium.

As Europeans, as Americans, as members of humankind, in fact, we must also pay particular attention to the problem of development. It has become fully recognized in the last few years that the traditional view of security, the physical protection of individuals, societies, and states, depends at least in part on people's economic, social, and environmental wellbeing. The 1994 United Nations Development Report included that fact in its term of "human security." Though we cannot say that there is a crude, causal link between poverty and conflict, we are obliged to recognize that a growing number of conflicts are now, at least in part, disputes about the control of scare resources. For instance, the Rwandan genocide of 1994 was designed by individuals fearful of losing power. They have been able to exacerbate well-established ethnic tensions and to recruit thousands of young Hutus who could easily carry out their plan because of the collapse in employment and social welfare, and the reduction of land holding. Some economic factors such as the devaluation of the Rwandese franc and the fall of the International Coffee Agreement affected the country. These problems led to a drastic reduction in social spending. The problem was even further amplified by low levels of participation in formal education – and we all know the role that education plays in sharing civic identity and transcending ethnicity. I want to congratulate here the Commission for making a very strong effort to help the developing countries to teach their population notions of human rights and respect for each other. I think this could constitute a step for the future. I must here add that where there is a failure of development, many people are led to think that they cannot survive in peace, and therefore are in danger of finding a great interest in war.

That is why I want to stress the importance of the policy we implement in cooperation and development and of the options we are taking right now. Development constitutes an important part of the strategy of conflict prevention. We must fight for a sustainable development. Some member states in Europe now prefer to look East rather than to look South, and year after year, the amount they devote to development and cooperation is going down. I refer for instance, but not only, to the problem of the volume of European development funding. Is it realistic and clever to "kill" the economies of the developing countries with unbearable levels of debt burdens and unfair international trade terms, given that we know how explosive a situation they are experiencing. For the prevention of conflicts, we must take a lot of factors into account: political, military for sure, but also agricultural, economical, climatic, demographic, all these factors are closely implicated in development and cooperation policy. We must be very careful in the options we are choosing. Either we make a real effort towards prevention, which still, in many quarters seems like a utopia, or the global political agenda will draw us into a disaster of inconceivable proportions.

THE RIGHT OF INTERFERENCE

The level of population displacement could become unmanageable. More than eighteen million people are displaced or refugees, and while the humanitarian aid budget may be increasing, there seems to be a commensurate increase in the political will to support the humanitarian aid budget. To be realistic, and to work for prevention, we must concentrate on three levels: prevention; our preparedness for present and future crises; and what we are doing here now, the quest for solutions. A framework for prevention already exists in Boutros-Ghali's Agenda for Peace, which has not the same implementation problem as all international arrangements, as we know very well within the Union and the European Parliament (much has already been said and written about this). The problem remains the same: the gap between the declarations and the will to put them in practice. Solving this will be the purpose of the next Secretary General of the United Nations.

We are swimming against the tide. The situation is deteriorating in various places of the world. The tendency towards ethnic-religious conflicts and the manipulation of ethnic and religious differences for political ends, the fact that in Europe there is currently a racist, xenophobic, self-centred movement with objective causes – economic, once again – but which is not being combated by our authorities, all these factors demand that we launch a humanitarian counter offensive. Otherwise, in spite of everything, we shall lose the battle for public opinion. If we lose that, then as most of the "politicians" and governments care only about the headlines from the previous day's opinion to set their following day's agenda, we shall loose our fight on humanitarian action and on prevention. Finally, we shall be lost ourselves and the humanitarian cause will be pushed back. We shall have no more budget, nor will we be able to plan innovative actions for prevention, and nor will we have the resources needed to find solutions and to implement the economic and social development which will bring about a more secure peace. As of now, in my own country, as in others, I can feel the threats to humanitarian action.

We must build the tools of the right of interference, that is to say, the right of protecting the minorities. We must remain modest and very ambitious at the same time. Modest because no individual can solve the problem and because it will last a long time. We need more coordination, between us, every country, between the institutions, between and across policies: foreign policies, development policies, environmental and economical. We cannot separate them or make them compete with each other. We have to work hard together. We must operate jointly. We need better cooperation between NGOs, institutions, European as well as international, and less competition and more professionalism and integration. We must be ambitious because we have to be capable of orchestrating and maximizing our mobilization of all sectors of society to put over the messages and to try and halt what is particularly unfavourable in a time of world crisis. No longer can massacres as in Chechnya or genocide as in Rwanda be considered as an internal affair. The unhappiness and fate of other men belong to all men. What we are dealing with, this new kind of intervention, will no longer be called humanitarian action but humanism to create.

I remember the words of our General Dallaire in charge of the troops in Rwanda: "We need to prevent. Let's work on building that. Inside a war the place of prevention is a joke."

11

Lessons in Living From the Dying
28 October 1997

Cicely Saunders

INTRODUCTION

When Dame Cicely Saunders delivered this lecture in October 1997, her friendship with the Montreal surgeon, Dr Balfour Mount, was almost a quarter century old. Inspired by her ideas, in 1975 he had established a Palliative Care Unit at the Royal Victoria Hospital and blazed a trail for others to follow within the mainstream of the healthcare system. The intervening years had seen the rise of palliative care as a modern field of specialization, growing out of the specific historical roots of hospice, gaining public health recognition, and spreading around the world.

In 1997, Dame Cicely was in her last decade of life. Now widowed, she was engaged in a final period of global travel, still eager to share her experiences, and willing to reach out to audiences of many kinds. She had founded St Christopher's in London in 1967 as the first modern hospice. There, clinical care, research, and education were combined in a triumvirate that could offer compassion alongside up-to-date and evidenced-based medical practice, and disseminate knowledge and skills to others. Aged seventy-nine and still wonderfully alert, she was perfectly situated in the Beatty Lecture to draw on a lifetime of experience, distilled into a compelling personal and professional story.

Her lecture is a tour de force, with that special combination of the heart and mind that was so key to Dame Cicely's approach to the care of the dying. It is also beautifully told. In a short space we learn much of her fascinating life: her three careers as nurse, social worker, and physician; the settings in which her ideas were forged and incorporated into practice; the deep personal encounters she had with patients and families facing the end of life; and her late marriage to the artist Marian Bohusz-Szyszko.

In my biography of this remarkable woman who did so much to transform how we care for dying people, I concluded that despite all my efforts to understand her, there is still so much more to be learned about Cicely. The lecture is a case in point.

Cicely Saunders. *Used with permission of McGill University Archives,* PR045593.

Here she demonstrates that ideas forged within a Judaeo-Christian tradition can transfer and translate to other cultures. She also reveals a sophisticated understanding of the relationship between living and dying in the face of serious illness and the importance of moving beyond terminal care as the orientation of practice. This balance between accepting death and embracing life is beautifully characterized and still speaks to us across the decades.

There are also some wonderful quotes and aphorisms in the lecture: "Whoever said, 'I wish I had spent more time in the office' as he was dying?"; "If you don't have problems, you don't have a hospice"; and "Truth lies in a relationship rather than in words."

In this lecture, Dame Cicely digs back to her earliest influences, from Alfred Worcester[1] and Herman Feifel,[2] to the pain specialists, to an influential nursing tutor, and, above all, to the stories she heard from patients in the nineteen years before St Christopher's opened. Yet she draws on current themes such Clive Seale[3] on the notion of heroic death, the ongoing deliberations surrounding euthanasia, and the work of the World Health Organization.

It is a privilege to re-visit this most significant lecture. It is a tribute to colleagues at McGill who have selected it for inclusion in this collection. It is further evidence, if we needed it, of the compassion, intellect, and insight of the lecturer. I hope it will be read eagerly, years after its delivery, to anyone concerned about the modern care of dying people, and what can be learned from them.

*

David Clark is Professor Emeritus of Medical Sociology and Wellcome Trust Investigator at the University of Glasgow. The author of many works on religion, family life, and end-of-life care, he is an historian of the modern hospice and palliative care movement, and the biographer of Cicely Saunders.

LECTURE

The following is the full Beatty Lecture delivered on 28 October 1997.

"I do not want to die, I do not want to die," said a man with much to live for. Yet three weeks later he was able to say, "I only want what is right." He had lived a lifetime in that three weeks, and made a journey into peace and acceptance against all the odds, completing his life as he died quietly at age sixty. Freedom and growth may come as we say yes to much of what life throws at us.

People move fast in a crisis and over the years I have seen growth through loss, healed relationships, and recovered faith. But I have also seen anger and resentment at the unfairness of leaving an unfulfilled life or unfinished responsibilities. I have seen fear and confusion, weakness and dependence, stark realities of the end of life. Nevertheless, without idealizing any of those I met on my own journey since I entered this field in 1948, it is the often unexpected triumphs that stand out and leave me with the conviction that there is much to learn about priorities from people who are facing life's end. Whoever said, I wish I had spent more time at the office, as he was dying?

The incentive, or rather, the commission to enter this field, came in early 1948 when, having been invalided from nursing with the back that remains tiresome today and forces me to lecture sitting down, I had become a medical social worker. In my first ward I met a man of forty, a Polish Jew from Warsaw, called David Tasma, who had an inoperable cancer of the rectum. I took care to meet him when he returned to the outpatient clinic, and when he collapsed five months later and was admitted to another hospital, I visited him many times during the two months before he died. We discussed the need for somewhere I could plan which would help people in his predicament; somewhere more suited to the need for symptom control, and above all, to give a chance to come to terms with the situation more easily than in a busy surgical ward.

Two phrases he used in our long talks formed for me the challenge I came to believe I had to respond to. Referring to a small legacy of £500 he said, "I will be a window in your Home." And again, "I want what is in your mind and in your heart." The first phrase gave me a commitment to openness – openness to and from the world, to all who would come and to all future challenges. From the second, although at the time it was a very personal exchange, came the commitment to everything of the mind; research, learning, full scientific rigour, always matched with the friendship of the heart, the vulnerability of one person before another. After he died, having made a private peace with the God of his fathers, I had the assurance that he had made his journey with his own quiet dignity in the freedom of the spirit. So openness, mind together with heart, and the freedom of the spirit are the three founding principles, not only of St Christopher's Hospice, but of a now worldwide movement. David Tasma, the Polish Jew who thought he had made no impact on the world by his life, started a movement founded on the Judeo-Christian ethic, which has shown it can flourish in different cultures, each initiative with its own characteristics, but with the common aim that people should be helped not only to die peacefully, but to live until they die, with their needs and their potential met as fully as possible.

After David died I spent the next three years as an evening volunteer in an early home for the dying, St Luke's Hospital. As a registered nurse I found myself in charge of a ward, carrying out the evening drug round. I saw oral opiates being given on a four-hourly regime, balanced to the patient's need and remarkably effective. For the first time I saw the constant pain of terminal cancer receiving constant control, patients free of pain and alert, not having to earn their morphine by having pain first; that constant switchback I had been accustomed to seeing as drugs were given as needed.

After three years the surgeon I was working for finally said, "Go and read medicine, it's the doctors who desert the dying. There's so much more to be learned about pain and you'll only be frustrated if you don't do it properly and they won't listen to you." With his help and my father's support, I enrolled as a first year medical student at the age of thirty-three. I continued as a volunteer for a further four years and then, after qualifying and some hospital experience, a clinical research fellowship enabled me to introduce and monitor pain and symptom control in another early hospice, St Joseph's, in a deprived area of London and at that time virtually untouched by medical advancements. The seven years' work there enabled me to lay the foundations of palliative care and raise the money to build St Christopher's, the first modern research and teaching hospice.

Seven years of listening to patients, 1,100 analyzed cases and endless networking, finally enabled the St Christopher's hospice to be built; nineteen years in all of learning what dying people are asking of us and can teach us in their turn. A whole body of research has grown from that early work both in this hospice and in many other centres.

There were other foundations. Dr Alfred Worcester put three lectures to the medical students of Harvard on "The Care of the Aged, the Dying and the Dead" into a book published in 1935.[4] I was introduced to it by a nurse tutor in 1953 and it was an inspiration. In 1927, Francis Peabody wrote in the *Journal of the American Medical Association* on "The Care of the Patient" and concluded, "The secret of the care of the patient is in caring for the patient."[5] There were researchers in the USA such as Beeching, Eddy, and Lasagna to meet, other early homes to visit, an admittedly sparse literature to discover, and many concerned nurses and doctors to contact. In 1959, Herman Feifel published a book of essays titled *The Meaning of Death,* including a chapter by Carl Jung on "The Soul and Death." Jung wrote, "We are never more convinced of this 'running down' than when a human life comes to an end before our eyes, and the question of the meaning and worth of life never becomes more urgent or more agonising than when we see the final breath leave a body which a moment before was living." He also said, "It would seem to be more in accord with the collective psyche of humanity to regard death as the fulfilment of life's meaning and its goal in its truest sense, instead of a mere meaningless cessation."[6]

In the same year, Renee Fox published *Experiment Perilous*, a description of a ward where the first research and treatment of some previously incurable and life threatening illnesses with steroids was carried out by a group of young doctors. The stresses and strains on both patients and doctors and their interaction, including the importance of humour, were observed over several months in a fascinating study of the sociology of medicine and science.[7] That same year Cruse, a foundation caring for the bereaved, began work in London and I published a series of six articles on the "Care of the Dying" at the request of the editor of the *Nursing Times*, London. Published the following year as a booklet, it sold many thousand copies.[8]

As Professor Patrick Wall wrote in an editorial in the journal *Pain* as it celebrated its first twenty-five volumes:

"Up to the 19th century, most medical care related to the amelioration of symptoms while the natural history of the disease took its course toward recovery or death. By 1900, doctors and patients alike had turned to a search for root cause and ultimate cure. In the course of this new direction, symptoms were placed on one side as signposts along a highway which was being driven toward the intended destination. Therapy directed at the signposts was denigrated and dismissed as merely symptomatic. By the second half of this century, a reaction set in as seen by such remarkable developments as the hospice movement. The immediate origins of misery and suffering need immediate attention while the long-term search for basic cure proceeds. The old methods of care and caring had to be rediscovered and the best of modern medicine had to be turned to the task of new study and therapy specifically directed at pain."[9]

But above all, those nineteen years were spent in listening to patients. So, also, in the years since St Christopher's opened in 1967 – though now I listen to staff and mainly meet patients at second hand – I continue to learn and, perhaps especially, observe the families as they face loss and share when appropriate. Above all, the lesson is, listen!

Science and evaluation has progressed alongside these many meetings. The psychiatrist Dr Colin Murray Parkes began his detailed study of the memories of the carers of dying patients in our locality as we opened and as our patients began to enter his cohort of more than 270 carers. He found much unrelieved pain, whether the patient died in a hospital or at home. As our patients came into the study he was able to show that people with serious pain problems were referred from the start to the hospice and were largely relieved.[10]

Robert Twycross compared morphine and diamorphine (heroin) in a double blind crossover study in St Christopher's in the 1970s and found no clinically observable difference between the two drugs. He also reported the absence of tolerance and drug dependence.[11] Clinical and evaluative studies have continued, always balanced with the development of patient care. As Francis Peabody wrote, "The treatment of a disease may be entirely impersonal; the care of a patient must be completely personal."[12]

So back to patients. Some accepting, many questioning. The total pain observed at St Joseph's Hospice in the 1960s, with its physical, psychological, social and spiritual components, has met the whole experience suffered by countless people and their families. The concept of "total pain" developed during my early years at St Joseph's Hospice was spelled out in an answer given to me by a Mrs Hinson in 1963 when I asked her to tell me about her pain. She said, without further prompting, "Well doctor, it began in my back but now it seems that all of me is wrong." She spoke of several other symptoms and went on, "I could have cried for the pills and the injections but I knew that I mustn't. Nobody seemed to understand how I felt and it was if the world was against me. My husband and son were marvelous, but they were having to stay off work and lose their money. But it's wonderful to begin to feel safe again." Physical, emotional, and family pain and the spiritual need for security and self-worth, all in one answer. That sometimes elusive search for meaning by people of many faiths, and none was as strongly expressed as by a dying primary school head teacher, Brenda Dawson:

"God, you need to ask my forgiveness.
Your world is full of mistakes.
Some cells, like weeds in the garden,
Are growing in the wrong place.
And we your children
Have polluted our environment.
Why did you let it happen God,
We prayed with faith, hope, love,
We perceived no change in our bodies or environment,
We are made sick by your world.
God you need to ask my forgiveness.
Was this why you sent your Son?"

There is a place and function for protest for our patients and their families. Lives can be desperately unfair as health fades, relationships sour and are broken, and parting becomes inevitable. Yet there can be a way through and if there is honesty about these negative feelings even they can have a positive outcome. For those who are involved as professional carers the anger that is part of compassion can be a force for change. The movement for hospice and palliative care has arisen around the world as a protest against the pain, isolation, and neglect suffered by dying people. The World Health Organization Centre for Cancer and Palliative Care has estimated that at a conservative estimate, their number on any one day has to be counted in several millions. There are other painful diseases, poverty, and starvation that afflict countless millions more. What is relevant in the gutters of Calcutta is totally inappropriate in Canada or the United Kingdom, but there is a common theme: human dignity should be recognized and enhanced by the assurance of worth. The hospice philosophy is summed up in the words, "You matter because you are you, and you matter to the last moment of your life, and we will do all we can not only to help you die peacefully but to live until you die." The message of Mother Theresa and the best resourced palliative care units are one and the same. Professors Ronald Melzack and Balfour Mount, with all their initiatives in better patient care, have illustrated this in Montreal.

As well as research, another difference is found in our concern with the families and friends of our patients, for most of Mother Theresa's are destitute and alone. In our home care patients and in both the day centre and inpatient group all workers in this field find themselves alongside many opportunities for reconciliations and forgiveness. At times it seems to be somewhat paradoxical. I recall one outstanding example from my husband's last stay in St Christopher's. We had been very aware of a small boy on his tricycle riding up and down the corridor of our ward of single rooms and came to know something of his grandfather, our patient. A thoroughly unpleasant man, he had abused his children and lived an aggressive life in many ways. He was not an easy patient and did not mellow with illness.

However, during the few weeks he was in the hospice, his daughter came daily and supported by an experienced social worker, used the time to work through her feelings for her father, to forgive him and to lay down her memories of hurt and abandonment. Determined to do better herself, she calmed her father's tempers and entertained her little boy, and resolved to give him a very different life from her own.

Our patient died on Christmas Day, and afterwards the nurse in charge called in the son, who had until then refused to visit, to join his sister, a single parent. Not only that, she enabled the son, too, to make a gesture of forgiveness for his father and to carry out his last shave as his body was prepared. I do not think religious language was used during all this time but who can doubt that a spiritual battle had been fought and won. A year later the daughter brought her little boy to join in caroling around the wards on Christmas Eve. The social worker who told me the full story I shared, only as another family in a ward were having a tense Christmas Day, are keeping in touch in case her support is needed again, but so far all goes well. From her own Christian background, an experienced social worker has helped this daughter to mature impressively on her own terms and in her own way. Need I emphasize how much we have to learn from her?

The spiritual needs of the dying are not merely appropriate rituals of their religion (if practised or recalled) but far wider, as relevant to atheists as to believers. They are: to find a meaning in life, to search and question, to be listened to with respect, and answered with honesty even where the answer can only be, "I do not know." People, both patients and families and all of us, need to be accepted and to give as well as to receive love. We may only be silent companions but as we accompany their journeys, we see growth through loss even in despair and that the travelling continues towards hope.

Ever since my first days as a volunteer in St Luke's, throughout my seven years in St Joseph's and since 1967 at St Christopher's, I have witnessed the resilience of the human spirit, how so-called "ordinary people" overcome adversity and make it the very means of what can only be called victory and growth. There is no hierarchy among such achievements. Who is to say who has done best, the young woman who fills a day centre with a party feeling for weeks on end and never shows how much it costs her, or the old reprobate who manages to stop grumbling for his last ten days? There is endless respect and not a little humour (often rather black) to be found in this field.

Most of my personal work now is in seeing all of our over three hundred staff and many of our eight hundred volunteers for annual appraisals and I have no doubt that they too are developing their potential for growth and character through their individual contributions. Again, I step back from idealizing what is going on. To everyone who is embarking on projects of this nature I want to say, if you do not have problems you do not have a hospice, and I might add, a university or anything dynamic and creative.

Maybe I sound as if all dying people come through their journeys with open eyes, or that I believe people should be told both diagnosis and prognosis. Treatments presume informed consent and I have seen much greater openness develop during my years of practise. I believe sharing among families is calmer and more creative than deception and that although some may hide truth even from themselves most will ultimately find it releasing.

It is a risky business to destroy an entrenched denial and we often have to wait our time, or never attempt it. Truth lies in a relationship rather than in words. I remember a man who, after weeks of caring, suddenly asked me bluntly, "Am I dying?"

I found I could only say, "Yes," without any softening words.

"Was it hard for you to tell me that?" he said.

"Well, yes, it was," I replied.

"Thank you," he said, "it is hard to be told but it is hard to tell too. Thank you."

It should be hard; we must care what we do with our words for they can hurt or heal, and open or close exchange and development. We should care what people do with what we give them; whether the moment or the manner was right. That man, the same speaker as the one with whom I began this lecture, who said, "I do not want to die," and finally, "I only want what is right," came close to me in a journey we shared during the next three weeks. He taught me much of what I know of what it feels like to be so ill, to be parting, of finding in losing. Such teaching is a gift to be used as we come alongside any kind of loss. Much has been built into palliative care, and not into palliative care only, but also into ordinary living and learning.

The review of my chapter in the first edition of the *Oxford Textbook of Medicine* referred to "the characteristic mixture of tough clinical science and compassion."[13] "Feelings are facts in this House," said one of the nuns at St Joseph's. We need both the facts of feelings and the facts of science if we are to learn and go on learning how to practise medicine in its widest sense. We need evidence-based medicine as much here as in the intensive care unit and any other ward in a hospital. We need it too in the home, where our patients spend most if not all of their time. Evaluative studies began as we opened; as I have already said, we have continued them. One comparative study between hospice and hospital matched patients has been carried out three times during our thirty years at St Christopher's and reveals that while pain control in hospitals in the vicinity of St Christopher's has improved greatly, family anxiety and the impersonality and urgency of a busy general ward are not so well addressed.[14]

In 1966, I was invited for a visiting lectureship by the graduate school of Nursing at Yale University and took part in a seminar with Dr Colin Murray Parkes and Dr Elisabeth Kübler-Ross and others. Colin, Elisabeth, and I had supper together one evening and he made a very interesting remark to us, pointing out that we were working in different time scales. At that time Elisabeth was carrying out her series of one-off interviews in teaching behind a one-way screen, I was working with patients at St Joseph's in days or weeks, and Colin was interviewing a series of widows from one to two years after their bereavement. We were all seeing acceptance and growth but responses to different time pressures led to different speeds of resolution. The husband of a very close friend of mine died of a dissecting aortic aneurysm just as she was returning home after the initial admission. On her return, she was left for half an hour alone with his body in the intensive care unit. That pause, enabling her to begin to absorb the enormity of her loss, did not soften an anguished journey of grief but she remains grateful to the nurse who made those moments of farewell possible.

Sudden death gives no time for important communications. Cancer usually gives us time to say, "I'm sorry, thank you, and goodbye." Seale, in his paper "Heroic Death," summarizes accounts provided in a survey of 250 individuals who had died of this and other diseases in the United Kingdom. His abstract reports on the interviews with their carers:

> "The analysis counters the view that the denial of death is widespread in conditions where religion no longer offers individuals a meaningful narrative for the dying self. Scripts for proclaiming heroic self-identity in the face of death are promoted by cultural experts and appropriated by many lay individuals. This

involves a struggle against external and internal enemies to gain knowledge, the opportunity to demonstrate courage and a beatific state of emotional accompaniment in which 'carers' and dying people participate. Unlike more traditional forms of heroism, this script deviates from celebrating solely masculine qualities and includes a female heroics of care, concern and emotional expression."

A quote from the paper states that, "I feel he had a lovely death, very peaceful. I'll never forget how he seemed to accept everything."[15]

The regional survey in the United Kingdom from which this paper comes is a unique study of many facets of the last year of life of 3,696 people. Among the reports from this work, one paper is concerned with the patients' view on euthanasia. Their carers were asked, "Looking back now and taking the deceased's illness into account do you think she or he died at the best time – or would it have been better if she or he had died earlier? What about the deceased? Did she or he ever say they wanted to die sooner? And (if yes) did she or he ever say they wanted euthanasia?" Twenty-eight per cent of the respondents, with a bias towards the younger carers, and 24 per cent of the deceased expressed the view that earlier death would be, or would have been preferable. However only 3.6 per cent were said to have asked for euthanasia at some point during their last year.[16] This figure is very unlike those quoted in national opinion polls where figures of 70 to 80 per cent are given; they illustrate what people who are facing the end of life are actually saying from the memories of their carers.

It is interesting that the House of Lords of England Select Committee on Medical Ethics, the New York Task Force on this subject, and [the Canadian] special Senate Committee on Euthanasia and Assisted Suicide all recommended the spread of palliative care rather than any change in the law. Interestingly too, it was a visit to the Netherlands after a year of taking evidence that finally propelled the decision by the very prestigious team of their Lordships. Kathleen Foley of Memorial Sloan-Kettering Cancer Centre, New York recently published an important article, "Competent Care for the Dying instead of Physician Assisted Suicide" in *The New England Journal of Medicine* discussing the Supreme Court's decision in this area. She summed it up to me last month, saying, "They said there was no constitutional right to assisted suicide, rather a right to the refusal of intrusive treatment and a right to palliative care."[17]

My husband, a professor of art, at age ninety-three and at the end of a ten-year battle with several life threatening illnesses, summed up his life thus: "I am completely happy, I have done what I had to do in my life and now I am ready to die." He became somewhat impatient but said firmly, "God will know what to do with me." Three days before he died he completed a delicate line drawing of one of his nurses. Three hours before he died the son of another patient came into his room to shake him by the hand and to thank him for the inspiration of his pictures all around the hospice. So many people I have known have reached a reconciliation or received important thanks which they would have missed had they been able to choose an earlier death, perhaps in distress or bitterness. The last word on this subject comes best from an elderly lady who wrote to the London *Times* some years back: "Human nature being what it is, euthanasia would not be voluntary for long." Many vulnerable people would so easily be undermined and the line between voluntary and involuntary euthanasia is, I believe, impossible to draw.

But to end with a hospice story which one of our patients told a local journalist last month:

"I found out I had cancer of the bones in 1988. The doctors told me if I responded to treatment I would be cured, but if I didn't, then my chances of survival would be fifty-fifty. They gave me radiotherapy, chemotherapy, and other medication in tablet form. I also had to have a blood transfusion together with the chemo. The treatments had a great effect on me and I felt much better. Eventually, though, they had given me as much radiotherapy and chemo as they could; any more would have just made me sicker than the cancer did. It was in 1994 that the doctors recommended St Christopher's Hospice. They said that it was a place that specialized in pain and symptom control. At first I was looked after by their home care team of nurses, doctor and chaplain, but then I had a bad patch and became an inpatient for seven weeks and three days. On the days that I wasn't feeling too bad, they would take me down to different classes. The very first day, I made a pot out of clay. My hands ached a little bit but the second time I tried it I liked it — and I've been doing it from that day to this. My hands are much stronger now. Not only do the things I make give me something to look back on and give me a thrill, but they also show that I haven't given up on life. It takes courage when you are ill not to give up, and I haven't. I have continued to do things even if it's just making animals out of clay. I have achieved something new. I have given lots of pots to my friends. The classes also give me a chance to be useful to others and to encourage people. The cancer is stable at the moment. After my bad patch in 1994, when I also had a heart attack, no one thought I would be here today. But now I'm being looked after at home again. I am still here, still not giving up."

Those I have met have shown me that they were not merely dying from a terminal illness, they were living with a life-threatening illness. They show us all there is no end to challenge and discovery in life, and I, like my husband, and some of those I have quoted, would add, and death itself is a gateway to a new way of being.

NOTES

1. Dr Alfred Worcester (1855–1951) was an American physician known as a pioneer of surgery, nursing education, geriatrics, and palliative care.
2. Dr Herman Feifel (1915–2003) was an American psychologist considered the founding figure of modern death psychology.
3. Clive Seale (born 1955) is a British sociologist who studies the prevalence of euthanasia and assisted suicide in the United Kingdom and the role of religion in end-of-life decision making.
4. Alfred Worcester, *The Care of the Aged, the Dying and the Dead* (Illinois: CC Thomas Springfield, 1935).
5. Francis W. Peabody, "The Care of the Patient," *Journal of the American Medical Association* 88, (1927):877–82.
6. Herman Feifel, ed., *The Meaning of Death* (New York: Blakiston Division, McGraw Hill, 1959), 3,9.
7. Renee Fox, *Experiment Perilous: Physicians and Patients Facing the Unknown* (Glencoe: The Free Press, 1959).
8. Cicely Saunders, *The Care of the Dying* (London: Macmillan, 1960).
9. Patrick Wall, "Editorial: "25 Volumes of Pain," *Pain* 25, (1986):1–4.
10. C. Murray Parkes, "Home or Hospital? Terminal Care as Seen by Surviving Spouses," *Journal of the Royal College of General Practitioners* 28 (1978): 29–30.
11. Robert Twycross, "Clinical Experience with Diamorphine in Advanced Malignant Disease," *International Journal of Clinical Pharmacology* 93 (1974): 184–98.
12. Peabody, "The Care of the Patient," *Journal of the American Medical Association* 88, (1927): 877–82.
13. Tessa Richards, "Buying British; an Oxford Initiative," *British Medical Journal* 286, (1983):1029.
14. Clive F. Seale and Moira Kelly, "A Comparison of Hospice and Hospital Care for People who Die, Views of the Surviving Spouse," *Palliative Medicine*, no.1 (1997): 93–100.
15. Clive F. Seale, "Heroic Death," *Sociology* 29 (1995): 597–613.
16. Clive F. Seale, and J. Addington-Hall, "Euthanasia: Why People Want to Die Earlier," *Social Science and Medicine* 39, no. 5 (1994): 647–54.
17. Kathleen Foley, "Competent Care for the Dying Instead of Physician Assisted Suicide," *New England Journal of Medicine* 336 (1997): 54–7.

Michael Ignatieff. *Used with permission of Michael Ignatieff, Creative Commons License* CC BY-ND 2.0.

12

Canada in the World: The Challenges Ahead
6 October 2005

Michael Ignatieff

INTRODUCTION

When Michael Ignatieff came to McGill to give the Beatty Lecture, his academic curriculum vitae included faculty positions at King's College Cambridge and the John F. Kennedy School at Harvard. He was already well-known as a public intellectual, author of an acclaimed biography of the British philosopher Isaiah Berlin, and for his support of the United States liberation of Iraq in 2003. In 2004, in his book *The Lesser Evil: Political Ethics in an Age of Terror* he had grappled with the use of violence by liberal democracies, arguing for a middle ground between pure civil libertarianism and cynical pragmatism.

Finding a careful balance between contending principles or ideas has been a hallmark of Michael Ignatieff's work, just as it was for Isaiah Berlin. In his Beatty Lecture, Ignatieff addressed Canada's role in the world in terms of balances: between support for the British Empire and building up Canada as its own country; then between supporting the United States during the Cold War and finding a distinct Canadian voice in international affairs; and in 2005, finding a balance between a multicultural Canada and a multilateral world, and reconciling past wrongs against First Nations people, Chinese, Jewish, Ukrainian, and Black immigrants with a future role for Canada promoting peace and reconciliation in countries riven by conflict abroad.

Re-reading this Beatty Lecture now, fifteen years after it was given and as an American who studies US-Canadian relations, I was struck by the insights Ignatieff offered on striking a careful balance in Canada's relationship with the United States. "Our relationship with the Americans works so long as we do not behave like free riders," he notes. "[W]e learned that the price of disagreeing with the Americans was not as high as we thought," he added. The latter in my opinion is true, but the price of disagreement may be higher when assessed over time.

"Getting them to listen means reminding them that it doesn't pay to take Canada for granted" may sound like fighting words, but if Ignatieff underestimated the full cost of disagreement with the United States in this Beatty Lecture, he overestimated the cost of taking Canada for granted. It could be argued that Canada's persistent underinvestment in its military, diplomatic corps, and international development assistance and past policy disagreements mean that Canada is not so much taken for granted by the United States, but forgotten as it is presumed in Washington that Canada cannot, or will not, contribute.

With this cautionary assessment of Canada-US relations in mind, one closing line in Ignatieff's lecture haunts me: "Maintaining a coherent national voice abroad is hard if we are divided at home […] we've got to get our story straight because our place in the world is shifting as we speak." After a period of four years of political polarization in the United States, Michael Ignatieff speaks to this moment in American history, too.

*

Christopher Sands is director of the Canada Institute at the Woodrow Wilson International Center for Scholars and an adjunct professor of Canadian Studies at Johns Hopkins University's Paul H. Nitze School of Advanced International Studies.

LECTURE

The following is the full Beatty Lecture delivered on 6 October 2005.

It is an honour to be asked to give this lecture. I was at the Steven Leacock lunch yesterday, and it said something wonderful about your community. Thanks to Leacock, humour is one of the traditions that ties the McGill community together. I have to warn you, however, that you are about to enter a humour-free zone. This is going to be an earnest and relentless lecture, just the kind my Scottish Presbyterian forebears used to like.

My subject is "Canada in the World: The Challenges Ahead." We are in a struggle to reinvent our country, to maintain our unity at home, and project our influence abroad. I am a historian by training and my instinct in the face of the dramas that we face as a country is to step back and think for a moment about our history. Before we can reinvent ourselves tomorrow, we need to understand how this country was made. One of my themes is the way in which the national identity and the nation-building of Canada was structured by forces outside us, chiefly by the forces and ideologies of empire.

I can detect three stages in this story. First, from Confederation until 1945, Canadian identity was essentially shaped by Imperial Britain. Then, during the period of the Cold War, our national identity was defined chiefly by our relations with Imperial America. And now in the present, when that imperial order may be passing, a multilateral order has failed to take its place. Part of our difficulty of defining our own place in the world has to do with the fact that while that old Cold War order has died, a new one has not taken shape. We are lost, but so is everybody else.

I have most to say about the present, but I am going to take you through some more remote parts of our story because I think we need to reckon with the nation-building of our past. So I am going to go back to Confederation. I am going to go back to John A. Macdonald and the National Policy. Macdonald famously said that he was born a British subject, and a British subject he would die. For Macdonald, Canada's role abroad and identity at home were both defined by its partnership in the most powerful force of globalization of its time, the British Empire.

Macdonald's masterstroke of nation-building, the Canadian Pacific Railway, was also an empire-building project designed to link Britain to its possessions in India and Australia. The railway would draw to Canada's shores the excess population of Britain, and Canada would be peopled by Anglo-Saxon stock. Canada's place in the world would be as the communications highway of Empire, its granary, and in time of war, its armory. Macdonald's vision of Canada tied us together from ocean to ocean. It settled the Prairies and it guaranteed our survival, and next to the United States our survival was by no means assured in the generation after Confederation.

But the nation-building project that Macdonald inspired left scars that have endured to this day. The West for example, was settled as a colony, its lands and resources administered by the Department of Interior in Ottawa. The freight rates that Western farmers paid were set in boardrooms here in this city. So, Western alienation is not a new phenomenon over the last twenty, thirty years, it goes back there from the beginning. It is a consequence of the failure to allow full self-government on the Prairies for the first fifty years after Confederation.

As a vision of Canada which saw it as a white Anglo-Saxon bastion of Empire, it had no place for the Métis, no place for the Aboriginal peoples of our country. The Macdonald who built the railway was also the prime minister who executed Louis Riel, and French Canada never forgave him.

The imperial image of Canada had no place for the French reality. It was in the West, with the execution of Riel, followed by legislation in Manitoba, Saskatchewan, and Alberta limiting the right to public education in French, that Quebecers' disillusionment with the Canadian federation began. That is also why the expression "the national dream," so often used by Pierre Berton, rings false for many Quebecers.

For the Aboriginal peoples of the plains, the national dream meant the cession of land through treaty, the reserves, a school system designed to turn them into Canadians. Residential schools inflicted scars that should teach us all that you cannot build a nation by forced assimilation. Residential schools did not just harm those who attended, it harmed us all. It was a nation-building project that did harm to our nation.

The third group of people, the fifteen thousand Chinese labourers who hacked their way through the Rockies, laid the steel that tied us together. If you were one of them, you expected that your country would show you a little gratitude and instead you were barred from citizenship and Chinese immigration was limited by poll tax.

These three exclusions, of First Nation's peoples, the Métis and the Chinese were mandated by imperial ideologies that restricted citizenship to those of British and white stock and defined national unity in terms of ethnic majority and dominance.

Ladies and gentlemen, these were bad ideas, and they did us harm, and truth requires us to acknowledge the harm they did to us all.

Now, none of these bad ideas was original to Canada. South of the border, anti-Chinese sentiment was, if anything, worse, and south of the border railway agents and the US cavalry waged a war of extermination against Aboriginal peoples. The idea that the nation must be under a dominant ethnic majority was a common place of nation-building ideology everywhere, in Bismarck's Germany and France's Third Republic. But these ideas of nation-building exterior to us flowing through our best minds in the nineteenth century were the procrustean bed on which Canadian identity was forged.

It was Quebec that set Canada free. English Canada has always believed that Quebec constitutes the main obstacle to the national dream. But we must understand that today's Canada owes a great deal to French Canadians' rejection of the imperial idea of Canada. The great Wilfred Laurier was the first Canadian prime minister who understood that the imperial connection might hold meaning for English Canada, but it profoundly alienated Quebec. It was during the conscription crisis of 1917 that the hour of truth sounded for the imperial ideology. An English Canada that found its patriotic raison d'être in the expression "For King and Country" was astonished to see Quebecers question why they should die in the trenches at the Battle of the Somme. Quebec nationalists like Henri Bourassa who opposed conscription forced the whole country to confront the fact that the imperial and English definition of Canada had no place for the reality of Quebec. It is ironic but true that Quebec nationalists were the ones who helped us to understand that Canada could not survive as a colony. To survive, it had to become an independent state.

It is Quebec that made Canadians understand that we could not survive as a colony and would have to become a nation. We need to remember how long that took. It was not until the Westminster Statute of 1931 that Canada acquired for the first time the right to have a foreign policy of its own. Even in 1939 when my uncle and my father went off to war, Britain declared war believing that its dominions would automatically follow suit. English Canada was still in the grip of an imperial conception of our identity, but Prime Minister Mackenzie King insisted that the

Canadian parliament decide the matter for us. Our entry into World War II was a crucial moment in our emancipation.

Our real emancipation as a nation began with Vimy in 1917, but was consecrated in the blood and struggle of World War II. When we honour our veterans in November, we should remember them as nation-builders because our nation was built in wartime sacrifice. We won our independence in the world through the sacrifice at Vimy, at Monte Cassino where my uncle fought, the Normandy beaches, and the liberation of Holland. The bravery and hard work of women at home in munition factories helped them and their children understand ourselves as a sovereign people. At war's end, we could demand a prominent place in the creation of the UN and NATO because we had paid for it in the coinage of power and sacrifice.

We had created the sinews of that independent national power in an Army, a Navy and an Air Force and to this day unpopular as it may be to say so, military capability remains the sine qua non of international independence and influence. World War II was also a nation-building experience in another and also darker sense of the word. We interned Ukrainians and other nationals from the belligerent powers in World War I, and in World War II we made the mistake a second time when we deported thousands of Japanese to the interior of British Columbia.

Canada again was not alone in being swept by these exclusionist ideologies. We were not alone in interning enemy aliens, but let us remember that Canada interned the Japanese before the Americans did. When the Americans justified their exclusion of the Japanese, they cited Canadian action as a justifying precedent. It is not a happy story. I love my country, but we owe it a duty of truth. The internment of the Japanese and of the Ukrainians in World War I, which prime minister Paul Martin just apologized for two weeks ago, shows that when we build a nation upon exclusion, we lay a heavy charge on the generations that come after us.

Let me now turn to the second phase, the phase that begins with the Cold War, nation-building in Canada between 1945 and 1989. The British Empire was gone. Canada was an independent state, but now our economic and political destiny was linked to the new empire to the south. American global leadership gave Canada its place in the Cold War world. The purpose of our foreign policy was to help America build a new multilateral order. It stood on three pillars: military deterrence of the Soviets and the Chinese, a defensive alliance of liberal democracies, and a rule-based international order structured around the United Nations.

When the United States provided clear leadership, Canada knew its way in the world. We were present at the creation of the UN and NATO, we fought with the Americans in Korea, we invented peacekeeping and downsized armed forces to fit that mission. In the Cold War, Canada also found a way to assert its independence. We recognized Cuba, and the Americans did not like it. We recognized China, they liked it even less. We disagreed about Vietnam, they liked it the least of all. And we learned that the price of disagreeing with the Americans was not as high as we thought.

Our problem is not that we cannot muster the courage to disagree. Our problem is to get them to listen when we do. Getting them to listen means reminding them that it does not pay to take Canada for granted. They need our oil, they need our electricity, they need our water, and they need our safe borders. The quid pro quo from our point of view is they ought to play by the rules. Lumber and beef are not side issues to Canadians, and the failure to solve these problems makes us think, "Can these folks be trusted?" Straight talking on these issues is crucial to any relation with the Americans. But we also need to convey the message that Canada is also willing to pay its way.

Our relationship with the Americans works so long as we do not behave like free riders. If we shoulder our proper share of the defense of North America, if we defend our sovereignty, we can agree to disagree. We can agree to disagree on issues like ballistic missile defense. But if we fail to do our fair share but reserve the right to give them little lectures from time to time, we will be dismissed as boy scouts. I have nothing against the scouts, but we live in a world of adults and in such a world, strength comes from capability, not from sermons.

In a world where the key public policy issue for every nation on Earth is, "What do we do about the Americans?" anti-Americanism is the form of patriotism that this country can least afford. We have an inferiority complex about the Americans that we have turned weirdly into a superiority complex, and my view is that an inferiority complex and a superiority complex are lousy ways to relate to the Americans. We need to build an identity beyond complexes, an identity secure not in some invidious or envious comparison to the Americans, but in a very centred sense that we are different. We have always been different. We always will be. We need to remember that if the twentieth century belonged to the United States, and it definitely did, there is no guarantee that the twenty-first century belongs to the United States. Proving your patriotism by being anti-American is going to look pretty parochial in a world where global dominance is shifting eastward to China and India.

Now, while we were learning to live beside the most powerful nation in the world, we were also undergoing the most revolutionary transformation in what it means to be a Canadian.

There are three distinct aspects to the story of what happened to our country beginning in the 1960s. The first was the decision to open our doors to multicultural immigration. The second was to do justice to Aboriginal claims. And the third, *evidemment*, was the Quiet Revolution in Quebec. These stories belong together, although we disaggregate them and tell them separately, but we need to bring them together because they change the master narrative of our country's history. The 1960s marked the moment when Canada backed into changing the way we were building the nation. All three transformations have profoundly enriched and deepened our sense of ourselves as a people. We went from the suppression of difference to the recognition of difference, from majority rule to minority rights, from exclusion to inclusion and we are profoundly better as a result of these tumultuous experiences. The story begins with a transformation of our immigration policy. My dad arrived on the Montreal docks as a teenager in 1928 with nothing and ended up as an ambassador of his country. I feel intense, if borrowed pride, about that story, but it is a Canadian story. There must be hundreds of people in this room who could tell a similar story about their own families.

But we need to remember the darker aspects of our relation to immigration. In the 1930s, we had actually turned away desperate Jewish refugees seeking a port in the storm of fascism. After the war, it was only after the war, only in the 1940s and 1950s that we began to become a place of refuge for the displaced and disinherited. We need to confront the fact that it was only after seventy-five years of building a white-only Canada, that we decided to build a rainbow Canada. Chinese, Japanese, East Asian and Aboriginal Canadians did not secure the right to vote in British Columbia until 1949.

This is the Canadian story we need to remember. In the late 1950s and 1960s, the barriers against Asian, East Asian, and Black immigration began to come down and we quietly dismantled a centuries-old assumption that Canada could only hold together if the common stock of the people was Anglo-Saxon and French. We embarked on a radical new vision of the nation based not on common origins, but on common citizenship. This revolution has had the biggest impact on our relation to the world.

Immigration collapsed the Canadian illusion that we were a safe haven from the troubles of a tormented world far away. The refugees from that world began showing up on our doorstep. Immigration also transformed the issues that mattered to Canadian foreign policy. Between 1867 and 1967, the core issue in Canadian foreign policy was European security. Not anymore. Now, the stability of Haiti, the future of Somalia, peace in Sri Lanka, the capacity of Nigeria to hold together as a state, and the fate of the Palestinians have all become issues which engage millions of Canadians because these places and their conflicts are our citizens' second homes.

The arrival of a multicultural Canada also coincided with the Aboriginal revival and the insistence that the Aboriginal presence be honoured as central to our identity as a people. We went from nation-building as forced assimilation, to nation-building as inclusion and we are still in the middle of this process. Difficulties remain, as anybody who lives in Davis Inlet or Attawapiskat will tell you. But there are also amazing achievements to celebrate: more Aboriginal peoples in positions of Canadian leadership, more in higher education, more land and territory restored to Aboriginal self-government.

Most important for our identity has been breaking the silence about the histories of exclusion on which our nation was built. What we did at home was profoundly influenced by what was happening abroad. The Aboriginal revival in Canada was part of a global Aboriginal revival as you can tell the minute you set foot in New Zealand, Australia, or Bolivia. In the same way, the multicultural revolution in Toronto, Montreal, and Vancouver was mirrored in London, Paris, Hamburg, Boston, and New York.

These two revolutions, the multicultural and the Aboriginal, coincided with the third and, for Canada, the most transformative of all, the Quiet Revolution in Quebec. The Quiet Revolution was a challenge to the English narrative of nation-building. English Canadians discovered that our national dream was not theirs and that our history was not theirs. Quebecers had bitter and very real memories of exclusion. Instead of thinking of Quebec nationalism as a threat, English Canadians need to understand how profoundly positive the Quebec challenge to Canada proved to be. It was Quebecers who took the lead in the reinvention of our country in the 1960s.

The entrenchment of bilingualism and equal language rights, the Charter, new social programs like Medicare and the Canada Pension Plan, anchors of common citizenship that all Canadians think of as their birthright were essentially invented by the brilliant Quebec generation that went to Ottawa in the 1960s. The generation that went to Quebec City instead contributed important things to the evolution of the Canadian model of government. We forget the key icons of nationalist achievement in Quebec, like taking hydro into public ownership, were profoundly in the Canadian grain. What René Lévesque did with hydroelectricity, Adam Beck had done in Ontario with hydroelectricty two generations before. This understanding of the functions and role of government is very distinctive to the political traditions of our country. Quebec nationalists were more deeply Canadian in their progressive vision of government than they ever wanted to admit.

The challenges Quebec faces as a society remain essentially the same as those confronting the rest of Canada. How to sustain the fiscal basis of the social programs that make us distinctive, how to invest in people, how to keep an economy inventive, productive, job-creating when we have commitments to social protection, how to manage the arrival of a multicultural society, and how to respond justly to the Aboriginal challenge. We talk as if our policy agendas were completely different. They are the same, and we are wasting time with division when we need to get our problems sorted out together.

The multicultural reality of Montreal has exposed the reactionary and outdated side of a nationalist discourse based on the fiction that the Quebec nation is composed of a pure laine and vieille souche monolith. The discovery that the Quebec nation does not include the whole population of Quebec explains, I believe, the defeat of the separatist project in the referendum. As Governor General Adrienne

Clarkson has said, "It was the arrival of a multicultural Canada that sounded the death knell of the two solitudes."

Instead of two solitudes, English and French Canadians have had to create a new identity corresponding to the reality we see in the streets of Toronto and Montreal. On both sides, people in Quebec and Canada are seeking a civic idea of Canada, based on a common attachment to the values of tolerance and respect. The central question for Canada and for Quebec is the same: what is the citizenship contract, the common values that connect Canadians of different origins to a common project? Individual rights are no longer enough. By liberating the citizen, we may impoverish the community. Our political challenge is to lead a dialogue on citizenship and on practical ways to guarantee equality and respect while avoiding the tyranny of the majority.

Canadians are struggling to adapt to a citizenship where majorities prevail, but they cannot dictate policy because all communities are equal. All are at the table, but they are no longer sharing the same myths and the same origins. This is the challenge we face now, to maintain democratic civility, plus the capacity to make some choices together when we no longer share the same myths of origin. We have had a revolution of inclusion all right, and now that everybody wants to be included the question is, how do we keep this show on the road? How do we hold ourselves together?

We talk obsessively about the national question, the linguistic question, the French-English question, alienation in the West, but the sleeping giant that is coming at us is social inequality. It is the class issue and when race and class combine, we do not have multicultural communities anymore, we just have ghettos. We have ghettos of race and religion, reinforced by the exclusions of class, and we betray the promise of Canadian life when we do. We have managed inclusion through rights, but the charter of rights and freedoms is not enough.

And we have got a bigger problem than social inequality. We do not agree now on the political rules of the game. The constitutional rules of the game are up for grabs. At Meech Lake and at Charlottetown, political elites sought to entrench new rules based on the recognition of Quebec as a distinct society. The rights of Aboriginal self-government and the rights of all provinces to constitutional vetoes. Canadians looked at those packages, both of them, and balked at the price. We know we need new rules, and we cannot seem to agree on what they are but at least we know one thing, we do not want another Meech Lake Accord and we do not want another Charlottetown Accord. We do not want to roll those dice again.

So while the stalemate continues, the strains on our federation grow. Beneath the current talk about fiscal imbalances, is a questioning of a logic of equalization between regions and provinces. We are questioning whether Canada is a community of fate, in which we share our wealth and work together to protect each other against misfortune. That is the big issue here looming just beneath all this back-and-forth about fiscal imbalance.

Now, how long we can manage the politics of inclusion without new constitutional rules is anybody's guess. We are a country that is testing to the limits the capacity to survive by agreeing to disagree. A few simple rules would help I think, until we can muster the political will as a community to do something better. Levels of government in Canada should begin to get it into their heads – and the feds need to learn this – that all levels of government in this country are equal. Equality means they should stay out of each other's jurisdictions. National unity, in my view, is not a synonym for asserting federal power. This country is too complex and it is too diverse to be run from Ottawa, Toronto, Montreal, or anywhere else for that matter. Canadians want strong provincial, municipal, and Aboriginal governments that represent their interest, but clear majorities also want to live in one country, not in ten balkanized principalities.

We are a country, not ten rival feudalities. To avoid balkanization, we need a federalism based on respect and recognition. Respect for the jurisdictions of others, and recognition that not all provinces are the same, but respect is a two-way street.

Quebec cannot demand that the federal government respect the jurisdiction of the Quebec government if at the same time its ministers insist that Quebec lead its own international policy. Quebec can always promote its interests in the economic sphere, but it is the Canadian federal government, with the support of other levels of government, that must speak for Canada.

Quebec admits, as one of its ministers says, that we should speak with a united voice, but it contests the idea that it should be a single voice. Nations that cannot speak with one voice, cannot protect their interests. And nations that cannot project their basic unity abroad and export their quarrels into every foreign jurisdiction and every foreign meeting end up being a laughingstock, and we have got to stop that. So, we need to have a conversation. Compromise is possible but let us be clear, foreign affairs is a clear federal jurisdiction.

Maintaining a coherent national voice abroad is hard if we are divided at home – and our difficulty is here, we have got to get our story straight because our place in the world is shifting as we speak. The Cold War ended with a victory for American policies of containment but once victory had been achieved, American leadership was lost and with it was lost the guiding star of Canadian foreign policy. America has been drifting, and we have been drifting ever since. Middle powers like Canada leverage influence by securing power within multilateral institutions. Canadian influence since the end of the Cold War has waned because the institutions on which our influence depends, the UN and NATO, have languished for lack of leadership by the US.

If we feel rudderless in our foreign policy and our projection of power and influence abroad, it is because we have always found our way in the world by exploiting our imperial dependencies to our own advantage. We did this with the British, we did it with the Americans, now the Americans do not know where they are going and we do not know either. This fact helps to explain the essential deep disarray at the core of our foreign policy. Nothing in Canadian foreign policy seems absolutely essential or necessary. We do not have a system of triage. We do not have a way to distinguish the vital from the merely important, or the fashionable. We do a little development, but not enough. We do a little governance promotion, but not enough. We promote UN reform but half-heartedly, knowing that we cannot hope for very much since we are not on the Security Council and the Americans do not care for a reform in any form.

So, what is the way forward? We need to decide, and this is a tough choice for us, that if the Americans will not lead, we will have to create alliances with the countries that will lead. The crucial fact is that the price of saying no to the Americans is actually going down, not up, and this gives us a historic opportunity. This is not an invitation to provoke them, to ignore them, or to defy them. It is an invitation for us to decide that we will not wait for them to lead. We must take advantage of this fact to build in concert with others, a rule bound multilateral order that seeks to reduce the inequalities in the global system, inequalities that now threaten our very national security. The inequalities between people in zones of danger and zones of safety, between those who have enough to eat and those who do not, those who live in safety and those who live at peril of their lives.

We cannot live in a world this unequal, this divided, and we cannot keep it at a safe distance from ourselves. We cannot do all of this, we need to focus. And how do we do so? As I was writing this my Hungarian wife found a wonderful poem by one of the great Hungarian poets Attila József, which struck me immediately. One of his poems ends with these beautiful lines: "Creating order in our common matters, this is our task, and we know it will be hard."

In other words, we must cultivate our garden. This is not a recipe for quietism or for withdrawal, it means we have to set our house in order. It means that Canada matters to the world less for specific policies than for our example to the world. If every democracy in the world is wondering how to create a new contract that will turn ghettos into communities, to turn those who are excluded into full citizens, if that is the central political task of every liberal democracy of our age, then what matters most is that we do it right. This is what we have to show to the world.

We must survive. We are a blessed country. We are rich, we are prosperous, and we are free. If we cannot make this work, there is no country in the world that can, and no one will. So how do we do it? I really do not know all the answers. I have only really offered you one in the course of this talk. My belief is you cannot get a community of political equals, a community of inclusion unless you speak the truth at all times, no matter how painful and difficult. The foundation of political community is political truth. We have to tell the truth to each other. We must tell the truth about our past, including all these painful stories. We cannot communicate to our fellow citizens who have been the victims of these kinds of inclusion unless we take this reality inside ourselves and understand, this is us.

For an English Canadian like me, the principal duty of being a citizen today is a duty of truth — the truth of history, the truth of the Aboriginal reality, the truth of the Quebec reality. Recognition must start with truth. And putting in place new rules depends on building a shared truth. That is why I have placed such emphasis on the painful passages in our history.

We cannot mean anything to the world unless we stay united. National unity is the precondition for any influence we hope to have in the world. Our unity matters not just to us, but to the world. We need to show that a politics of inclusion is not a politics of chaos, that our respect for difference can go hand in hand with rules and boundaries for tolerance. We need to show that we can maintain national unity without caving into every regional interest, but rather creating and sustaining a vision that Canadians do want something more than living in regions. They want our country, and they deserve nothing less.

We need to remember finally, simple things, like why we need a country. Why in all this loose talk about a globalized borderless world, national identity matters so much. Because nations are what keep us free, that keep us safe, that give us purposes larger than ourselves. Individualism is not enough. The good life is not enough. We need the bigger frame, the larger meaning, the purpose that gives a sense to our lives. And the name of that purpose, the bigger frame, the larger meaning is Canada.

13

Building Social Business: The New Kind of Capitalism that Serves Humanity's Most Pressing Needs

1 October 2010

Muhammad Yunus

INTRODUCTION

It is with great pleasure and pride that I introduce Dr Muhammad Yunus' extraordinary 2010 Beatty Lecture, "Building Social Business." This lecture, a moving account of how one person can change the lives of millions, is a glimpse into the enormous impact Dr Yunus has had on the world. As the pioneer and earliest practitioner of microfinancing, he and his work with Grameen Bank were awarded the Nobel Peace Prize in 2006. But while Dr Yunus' enlightened economic leadership demonstrates truly trailblazing originality, it is his unshakeable conviction that any person can become an agent of change, regardless of economic or social status, gender, age, or circumstance, that ignites our imagination.

In 1974, Dr Yunus stepped out of the classroom and into his community, where he studied need on an individual human level. What he saw was not new: that poverty begets poverty, and lack of opportunity is too often mistaken for lack of ability. But by keeping an open mind, he reimagined a situation that seemed beyond hope. With just $27, Dr Yunus launched the concept of microcredit, cracking open the misconception that any person or situation is hopeless. He proved that when individuals become advocates of change in their own lives, they can contribute to their greater communities. And perhaps most importantly, he showed us that conventional thinking is one of the greatest obstacles we may face.

The idea of manifesting change from within has been one of the driving touchstones of my career. When I launched Lightspeed in 2005, I knew I wanted to create a cloud-based commerce platform that empowered small retail and restaurant businesses to write their own stories. I knew these businesses were the cornerstones of their communities, and that we all do better when our local merchants are thriving.

Muhammad Yunus. *Used with permission of Stephane Desjardins.*

But I never imagined the full impact of individual agency on social structure until I saw it in action, time and time again. When people are empowered to work, they join not only a cycle of economic success, but a cycle of contribution and social investment that shapes the world around them.

Today, as we attempt to navigate a global pandemic and its consequences, we see yet again that no person or business is an island. We are connected as global citizens, and the power to survive and thrive lies in our collective ability to support one another and prop each other up. We are not just consumers; we are stewards of our economy. We are not just entrepreneurs; we are guardians of our shared social responsibilities. Our businesses are vehicles for change in the face of mounting environmental, economic, and humanitarian challenges around the world.

In his lecture, which feels less like an academic treatise and more like a conversation with an inspiring friend, Dr Yunus reminds us that we each have more power and influence than we imagine. And while his groundbreaking body of work does and should inspire awe, his greatest gift to us is surprisingly small in scope. He shows us the power of thinking small: how just one person or business can make a difference. Big issues do not necessarily call for big solutions from one, but small actions from many.

By focusing on just a fragment of the bigger picture, one that is within our grasp to change, Dr Yunus' message contains timeless, infinite hope: we each have the ability to lift each other up, and the power to help build a better world.

*

Dax Dasilva is the founder and CEO of NYSE and TSX-listed technology company Lightspeed, a leading provider of cloud-based, omnichannel commerce platforms based in Montreal, Quebec. In 2015, he also founded Never Apart, a cultural non-profit organization determined to bring about positive social change and unity through original programming with global reach and impact. He is also the author of *Age of Union: Igniting the Changemaker*.

LECTURE

The following is the full Beatty Lecture delivered on 1 October 2010.

It is a great honour for me to be invited to give the Beatty Memorial Lecture. I have been told many times what a prestigious lecture series this is so I feel especially privileged to be selected, on this particular occasion, to give this lecture.

I was introduced by the chancellor as having done something heretic. I liked the word heretic in introducing the concept of lending money to the poor people. I did not do it because I was worrying about it, or because I was doing research on it. It is not like the way people devote their time and energy to a particular issue and then go into action for that. In my case, it is quite different. It was quite an accidental thing. I had no idea I would ever get involved with anything to do with lending money, but I ended up doing that, and even at that time I had no idea that it would lead to anything. Simply put, forces pushed me in that direction, which became a lifelong involvement in that subject. The circumstances in which all these things happened was because of the terrible economic situation that prevailed at that time in Bangladesh while I was teaching at Chittagong University. This was the mid-1970s and we were going through a terrible economic situation, right after the War of Liberation. Bangladesh became an independent country at the end of 1971 with a lot of devastation, a lot of killings, and bloodshed. So when I came back from the United States where I was teaching, I saw a situation that was pretty terrible and it became worse as years went by, resulting in famine in 1974.

At this time I was teaching economics at the university. When you teach economics with a lot of enthusiasm and energy as a young teacher, you feel totally confident about the validity of all the things you teach your students. But then when you walk out of the classroom and see massive famine all around the country, you start questioning yourself. What good is your economics that you teach in the classroom? Because it has no relevance to the world outside of the classroom. So gradually, you start losing faith in what you teach. Your voice becomes more muffled. You lose your strength in insisting on the validity of all the things that you say to your students. And as a person, you feel very useless, useless in the sense that you are not of any use to the rest of the society in the dire emergency that prevails around you. Out of this emptiness that you feel inside of you, you try to come up with something in desperation of the circumstances.

Since I had no other alternative, or other options, I thought, why don't I just walk out of the campus and be with the people right outside the campus, in the village, and see if I can make myself useful as a human being, to any one person in the village, even for a day? I do not claim that I have any special ability or a special quality to make myself useful to many people, so I thought one individual would be good enough for me. So that is the way that I formulated my ambition and started walking into that village every day to try to see what could be done.

As I started doing that, I started learning a lot of things that you never learn from the textbooks. In a way that village started appearing like a university to me because that was a real learning for me, and I started enjoying it. I felt that I was being useful to other people. As I was doing it, I started noticing something which I never felt so directly before and this is the loan-sharking in the village. It is such a terrible thing. Unless you come face to face with the individual situation, you cannot realize it. You can see it in a movie. You can see it in a play or a novel. You read about it all the time, about the torturous human behaviour of loan sharks. But it does not really get into you until you see the real situation of a person who was a victim of a loan shark.

Seeing it in very, very close quarters, I thought I should try to understand this situation in the village more clearly, the way it operates. I made a list of people who were borrowing from the loan sharks and what amount they borrowed, and how the loan sharks established their links with these people and tried to squeeze everything out of them. When my list was complete, there were forty-two names and the total money they had borrowed was $27. I could not believe that people had to suffer so much for such a small amount of money. I was in shock that it was right there in front of me. I saw that people had been enslaved by the loan sharks just because they needed a tiny amount of money. The loan sharks happened to lend them that money. Suddenly it came to my mind, that the problem is difficult, very complicated, intricate, but that the solution is so simple. I could solve it right away. I did not have to wait for any consultation or to go back to my textbooks to find out how to solve it. The idea was very simple. I thought, instead of loan sharks lending this $27 to forty-two people, why don't I lend this $27 to forty-two people and delink the people from the loan sharks? As I came up that night with that idea, immediately I acted on it. I did – exactly like that! I gave the money to the people to return the money to the loan sharks so that they became free from this relationship they had built between them. It created such a sensation in the village. I did not expect this, I thought this was just one of the many tiny things I had done, this is one more tiny thing, but this one thing got out of proportion in terms of the reaction from the people. They started looking at me as I went around the village as if I had done some miracle. I was even kidding with myself that if you can become an angel with $27, it is pretty cheap.

I thought, if I give another $27, I would probably become a super angel. I thought, if you can make so many people happy with such a small amount of money, why shouldn't you give more of it? I thought, how can I give more of it? It sounded like it clicked with people's needs. That kind of pushed me in a direction. I thought, I can still give money from my pocket, but I should find a way so that it becomes more institutional rather than personal. I thought about the bank located on the campus. I thought, why don't I go to the campus and tell the bank manager, here is an opportunity for you. You can lend very small amounts of money to these people and you can become a hero for them because they like it so much. Instead of going to the loan sharks, they will come to you and the bank will not miss anything because it is such a small amount of money. So, I told the manager and I thought he would immediately jump at the idea and accept it. You may laugh, and that shows how innocent I was about banking. I was thinking in a completely different way, and I was surprised that he was shocked by my suggestion. He said, "This is impossible.

How can I lend money to the poor people?" He explained in detail how they are not creditworthy, how it is impossible to deal with them. The more he argued, the more I argued back, but it did not make any difference to him, he maintained his position. But I did not give up. I started talking to his senior officials in the hierarchy of the banking system, I went up to whatever level I could reach out to. Everybody told me the same thing, it cannot be done. This went on for months, but I did not give up. Finally, I learned something from these discussions, and I offered myself as a guarantor.

I said, What if you accept me as a guarantor, and I sign all your papers and I take the risk and you give them money? This time they could not quite throw me out of their windows because I spoke their language, and they saw that this time, if they reject me, I will continue to criticize them. So, I think they thought, why don't we give some money to him and it will completely flop and he will never come back again because it will not work. They were totally confident that it would not work so they agreed. They agreed because they knew that I must pay the money back and they will be safe. Since I must pay the money, I will never come back to them again. I was happy that they agreed, and I took the money and gave it to the people.

I came up with some simple ways to make it easy for people to pay back their loans, and it worked. The more it worked, the more I got very excited and wanted to do more. I kept on adding more people every round. The more it succeeded, the more the bank became reluctant because they were expecting it to fail. Now it is working, and I am taking more money, and I keep on signing. I did not care where I signed, I just kept on signing. They got worried because they assumed it will fail at one time and at that time there will be big money involved. The bankers were creating a lot of problems along the way. Then I thought, in the beginning I had no idea what this was all about, I never did any lending at all and I had no idea how banking works, but now I do. Even if the bank did not believe in it, I became a total believer in it. I thought, why don't I create a separate bank for this instead of trying to persuade this bank which does not believe in it? I started a new campaign for myself to get a new bank license to create this bank. I also insisted that there should be a new law creating this bank so it is not being created under the existing law. I felt that if we do it under existing laws, sooner or later, it will be pushed in the same direction as the conventional banks.

Because after all, I felt that the law is a kind of a mold. If you create that mold, no matter what you do, once you have entered that mold, you take the shape of the law that you created. I was looking for a new mold and it was not easy to get a law passed for something that you want to do. But I was lucky and in 1983 we got the law and we became a bank by ourselves. We began in 1976 and by 1983 we became a bank. Once we became a bank, we kept on expanding our work very easily because now we knew how to do the job and, merrily, we kept expanding. Today after thirty-four years, we work all over Bangladesh. We have over 8.3 million borrowers and 97 per cent of them are women. We lend tiny amounts of money for income generating activities so that they can improve their income and get to use their talent and creativity. Women love it because, otherwise, they had never had any source of income, they were always depending on their husband's income. By depending only on that income, the relationship between a husband and wife remains a difficult thing because he controls everything. When a woman starts earning money, she has a different kind of status in the family than she previously had.

We made sure right from the beginning that the bank is owned by the borrowers. At that time, we were a very small organization, so owning by the borrowers was a simple thing. Today, all these eight million plus women own the bank because that is the way we developed it. In a way, we created a bank which is completely different than the conventional banks. Conventional banks concentrate on lending money to the rich. We lend money to the poorest. In many countries, including Bangladesh, they lend to the men, but we concentrate on giving money to women. Conventional banks also work always in the city centre and ask their clients to come and talk to them. We reversed it. We made the principle that the people should not go to the bank, the bank should go to the people. We go to meet all those 8.3 million borrowers at their doorstep to do the business. We also made it a weekly cycle so within one week we meet all these 8.3 million borrowers at their doorsteps in all the villages of Bangladesh. It is an amazing kind of exercise to meet them, do the business, get the money back and put the money in. It goes on – rain, shine, flood, drought, does not matter. It is a routine, a clockwork thing, that continues and gives tremendous strength to this whole network of people.

So if you compare Grameen Bank and a conventional bank, you may feel that we deliberately created rules that are just the opposite of the conventional group of banks. You can say that whenever I needed a rule, a procedure, I looked at the conventional bank and learned how they do it, and I did it the opposite way. I did not have to think of anything new. It happened exactly like that.

We continued and then people said, Well, this is microcredit. The work that we do started being described as microcredit. So, the new word came into the dictionary, microcredit. It did not exist before. People said that microcredit is a good idea that works for the poor people, but only for the entrepreneurial poor people. I said, I don't understand that, what do you mean by entrepreneurial poor? We are working with all the poor. People said, No, unless they have the entrepreneurial ability, they won't be able succeed, and they will fail. I said, Look, I don't understand your idea of entrepreneurship if you feel that entrepreneurship is limited to certain people. To me, it is completely the other way around. I feel that entrepreneurship is already built into every single human being. We do not see them as entrepreneurs because society never gave them the opportunity to bring that capacity out. Once you provide that environment, this brings their capacity out and they become an entrepreneur. They did not pay much attention to what I was saying. I thought I should demonstrate it instead and show that all people have entrepreneurial ability.

About four and a half years back I started lending money to the beggars exclusively. We always did lend money to beggars, but we were not focused on beggars. This time, we made a separate program at Grameen Bank absolutely dedicated to the beggars. We go to the beggars, talk to them, and give them an idea that, as you go from house to house begging, would you like to take some merchandise with you? Some cookies, some candies, some sweets, some toys for the kids. We made it sound very simple. We told them, Look, you are going there anyway. It's not extra work for you.

They loved the idea. They said, You give us more options, whether to ask for some food to eat or some money as charity, or now to say, Would you like to buy something from us? They can give us either some money or food, or buy something, or do both. No problem. The beggars understood the whole issue and they started taking. I said, We will give you a loan to buy all this stuff so that you can take it and sell it and make money. I thought there would be about one thousand or two thousand beggars in that program and we would find out whether they really have this entrepreneurial capacity. It became so popular that soon we had over a hundred thousand beggars in that program.

I was amazed as they kept coming forward. Our staff enjoyed it very much, they were so happy to see a beggar taking money and getting into business. We did not train them or anything, we just explained to them that this is what you can do, so find out what people like and sell it to them. We made it very simple for them. We said, There is no interest on your loan so that this money will never grow no matter how long it takes. We told them that there is no time limit on their loans so no one can tell them that they are in default. Defaulter is a bad word in banking and this way nobody can blame them that they are defaulters because they have no time limit. They can spend the rest of their lives not paying back and they are still as good clients as any other.

So our staff became very happy because they did not have to worry about it and instead they thought, let us give it to her and if she pays us back anytime and whenever she feels like it, she will take more money and continue to expand. Today all these borrowers, all those beggars that joined, they are on a second loan, a third loan, and a fourth loan, meaning they are paying back without having any restriction whatsoever. More than twenty thousand beggars are now out of begging completely. They became door-to-door salespersons. My colleagues ask, How long will it take for the rest of the beggars to come out of begging? I said, Look, don't pressure them, they are now part-time beggars because they are mixing begging with selling at the same time. They know which house is good for begging and which house is good for selling. I tell them, Look, they didn't go to the Harvard Business School but they understood the market segmentation and how to play your game. I said, Don't get too anxious about it, after all they are trying, and begging is their core business. You don't close down your core business overnight. You must be absolutely sure that your core business can be now given up when a new business has developed.

It really happened that way. I give this example because it again shows you something, the capacity of individual being. I think we neglect people. We think they do not have capacity in something, we have to take care of them. Sometimes taking care becomes so obsessive that you destroy them. It is not a good idea at all. You take care to make sure they can take care of themselves, not take care for the seeking of take care. That is a distraction. So I will come back to that subject later on, but this is something that we felt very good about.

One of the things that we wanted to make sure of was that the children of Grameen families did not remain illiterate like their parents. We wanted to make sure that 100 per cent of the children went to school, right from the beginning. It became a tradition, a culture of Grameen Bank that all children are in school. Our staff made sure that it was done. It is not simply lending money and collecting it back, it is taking responsibility for the family and their children. We saw that the children went to school and that they did not stop at primary education, but that they continued to high school and many started enrolling in higher education. Then higher education became difficult because their parents could not afford it, so we immediately introduced education loans. Now thousands and thousands of students get into higher education because Grameen Bank provides all the loans to support their maintenance, tuition and books, and whatever they need.

Today there are more than fifty-two thousand students in medical schools, engineering schools, and universities. You have a completely new generation coming out of them. We want to make a break of the traditional cycle of poverty, which includes illiteracy and lack of jobs, lack of income, and lack of health. We want to make a break so that this generation is the last generation in that cycle. A new generation is coming out of them that will be completely new people. We are creating a new cycle and taking them forward in a new life, in a new direction.

If you go and see them, you cannot but conclude that there is nothing wrong with these poor people that you work with. They are as good human beings as anybody else, simply society never gave them a chance. When you see an illiterate mother standing next to her daughter who is a medical doctor or a son who is an engineer, you cannot avoid asking the question or thinking that her mother could have been a doctor too but that she never had the opportunity to go to school. She never learned how to read and write. Is it her fault or is it somebody else's fault? She has the same capacity or maybe more capacity than her daughter. Her daughter became a doctor, but she remained an illiterate person.

I extend that idea by saying that poverty is not created by the poor people. Poverty is created by the system that we have built. So if we were to take people out of poverty, not only do you have to work with the poor people and provide these opportunities but you also have to work to change the system. As long as you keep the system as it is, it will keep on creating poverty. Unless you close down that faucet which brings out those in poverty, poverty cannot be eliminated. You eliminate one, they create two. Poverty is not in the person, poverty is imposed on the person externally. If it is an external imposition, we have to lock it up where it is coming from so that it does not come in from outside.

I just gave you this long story about Grameen Bank for the simple reason that after thirty, forty years of our work, conventional banks still have not changed. You go to them and they will say the same thing, Poor are not credit worthy. Whereas the whole world is brimming with people now who take this loan called microcredit. It is not a Bangladeshi phenomenon anymore, it is a global phenomenon. The poor pay you back much better than anybody else. Our repayment rate, despite our difficulties in Bangladesh, with floods and disasters and so on, never faltered, it continued. Bangladesh is known as a country of disasters and when disaster happens, it is the poor people who are at the frontline of this disaster and lose everything. Grameen Bank did not close down because of that. Grameen Bank flourished because we built it up in a way that we absorbed disaster and helped people to overcome disaster, and it continues this way.

Funnily, we were challenged that Grameen could not be replicated in a country like the United States, which is a rich country with a welfare system where people are not looking for tiny money, they are looking for big money. I said, That's what you think, if you go deep into it, you'll see it completely differently. They said, Why don't you show us that it can be done here in a Grameen way? So we started a program in New York city in 2008, in Queens, and called it Grameen America.

We took the challenge and they provided us with the money. We repeated exactly the same thing we do in the villages of Bangladesh, nothing changed. We actually sent some people from Bangladesh to run the program, though they never had been to the United States in their lives. They were very worried and said, What do we do? We don't know anything about America. I said, That's your advantage. You just do what you do in Bangladesh, blindly. Don't even think that you are in America. They did exactly that and it worked beautifully.

The funny thing was, we started in January 2008, but in the latter half of the year, the financial crisis came and very strange situations started happening. Huge banks collapsed and melted away whereas this tiny bank with tiny loans flourished in the same neighbourhood. And I said to a journalist, "You should ask me now, who is creditworthy? Because thirty, forty years back, you told me that the poor people are not creditworthy. Now tell me who is creditworthy? It is the big, rich people who are not paying back while the poor people in your same neighbourhood are paying back 100 per cent with no collateral."

But still, the system does not change and that system denies access to more than half the population of the world, probably two thirds of the population of the world. When debt is not available, this service is not available. They have hardly taken a step to move forward. When the big banks started collapsing, government has to come forward to bail them out because their argument is, they are too big to fail. Meaning that if they fail the privileged people will lose all this opportunity to continue their lives. It will create a problem, a financial crisis, an economic crisis.

But for two thirds of the world's people, banks do not exist. It is not a question of collapsing, for them, banks do not exist. We do not worry about them. We leave them to pay their loan sharks 500 per cent interest, 1,000 per cent interest, 1,500 per cent interest. Who cares? And that becomes a trillion-dollar industry. We do not worry about it. Pawn shops flourish everywhere. We do not care about it. That is where the system goes wrong. You do not apply your talent or your creativity to create a system that can embrace everybody. Everybody has to get into the system. Then I talk about the concept of business itself. I said the whole concept of business is also grossly mistaken because economists misinterpreted human beings. Economists imagined that all human beings are just money-making machines, nothing else. All they do in their lifetime is make money, that is the goal of their life. That does not sound like a human condition, a human desire. It is artificially created by the theory that we built. We are trying to fit into the theory rather than theory fitting into us. Because a human being is much bigger than just being a money-making machine. We are not robots, we have many more dimensions than this simple selfish dimension which we are given recognition for within economics.

I said, we are selfish, but at the same time, we are selfless too. Both things coexist in all of us. There are no two kinds of people. One that is a selfish kind of person and the other a selfless kind of person. The same people have the same thing in us as anybody else. But the economists do not want to recognize that selfless part. They tell us that if you want to be selfless, work outside of economics, become a philanthropist, give away your money if you want to be so charitable and help other people. I said, Why should I? Why should we call it economics and social science if that cannot accommodate me as a whole? Take only a piece of me and build a whole theory that says, You do it this way. I said, That doesn't make sense.

All the trouble, all the problems that we created around us came from that misinterpretation. This financial crisis, and the environmental crisis, and the energy crisis, and all the social crises we have are all manifestations of a fundamental flaw in the framework of theory that we practice. Unless we eliminate that flaw, we'll keep on bumping into this problem and the crisis will become bigger and bigger.

So, I started creating some businesses on my own, not because I was thinking that way, I was just creating many businesses, which now are based on that selflessness that I was talking about. People kept asking that question. Then I realized, yes, this is a different kind of business. Over time, I created over forty such companies. I do not own any shares of any of these companies. They have become large companies, but I do not own a share. Every time I see a problem, I create a business to solve that problem. As there are many problems, I created many businesses. One that I created became quite big. Many of them became quite big.

One I want to mention is called Grameen Shakti or Grameen Energy. We sell solar home systems because Bangladesh does not have much electricity, in fact 70 per cent of the people have no access to electricity. We thought this was an opportunity to bring solar energy before expensive fossil fuel electricity came in. People said that it could not be done in the villages of Bangladesh, it is too expensive for them, but we came out with a business model that was attractive for them. Instead of paying up front, we said, You can pay it in monthly installments, over two or three years so that it becomes easy for you. We started selling five solar home systems a month, and then ten solar home systems a month. We wanted to get to one hundred solar home systems a month. Now we have come to a stage where we sell more than one thousand solar home systems per day. It is a huge thing. We need to buy so many solar panels from countries like Japan, Germany, and China. We keep buying them because people are asking for more and more solar home system.

We decided to set up a whole factory to produce solar panels so that we can make them more cheaply, as a social business. So, all these businesses relate to that kind of business that I am talking about, not for making money, but for solving problems. It is based on that selfless part of us that is in all of us. I call it social business and I gave you examples of that. It is much better than charity. I could have given this solar home system as a free system but I would then have to go to the donor every time I give a solar home system. I would need somebody to donate $300 so that I can donate a solar home system. So, how many solar home systems could I have given? Five, ten, one hundred, two thousand? That is all. Donor says, Okay, you stop it, I can't give you more money for free distribution of solar home systems because in charity, once money goes, it doesn't come back. You are limited by the amount of funds you can raise.

Fundraising is a very torturous work, you know that. Many organizations who are engaged in charity work do wonderful work and they are very dedicated people. Their frustration is that their whole organization devotes 80 per cent of their time to fundraising and only 20 per cent of their time in doing the actual job. Sometimes it gets more difficult to get this money because donors become reluctant and they will ask 101 questions.

Charity is important but if you can convert some of your charity work into a business format, then it runs by itself and creates its own fuel all the time and continues. That is the solar energy thing that we are talking about here. I do not have to worry about money because people are paying. The more money that gets paid back, the more I buy and sell. In the meantime, I try to reduce the cost so that I can sell it to more people who could not afford it before. That is the beauty of social business – that you can keep it as a way that it keeps running.

In charity, money does not come back but in social business money recycles all the time. You create a machine which runs by itself and does not have to bring fuel from outside anymore. This is what I have been talking about and what created a lot of these social businesses. One of them was with the big multinational company Danone. We created Grameen Danone, a social business company to produce yogurt. We did this to address the problem of malnutrition among the children. We put all the micronutrients which are missing in the children into this yogurt, such as vitamins, iron, zinc, and iodine. We sell it very cheaply so that poor people can afford it. When the children eat this yogurt, they gradually get back their nutrition and become healthy. Today it is a very successful company in Bangladesh and we are expanding. Since it is a social business, expanding is not difficult. What do we do? We go to the bank, borrow money, invest it, or find new or the same investors and we continue.

We created other companies too, like a joint venture with BASF, a German chemical company. Now the Grameen BASF company produces treated mosquito nets to protect people from malaria. Bangladesh is a malaria country, at least in some parts, and it also has dengue fever. We make the nets very affordable to buy. In the social business, you do not want to make money – all you want to do is to stop malaria. You are devoted to the cause and you continue.

We have another large social business, a joint venture with Adidas. I challenged the company's CEO that as a shoe company, it is their responsibility to produce affordable shoes for even the poorest person. Their goal should be that nobody in the world should go without shoes. Nobody should be barefoot. They took the challenge and made a joint venture with us called Grameen Adidas. They asked me how cheap the shoes should be to be affordable to the poorest people and I said, maybe under one euro. They were shocked and asked, How can you produce Adidas or Reebok shoes for under one euro? But they did not give up. They worked and worked and finally found a formula to produce durable, attractive looking shoes at under one euro so that everybody in Bangladesh can afford shoes: every child, every woman, every man. People suffer from parasitic diseases by going barefoot and these shoes give protection. It is a health intervention.

I will not go on listing the many companies but you can see this is an idea that can solve any problem. People ask me, Can we design social businesses for any kind of problem? I say, Of course, any social problem. It is a question of creativity. The moment you put your mind to it, you will come up with some solution. But today we do not put our mind to it. We are very privileged in the world. We have the most powerful technology to change the world today and which every day becomes more powerful. Imagine what different things will happen in the next ten years in our lives.

When I was a student, the Xerox machine was the biggest thing. Probably you have not seen one unless you are of my age. Then the fax machine came. It was the miracle of miracles. The Bangladesh government immediately imposed that you had to get a government license to buy a fax machine, it was that important. That fax machine today is in every home, with every computer, and every telephone. Then the mobile phone was a miracle. In 1995, there were only half a million landline telephones in Bangladesh. We created a mobile phone company called Grameen Phone to bring phones into the hands of the poor. Everybody was shocked. How can poor people have a telephone, what are they going to do with it? Even the regulators when we applied for licenses to get this company asked us, You want to give this phone to the poor women? I said, Yes. They asked, Who is she going to call? I said, She's not going to call, but people will call her using her phone and this will be her business. She'll be selling the airtime to the people in the village to make money. They said, That's impossible, this woman is an illiterate woman, and she doesn't know how to read numbers. I said, You misunderstand them. There are only ten numbers in the world. If pushing these ten numbers brings money, she will learn it in ten minutes.

When we got the license, we expanded our network to the village before the city in order to bring phones into the hands of the poorest women. Grameen Bank gave her a loan, she picked up a phone and started selling the phones in the village where phone service does not exist. She has the only phone. Everybody lines up in front of her house to make a phone call and she enjoys that. After six months, I went around to meet all these women who took the phone for the first time to see if they have understood how to run this business. They were bubbling with enthusiasm. I asked someone, Do you have any difficulty in dialing the numbers? She said, No problem, I know everything. Do you want me to call somebody? Give me your number, I'll call you. I said, No, it's okay, you know. Another stood up, she said, You didn't give her a number, you give the number to me and I'll dial it. Before I dial it, blindfold me. If I cannot dial it blindfolded, take my phone back, I'm not worth it. I was astounded. I could not believe this illiterate woman was challenging me, saying "Blindfold me and if I cannot dial it blindfolded, I will return your telephone."

I wished that a bureaucrat from the regulatory agency was there. How easy it is to underestimate the capacity of people just because you are somewhere else. People have that capacity, we are just not unleashing it. Social business is a way to expand that. Technology makes us powerful. We can create enormous varieties of social businesses. Taking people out of welfare could be a wonderful social business. Putting people on welfare is a very important thing but keeping them there is totally unacceptable. We must make efforts so that they become full citizens of the country rather than depend on charity of the government and charity of the other taxpayers.

I was exposed to this situation very drastically in Glasgow, while I was speaking there. I was told that there are thousands of families in Glasgow who are in fourth generation unemployment. I could not believe that in a civilized society, you can have fourth generation employment. You are condemning those people to a situation where they lose all their human capacity. I told them that the responsibility of any society is to make sure every human being, every citizen, has the capacity to unleash the energy, unleash the creativity they have. Every human being is packed with unlimited capacity. To ask them to not use that capacity is criminal. I said, Why don't we create some social business to take these people out of that prison that you created for them?

I am sure that in a welfare system this problem is not unknown, but welfare is only part one of the solution to help people to overcome their problems. Part two, the most important part, is to get them out of a welfare situation. We created a nursing college in Bangladesh because we saw that the need for nurses in Bangladesh and outside is tremendous. I said, Young girls are sitting around in the villages, getting married, having children, nothing else to do. Why don't we pick up these girls, put them in a decent nursing college, give them a world-class nursing education? They can become important citizens of the world by delivering health services.

We take the students, girls from Grameen families – and from the poorest families who were able to go to school because of Grameen Bank – and we take them to nursing college and Grameen Bank gives the education loan to them. They pay the tuition for the nursing college. The nursing college covers all these costs and gives them the world-class education and then they find jobs in Bangladesh and elsewhere and become part of this whole healthcare system.

I am very grateful to have a collaboration between Grameen and McGill University. One of the things that we will be creating through our collaboration is a Grameen-McGill nursing college in Bangladesh. We can create nurses out of these girls who can compete with anybody anywhere. They lack nothing in capacity, but simply the facilities were not given to them and so we are creating this facility. We joined hands together because McGill University has that world-class capacity. The whole world knows about McGill University and their healthcare system, and their nursing colleges. We want to bring that knowledge to them, so that they become part of this whole high-class education. They will be different people. There is nothing wrong with them, simply they did not have the opportunity.

We can create many of these opportunities all around. Every single individual can do that. It is not only Danone, BASF, or Adidas who can do that. Every single individual can create a small social business to help five persons. My beginning was to help those people with it for $27. That is what changed everything that I do and created this whole idea. Anybody that wants to solve this specific problem can do it in a social business way, with the goal not to create a business to make money for themselves. They can earn money from other businesses. At the same time, they can do this social business. It is a question of creative ideas to come. If we bring together social businesses, creative ideas, and technologies, nobody should remain a poor person. There is no reason to be because it is not part of a human being.

We look forward to a day, very soon, when we can put poverty in the museum. When there will be nobody left in the world who is a poor person. If you want to see a poor person, you will have to go to the museum to see them.

14

The Challenge of Regressive Democracy
12 October 2017

Charles Taylor

INTRODUCTION

One of Canadian philosopher Charles Taylor's great gifts as an expositor has always been to make demanding, wide-ranging systems of ideas clear and accessible, and this reflection on democracy is no exception. What he diagnoses – with deceptive effortlessness – is indeed a major global crisis. The word democracy has become a talisman. We seem to think that it is the natural default position for any intelligent human being (which of course prevents us from doing the hard work of learning about the hard work, across the centuries, of uncovering more and deeper meanings for the word). We miss the subtle differences between different senses of the word people, so well sketched by Taylor – a McGill professor emeritus – in these pages. We pontificate about the transcendent authority of majority decision-making, we confuse democratic participation with direct plebiscite, we fail to ask where the skills of democratic process are learned and refined or even to recognize that there are skills involved at all. As Taylor observes, we are impatient with the idea that democracy may mean a continuing argument about public goods rather than a sure-fire method of stopping or preventing argument by appeal to majority opinion.

Taylor very rightly pinpoints the need to think afresh about civic identity and liberty. Talk about democracy which ignores the basic vision of human beings as reflective and creative citizens will be a recipe simply for passive and consumerist politics of the kind we are too familiar with these days – the politician as sales representative, assessing the market demands of an undifferentiated public, the politician as entertainer, reinforcing our comfort zones. Any democracy wanting to avoid regression in Taylor's sense needs to think about how it supports and nurtures decision-making in local communities, and an educational culture that encourages people to ask awkward questions about accountability.

And this suggests that one further notion that might throw light on Taylor's argument is that of lawful democracy – a system in which universal protection

Charles Taylor. *Used with permission of Alex Tran.*

and redress are embedded, because all levels of society are held answerable to a foundational commitment – a commitment to the freedom of any and every participant in society to make their voice heard without fear. Absent this foundation in law, democracy will readily degenerate into a majoritarian tyranny of race, class or financial interest. It is why attacks on an independent judiciary or an undermining of the credibility of legal professionals constitute very bad news for democratic societies. States on both sides of the Atlantic have had good reason in recent years to be anxious about trends in this regard.

But – and here is perhaps the central paradox of democracy – the law-governed concern for the freedom of every voice rests on a radical act of faith, faith not in an ideal called democracy but in a reverence for human beings as such, educated or uneducated, rich or poor, old or young, physically fit or physically challenged, of every imaginable background and culture. A principled democracy needs this tough and non-negotiable basis, even though it can make for formidable practical difficulties at times and intractable arguments about the good of individuals and communities. It needs what some would call a myth, others a metaphysic; it is why – as Taylor would agree – it needs traditions of religious commitment alongside the discourse of secular emancipation to remind us to take all human agents with the seriousness their human status demands. Liberal democracy has historically and understandably resisted any legal enforcement of faith; the mistake has been to conclude that faith has nothing to say in the public argument about the legitimacy of a social order and the foundations of the risky democratic enterprise of giving voice to all.

Over many years, Taylor has modelled a deeply erudite, nuanced, imaginative engagement with the foundations of social philosophy and the complexities of our unevenly secularized culture in the West. In his diagnosis of the perils of democratic language and practice in our era, he once again shows himself to be an indispensable voice of both sanity and depth in our public debates and we have good cause to be grateful.

*

Rowan Williams retired as Master of Magdalene College, Cambridge, in 2020 having previously been Archbishop of Canterbury from 2002 to 2012. His most recent book (with Mary Zournazi) is *Justice and Love: A Philosophical Dialogue*.

LECTURE

The following is the full Beatty Lecture delivered on 12 October 2017.

It is a great pleasure to have a discussion with you tonight on a very important issue on which we are all very confused, and I am not a total exception to that, but I am going to try to see if we can clarify a little bit. I am talking about the crisis or crises of democracy that we are now living. Let me introduce it by saying that we have often had the idea, or the idea has often surfaced, that there is some kind of inevitable escalator in history which is pushing towards more rational, more humane, more democratic forms of society and government. In the last century, we have had moments when we have really believed in this, when this seemed to be plausible. I am thinking of 1919 at the end of World War I, the war to protect democracy or defend democracy. After 1945, various decolonization movements in the various European empires also encouraged this thought.

More recently, in 1989, the collapse of the Berlin Wall and the collapse of Communist regimes really gave it a fresh impetus, and it looked in the 1990s like we were on a roll. It did not happen. This roll did not happen. On the contrary, we are in a rather grim situation today. I think that we have to recognize that this hope of what let us call the escalator view – that somehow things are moving that way – is really an illusion.

I want to try to explain why I think it is an illusion. Because of certain inherent dangers and tendencies built into democracy, which does not mean that we are justified in being just as pessimistic now as we were optimistic in 1989. No, but it does mean that we have to recognize these dangers and try to combat them.

Democracy is not an escalator going up. Democracy is a perpetual struggle to maybe keep what we have and maybe advance a few more inches and not suffer retreat. I want to talk about three ways in which democracy is vulnerable, if you like, to regression. That is why I use the word regression or you might even say degeneration. I mean losing its quality as democracy. The first one of these I want to talk about is that democracy can begin to lose its quality as democracy if we drift towards elite control. Or to put it in other terms, if the non-elites play less and less of a role in society. Non-elites is of course translated into the Greek word *demos*. What the Greeks meant by the demos was not the whole population, but the non-elites of the society. It is a very remarkable fact about modern European languages that the word for people – *peuple, Volk, narod* – always has these two meanings. It has a meaning on one level of the whole population, all the citizens, that the ensemble of them make the people, in one sense. In another sense, this Greek idea of demos recurs. When I say I want to mobilize the people against this unjust law that has been passed by government, I am talking about the people as the people who do not wield the first level power, the non-elites.

Democracy is actually going to be understood as an interplay of two concepts with the same word, the concept of the people as all-embracing and the concept of the people as those who are disadvantaged and forgotten because they are not part of the elite. You can see that in a certain sense the introduction of what we think of as modern democracy passed through a certain semantic shift.

Aristotle thought of democracy as rule by the common people over and above the elites. That is what the word meant in European discourse up until the end of the eighteenth century and the founders of the American Constitution did not want democracy. They wanted a republic. In other words, they wanted to have this kind of balance between the people and the elites. The word democracy begins to take over in the nineteenth century for this mode of government precisely because this issue of elite rule and combating elite rule became tremendously important. So in order to keep ourselves from being confused, we have to see that there are two meanings of democracy.

One, when legally and by the established law and so on, power, ultimate power to elect, is in the hands of the whole people as against the aristocratic or oligarchic or dictatorial rule. That is one sense of democracy, but in another sense, the notion of the demos comes in and people can ask the question, Well, are the non-elites really playing the role that they ought to be playing? Do they have this share of power which goes with their numbers? There, as against the first concept of democracy, which is pretty well an on-off, either the laws give the vote to everybody or there is some mode of control from on top. You can say that this country is a democracy, that country is not. Among the countries that we think of as democracies in that sense, there are big issues arising as to the degree of elite control. This is something which can never be resolved once and for all.

If you just look quickly over the history of the last two centuries, you see that there have been periods of this very severe imbalance, in which elites have had more than their proper share of control, but it has been on the basis of very different qualifications. In the early nineteenth century, in America, property and commercial success was what made you part of the elite. Then in a certain sense, there were movements of Jacksonian rebellion and so on, in which there was a pushback against this, but then the economy changes. We get an economy based on large industry and large corporation, and the robber barons, and we get a situation of great inequality arising.

Then in the twentieth century, in the 1930s and in the aftermath of World War II, there is a pushback against this overwhelming power. We have trade unions and democratic governments and so on. After 1970, we find ourselves slipping back again. One of the indices of this is that as the division or the distance between rich and poor becomes greater and greater and greater, we get the power of finance playing a role.

There is not and there will never be a final resolution of the problem of equal distribution of power. What there is – and that I think is very important – is a sense people have of what the direction is. Are we moving towards a more democratic, in this sense, equal distribution of power? Are we moving towards a more democratic society or are we being pushed away from it? It is very clear that in the thirty years after World War II, during what the French call Les Trente Glorieuses, the years of great prosperity after the war and also various gains of popular legislation and the welfare state and so on, people had a sense of the direction that they were moving towards.

Since 1975, 1980, the sense is very powerful that we are sliding away. Now, I think we have to understand that this kind of move has its own tendency to enhance itself as a spiral downward. If you think of the situation since the 1980s in most democracies, I think you can see a steady growth of the sense – I want to introduce a word here, citizen efficacy – the sense that people have that as a citizen they can really do something. It is a subjective sense, a sense that either we cannot do anything, or all the parties are the same. It is all corrupt, they control everything, or the sense that, yes, we can do something.

This sense of citizen efficacy has been slipping. This kind of move can have a self-feeding quality. That is, if people feel that they cannot really do anything serious in politics, they will both tune out more and more and, in many cases, stop voting. We see a steady direction – a general and clear trend – in all Western European democracies since roughly the 1970s or 1980s, for a lesser participation in the vote.

But of course, that enhances the imbalance of power. When a large part of the demos does not vote, it gives greater power to the elites. Then the tuning out of politics in general gives greater power to money because you need to reach people through television and so on. Then again, the imbalance of power gets intensified. We have here a real danger. It is not something that can just be easily reversed. It is a trend towards degeneration, the lowering of democratic morale, which can feed on itself.

It is also the source of great dissatisfaction. You can see this in the sense of decline in felt citizen efficacy. You can see that for a lot of people there is really a sense of decline, of a disempowering of themselves. You can see that in the slogans. For instance, Obama's slogan, "Yes, we can." Yes, we can be an answer to the feeling of, no, we can't. We're helpless, right?

If you think of the movement of the Indignados in Spain, one of the parties that emerged from this is called Podemos. What is Podemos? It is, "Yes, we can," in Spanish. The same idea. So that is one of the paths of degeneration that I want to talk about here.

The second one is when the notion of the plebs, of the people of the demos, in the sense of demos, is captured by a restricted definition of who the people really are, so that we get a discrimination between the real people and certain others who are in the population but are really outsiders and do not belong to the real people.

That is of course what we see today in contemporary populism almost everywhere in the Western world, that kind of development of a narrowing definition of the people to the real people, to the core. It happens for various reasons. An important part in many Western societies has been immigration. Particularly in European societies that were not used to immigration, there could be this reaction of, "They are not really part of us, they do not really belong to our culture." To some extent in Quebec, we have got something similar. But I think we must see that the flip, that move towards a kind of nativist outlook is, in a sense, built into modern democracy for a reason that I do not think we adequately focus on normally. That is that democratic societies are a very peculiar kind of society. They require a very strong sense of common identity, that we are linked together because we have important common moral beliefs about democracy and so on and because we have a history together of forging and upholding these democratic principles. There is usually in a sense of identity a level of principle and a level of identification of "us" as a particular project, an American project, a French project, of realizing democracy.

Now, it is essential you could not have a democracy without a very strongly felt common bond. Just look at places where it does not exist. Attempts to get a vibrant democratic life with elections in the European Union has really not got off the ground because there is not one European people. There is not a people who identify primarily and have a very strong identification with that whole. Or there can be societies which are split, as was threatened in the case of Canada between two segments. One segment of which many people were saying, "We do not belong. We are not really respected. We are not part of this." So, we had a great movement for independence in Quebec. We see now in Catalunya something similar is going on. Moreover, democratic societies really require a certain amount of solidarity, of help, that those who are in a good situation give to those in a bad situation. Even the United States, where I suppose the sense of solidarity is the weakest of any Western society, society has demonstrated that when you get these huge catastrophes, the hurricanes for example, we should help each other.

Most of all, they need to generate the trust, the trust that all of you when we are deliberating together will think of the general good. So it is very important to have this emotionally powerful sense of the people here, the people as the whole people. But that emotionally powerful feeling can easily slip into being the people are the original people, the real people, the people who were originally here or they can be infected by – this is something very hard to pick out, but I think it is evidently working, conceptions of inherent hierarchy or precedence. Take the fact – it will be extraordinary to our children – that in the whole development of democracy, male universal suffrage came well before the extension to women and went a very conflictual way in different times in different places. For example, only very recently in the Swiss cantons and only in 1940 in Quebec. Because it is an inherent hierarchical sense that the real operative agent in the family is the man, that hierarchical sense somehow just, we would say today, blinded people to the fact that democracy as manhood suffrage was incomplete. But you could see other such notions of hierarchy or precedence operating today, like very powerful notions in the United States, which you see being exploited by Donald Trump in that movement, that it is a very subtle notion of hierarchy. It is a notion you might see of precedence that certain people deserve to be served first if you like, natives rather than people who arrive. In the South, whites as against Blacks. Still, for many people, men as against women. Original Americans, et cetera. Original Anglo Saxons, Scots, Irish Americans versus others and so on. So when these begin to play a role, you get the basis for the very thing democracy thrives on, which is a strong sense of common identity, that gets captured and narrowed and becomes something destroyed from within by dividing people.

Put these two things together, and that is what we are living with today. That is, the neglect of non-elite power and the lessening of non-elite power in the sense of dissatisfaction arising from the lack of felt citizen efficacy on the one hand, and the sliding of the sense of who is lacking that efficacy, who is the demos into a narrower confine. You get the basis for the kind of mobilization that Marine Le Pen pulled off in France, that Trump pulled off in the United States, and that Geert Wilders pulled off in Holland. You can go down the whole list. The appeal is that you have been neglected and there is a certain economic basis for this. You have been neglected by these elites who are more interested in serving these people that should be second, or maybe do not even belong to us, than in serving you. You have to rise up and put an end to this. That, of course, itself can produce a spiral, a spiral you can see happening in certain European societies, particularly France, where the populations that are being pushed to the edge develop a counter identity and say, No, we are not really French. We are Muslim, we are not French. These then play off against each other and threaten to destroy the society.

Let me mention the third mode of decline: this is when democracy gets misinterpreted as majority rule. You can see this can arise easily about the second slide. If you are thinking of the people as this group and then you think that it is this group which is the demos which must be ruling, then there is no need to think of negotiation, or discussion, or sawing off certain differences with the rest of the society that is not really belonging to the people.

Successful democracy gets reinterpreted as majority rule in the sense that this majority movement is now in power, but the others are not treated as fellow citizens, as people you have to negotiate with. The obvious manifestation of this is a decline in the civic language. You get extreme language, branding people as enemies that cannot be talked to and so on.

Now you in a sense are seeing in the West a kind of perfect storm, if I can put it that way, in which these three kinds of degeneration are, as it were, working together. Certainly, the sense of a loss of citizen efficacy is feeding the various modes of populism that is defining the populace as narrow. That, in turn, is feeding the idea that what we are dealing with here is enemies, outsiders, so what we need is the people to rule us, for them to ride roughshod over these outsiders. Whereas, a real democracy in the proper sense is a deliberate community in which we nourish the sense of mutual recognition that can allow for a real discussion, in which people respect each other. And it can arrive at some kind of general conclusion for the moment, a conclusion determined by the majority but it is understood that the discussion goes on with these other people, they are not enemies, they are people that temporarily lost the battle.

All right, you might very well ask, "What are we going to do about it?" I only have thirty-five minutes. That is very bad in one way, but I am tremendously relieved in another way. I think that we owe it to each other to look at some of the things that we have to tackle in order to fight back against this triple slide, where the different elements are, as it were, supporting each other.

The first is we have to look at what produced the discontent on the economic level in places like the Rust Belt or various parts of England that voted for Brexit. The Rust Belt is a major factor here. The parts of the French working class that have moved over from communism to support Le Pen are precisely the areas that are deindustrializing. We may have to look at something much more radical. I don't mean in a sense of rallying people on the barricades, but much bigger changes than we have thought of before.

Is it going to be possible in an age of globalization and automation – extreme automation to ensure self-respecting jobs for everybody without changing very considerably the way we remunerate work, the way we can help to support voluntary work, the way in which communities can determine their own needs and set up programs of contribution, voluntary participation, which are funded from the centre, but are not necessarily paid work? All these things need to be thought through. I am just at the beginning of my thinking. That is one area we have to tackle. That is tackling the, as it were, economic sources of this slide, which as you can see, are typified in the Rust Belt.

Second, a very important feature of any real solution is the re-creation of a sense of deliberate community, which requires really working very seriously on our public sphere. By public sphere, I mean the sphere in which we discuss with each other and exchange ideas and exchange propositions. This is really in a very sick condition for two reasons which we all recognize.

One is that we no longer have media that are read and contributed to by the whole spectrum, but we have media now which constitute echo chambers. Fox News against MSNBC, et cetera, where like-minded people get their information, get their opinions and never hear what happens elsewhere. Fox News gave a report of the terrible attack in Quebec on 29 January, but their report was that the assassin was Moroccan, whereas in reality some of the victims were Moroccan. I don't think they ever rectified it.

People who listen only to Fox News are a very great mixture, as Aristotle would say, of pity and horror. Contemplate it. People who listen only to Fox News never get any access to reality. Then that is exacerbated, I think, by the way in which social media works, where people get a certain set of friends and where a certain set of ideas and supposed facts circulate, which in some cases are just totally non-facts and again never get called.

Again, we have a very deep set of problems here about how to recreate a public sphere, which is a genuine exchange across difference. There are other things too that we must look to, but these are two very general problems that we have to tackle. I am glad I do not have to give you the detail on these today because I do not have it and I am still struggling, but this is the direction that our thinking has to struggle.

So is this a pessimistic message? Well, if you believe in the escalator, it sounds devastating. If you cease believing in the escalator, that things are automatically going up, it can even be exhilarating because these are things that can be fought against, that we can fight back against. I mean the case of the Emmanuel Macron election is a case that can be faced and defeated. But we have a lot of hard thinking to do if we are going to move the needle back so that people have the sense that, yes, we can and we are moving towards a more democratic society – one that is again sliding away.

Difficult Women, Bad Feminists, and Unruly Bodies
11 October 2018

Roxane Gay

INTRODUCTION

It is a challenge to find a singular descriptor for Roxane Gay. She is a prolific author of fiction, graphic novels, memoirs, essays, works of short fiction, opinion columns, and comics. She is also an editor, publisher, professor, podcaster, advocate, social commentator, social media influencer, and cultural critic. Her debut novel, *An Untamed State* (2014), was long-listed for the Flaherty-Dunnan First Novel Prize. Her collection of essays in *Bad Feminist* (2014), short stories in *Difficult Women* (2017), and her memoir *Hunger: A Memoir of (My) Body* (2017), are definitive and deeply personal works in social and cultural commentary on the intersection of gender, race, sexuality, and sexual violence.

In this 2018 Beatty Lecture, Gay reflects on the #MeToo movement. This moment of reckoning not only precipitated the downfall of Harvey Weinstein and other powerful men who were finally held accountable for their decades of sexual abuse and violence, but also exposed the traumatic normalcy of these experiences for so many women. It is a movement built on the foundation and necessity of solidarity across class, racial, and national lines. The hashtag, and later the movement, went viral precisely because the experiences of sexual abuse, harassment, violence, and trauma are so horrifyingly common that the confession, "it happened to me, too," has come to be a near-universal feature of women's realities.

The #MeToo movement, Gay argues, highlights the unequal power relations that define our quotidian experiences as gendered subjects: the value given to the desires, reputations, and feelings of the powerful; the utter disregard of the needs and safety of the powerless; the sleight of hand in our cultural currency that cements the rift between who is believed, who is given empathy, and who must suffer alone and in silence. "Women should not have to think of ourselves in terms of resilience

Roxane Gay. *Used with permission of Joni Dufour.*

or our ability to endure," Gay writes. "We are capable of so much more, but we are too busy dealing with bullshit to demonstrate the full extent of our powers."

Throughout her inspired lecture, Gay conveys the importance of examining the systems that produce sexual violence and misogyny. Individual firings, downfalls, lost opportunities, cancellations, and arrests are important, but will not catalyze the radical social transformation required for all women – especially women of colour, undocumented women, incarcerated women, queer women, and women with disabilities – to feel safe and valued. This central message of the lecture continues to be relevant.

We need, perhaps now more than ever, voices like that of Roxane Gay and her honest and unapologetic dissection of structures of domination, masterful skill with language, and bone-deep commitment to equity and social justice.

*

Debra Thompson is Associate Professor of Political Science and the Canada Research Chair in Racial Inequality in Democratic Societies at McGill University.

LECTURE

The following is the full Beatty Lecture delivered on 11 October 2018.

This past year as #MeToo has gained cultural prominence, we have seen how necessary change can be excruciatingly slow, and that can be infuriating. When Harvey Weinstein and then several other men were finally held to account for decades of misdeeds, it finally felt like the beginning of something. For once, it seemed, women might not only be heard, but believed. Justice felt like a real, tangible thing, rather than a vague, illusory ideal.

But, over the past several weeks, we have heard from men who transgressed against women and fell from grace. In "Exile," by former WNYC radio host John Hockenberry, which appears in *Harper's*, he is mournful for the life he lost after he was accused by multiple women of sexual harassment. He is aggressively self-pitying throughout his essay, airing any number of grievances about the injustice of how he has been misunderstood. Then at one point in the essay, he misunderstood *Lolita* and declared that romance was dead, as if sexual harassment in the workplace is some kind of grand romantic event or overture that modern women who dare to stand up for themselves have cruelly forsaken.

Jian Ghomeshi, the former CBC radio host accused of sexual assault and harassment, also wrote a terrible essay, utterly lacking in self-awareness. In his "Reflections from a Hashtag," published in the *New York Review of Books*, Ghomeshi takes an almost pithy tone as he reflects on his life since he was accused of various crimes and sexual misdemeanours. He presents himself as the misunderstood hero of his own narrative, the rational man in an irrational world. And those are just the essays and publications I once respected. Even more impoverished accounts have been published elsewhere. Men writing about how their lives have been derailed with no clear understanding of the lives they themselves have derailed with their own actions.

Starkly lacking in any of these accounts is accountability or genuine recognition of the wrong done. These men display entitlement, and rage, and contempt for being seen as they truly are. The people who publish such pieces treat the perpetrators of sexual misconduct as intellectual curiosities. They reserve their empathy for these broken men. They reserve their empathy for themselves rather than for women, because as a culture, we expect women to suffer. We gild women's suffering with both inevitability and nobility. Time and again, women splay themselves. Women cut themselves open and share their painful stories. They bleed for this world that remains largely indifferent to their pain.

#MeToo was a reckoning, one that has been a long time coming, but far too many men are unwilling to face this reckoning and to recognize their role in bringing it about. Men are unwilling to reflect on how they treat women, how they understand consent and how they do not. Instead they say, not all men. They suggest that they are the good men. They tell women that harassment or assault is not so bad. Not really. Boys will be boys remains a popular refrain. I marvel that women still deal with men at all, when there is such a lovely alternative. I am talking about the joy of lesbian sex to be crystal clear.

I am often asked about hope. I am asked if I am still hopeful despite what I know of the world. I am asked if hope is possible in these troubled times. I am asked how to hold on to hope. I always respond as best I can, but those responses feel hollow because they are. I am not the kind of person who thinks in terms of hope. Certainly, I want to hope because I need to believe there is something better beyond the present, but I am more realist than optimist. Hope is too ephemeral, too inconsistent, too fleeting.

We are in a brutal time. In the United States, Supreme Court nominee Brett Kavanaugh faced accusations of sexual misconduct. Every day there is new information about men who have abused their position, or acted inappropriately, or committed crimes against women. Dr Christine Blasey Ford testified in front of a panel of mostly men about the sexual assault she endured at the hands of Brett Kavanaugh. She took a polygraph supporting her version of events. She spoke her truth in front of the nation. Her entire life exploded because she had the courage to come forward out of a sense of what she called a patriotic duty. She considered the greater good and still there were people who doubted her, who did not find her credible. And if they did find her credible, they did not think that what she endured merited Kavanaugh losing a career opportunity.

Judge Kavanaugh did not need to write down his woes in a bad essay. He was able to share them in front of an international audience in real time. When he spoke on his own behalf, he was all rage and righteousness, ego, and entitlement. He cried, he glared. It was a grand and grotesque performance. Kavanaugh interrupted nearly every democratic Senator who questioned him. A year after the allegations against Harvey Weinstein were first reported, a federal judge behaved as a self-indulgent brat, unwavering in his conviction that he deserves to be on the Supreme Court. In his statements to the committee, Brett Kavanaugh said that the allegations against him had ruined his life, even though he was very shortly after that confirmed to a lifetime appointment on the Supreme Court. The bar for a man's ruin is apparently quite low. May we all be so lucky as to have our lives so ruined.

The bar for women's ruin however, has no limit. That is a painful truth to live with day in and day out. And it is a disgrace. Womanhood should not be primarily defined by suffering however gilded it may be. As of late, people have offered up all kinds of moving words about the strength of women in a world dominated by the whims of men. The truth is, I often hate those words. I hate that they are needed. I hate that we are supposed to find inspiration in women merely surviving things they should never be expected to experience. I hate that this culture must constantly be reminded of the magnitude of what women withstand. I hate that even knowing the magnitude of what women withstand, this culture seems to think that we can handle even more. Or worse, they simply do not care.

Women should not have to think of ourselves in terms of resilience or our ability to endure. We are capable of so much more, but we are too busy dealing with bullshit to demonstrate the full extent of our powers. We should be able to move through this world freely, safe, and strong in our bodies. We should be able to thrive unfettered by the chronic malignancy that is misogyny.

I am also often asked to define feminism and I love saying that I no longer answer that question because – let us be real – it is 2018, and either you know what feminism is or you do not. Either you know that women deserve to be treated with equality and equity, to be seen as human, or you do not. If I absolutely had to offer up a definition though, I would say that feminism is working to ensure that women are free to focus our energies on more than mere survival. I look back at this past year and I wonder when that might happen and what more it could possibly take.

As a writer who engages with race, gender, sexuality and culture, it often feels like I am writing the same thing in slightly different ways over and over. Not because I lack imagination or a breadth of intellectual interests, but because so little truly changes for women or people of colour, or the LGBT community, or the disabled. What we call progress is marginal change at best, and that marginal change only comes because women fight tirelessly to bring it about. And however incremental change is for women in the United States, the pace of change is far more glacial for women in many other parts of the world. We march, we share our personal stories, we cannibalize ourselves, we vote though let us never forget that in the United States, only 47 per cent of white women voted in their own best interests in the last election. We run for office sometimes. We take stands great and small in our personal lives. We try to advocate for ourselves and for each other. We live and love. We fight. We hope. And still the sociopolitical structures that shape our lives remain immovable. We talk about resistance when what we need is a revolution.

It has been a year of #MeToo. A year of reckoning. I feel like I am supposed to offer an uplifting message about how far we have come when in truth we have not come far at all. Yes, we have had a vigorous and necessary national conversation about sexual violence and harassment. Over this last year, we are starting to see men face consequences for the harm they have done. Bill Cosby is sitting in a prison cell and will probably rot there for the rest of his life. Harvey Weinstein will eventually face trial and hopefully, if he does not buy his way out of it, incarceration. More powerful men will lose their jobs and face the opprobrium of the court of public opinion when the truth of who they are is revealed. But, how are we going to create lasting change? How will we ensure that the justice system better addresses sexual violence? How will we encourage the justice system to include restorative justice and sentencing guidelines? And more importantly, what will change for women? What especially will change for the most vulnerable women among us, the undocumented, women of colour, working class women, single mothers? What will change for women who cannot afford to come forward when they are harassed or assaulted?

As I consider this past year, what strikes me is how #MeToo has mostly benefited culturally prominent, mostly white women. Those women deserve justice as much as anyone else, but they are the few among a great many women who deserve justice and acknowledgment. What will change for men who feel entitled to women in whatever ways they see fit? A few men have indeed fallen from grace. A few more men are worried they will be next because they know how they have crossed lines. A majority of men do not realize that they too are part of the problem because either they have committed sexual transgressions or they have looked the other way, or they have not believed women.

It has been a year of #MeToo but it has also been more than a decade, because before the hashtag, activist Tarana Burke began the #MeToo movement after meeting a young girl who had been sexually abused. During that encounter Burke wanted to tell the young woman, "me too," but she could not. Eventually she created a nonprofit called Just Be, dedicated to helping victims of sexual harassment and assault. She created a space where people could say "me too" so victims of sexual violence would always know that they are not alone. Today we do know we are not alone. Today we honour that space that Burke created as best we can. We know sexual harassment and violence are practically epidemic. We know change is needed. As we move forward, we need to figure out how to hold this space that #MeToo has made for empathy and solidarity, while working to create a culture where someday this space will not be needed. That, if anything, is what I hope for.

Permissions

"The interplay of East and West, points of conflict and cooperation" © 1957 Barbara Ward. Published here with permission of W. W. Norton & Company, Inc.

"Asia Today: Revolutionary Change in the Twentieth Century" © 1968 Han Suyin. Published here with permission of McGill-Queen's University Press.

"How Long Have We Got?" © 1971 Peter Ritchie-Calder. Published here with permission of the Estate of Peter Ritchie-Calder.

"Genetic Engineering: Ambush or Opportunity?" © 1972 Robert Sinsheimer. Published here with permission of the Estate of Robert Sinsheimer.

"The Emergence of Intelligence in the Universe" © 1975 Fred Hoyle. Published here with permission of the Estate of Fred Hoyle.

"Interpretation in Music and in Life" © 1975 Yehudi Menuhin. Published here with permission of the Estate of Yehudi Menuhin.

"A Swing to the Right? Socio-political Changes in the Western World" © 1981 Ralf Dahrendorf. Published here with permission of the Estate of Ralf Dahrendorf.

"Apartheid: Dying or Resurgent?" © 1982 Gwendolen Carter.

"The New World Order" © 1993 Mikhail Gorbachev. Published here with permission of the Gorbachev Foundation.

"The New World Order" © 1993 Pierre Trudeau. Published here with permission of the Estate of Pierre Trudeau.

"The New World Order" © 1993 Valentin Boss. Published here with permission of the Estate of Valentin Boss.

"The New World Order" © 1993 Reuven Brenner. Published here with permission of the author.

"Right of Interference: Progress and Failure in Conflict Prevention in an Age of Global Anxiety" © 1996 by Bernard Kouchner. Published here with permission of the author.

"Lessons in Living from the Dying" © 1997 by Cicely Saunders. Published here with permission of Cicely Saunders International.

"Canada in the World: The Challenges Ahead" © 2005 by Michael Ignatieff. Published here with permission of the author.

"Building Social Business: The New Kind of Capitalism that Serves Humanity's Most Pressing Needs" © 2010 by Muhammad Yunus. Published here with permission of the Yunus Centre.

"The Challenge of Regressive Democracy" © 2017 by Charles Taylor. Published here with permission of the author.

"Difficult Women, Bad Feminists, and Unruly Bodies" © 2018 by Roxane Gay. Published here with permission of the author.